TOO GOOD TO BE TRUE

TOO GOOD TO BE TRUE

THE STORY OF DENISE REDLICK'S MURDER

Janet Parker Beck

NEW HORIZON PRESS
Far Hills, New Jersey

Library of Congress Catalog Card Number: 90-53558

Janet Parker Beck
  Too Good To Be True

ISBN: 0-88282-066-4
New Horizon Press

■ CONTENTS ■

Contents

■ AUTHOR'S NOTE ■

These are the actual experiences of real people. The personalities, events, actions and conversations portrayed within the story have been reconstructed from extensive interviews and research, utilizing court documents, letters, personal papers, press accounts and the memories of participants. In an effort to safeguard the privacy of certain individuals, the author has changed their names and, in some cases, altered otherwise identifying characteristics. Events involving the characters happened as described; only minor details have been altered.

PART ONE

The Disappearance

Prologue

One of Jose Rodriguez's first tasks on Tuesday morning was to thoroughly clean the interior of the white Ford Econoline. Rodriguez was used to finding fast food wrappings, empty coffee cups and other bits of trash carelessly left in rental cars. A couple of times he retrieved some valuable items—one time a briefcase, another time a gold necklace. He had passed the belongings on to his manager and assumed they were eventually reunited with their forgetful, but grateful, owners.

But this time, something peculiar caught Rodriguez's eye.

"Hey, take a look at this," he hollered to Charles Cantrell, the lot manager who was running a vacuum in the cab of the van. Cantrell jogged around to the back and peered inside the open rear doors.

Rodriguez didn't have to explain why he had called his manager over.

Near the rear wheel well, on the cold metal floor, was a large, oval-shaped, dark red stain.

"Looks kinda like . . . blood, I guess," Rodriguez slowly said. Cantrell had to agree. He fought off the uneasy feeling in his stomach.

Neither of them spoke for a few seconds.

"Probably went on a hunting trip," Cantrell finally speculated out loud, looking past Rodriguez toward the traffic on El Camino Real. "Bet whoever rented this thing took something he shot home with him."

3

"Yes, bet he did," answered Rodriguez who had been hunting but didn't have the slightest idea what kind of animal anyone would be shooting on the San Francisco Peninsula in mid-November. He crouched over, stepped up into the back of the van. On his hands and knees he looked around for some animal hair or fur. He didn't find any.

Rodriguez walked over to a shelf filled with soaps, waxes, rags and sponges. He grabbed a stiff scrub brush and two containers: a white wall cleaner and a bug and tar remover.

For a long while, Rodriguez scrubbed at the large stain on the floor of the van. Finally, Cantrell agreed with him that the stubborn blotch wasn't going to disappear completely although, by then, it was slightly lighter in color.

When the two lot workers were finished, the van was returned to the fleet's active inventory, ready to be rented again, along with two similar vehicles that had been returned that day. Neither of the Budget employees made special note of the curious stain in the vehicle inspection record for the Ford Econoline van.

In all, Rodriguez and Cantrell cleaned fifteen cars, vans, trucks and trailers that day. Cantrell would specifically recall that of the fifty vans in the Budget Bay Area fleet—including a half dozen that are kept on the San Carlos lot—the van with the suspicious red stain that day was the one with the upside down Ford emblem on the steering wheel.

But after that chilly November morning, Rodriguez and Cantrell didn't give another thought to the seemingly indelible stain on the floor of the Ford Econoline van.

■ CHAPTER ONE ■

Where Is She?

Sunday 3 P.M.
No one would have expected Kathleen Wade to remember him.

But she did.

He was tall, slim, about thirty, with a thin moustache and slightly receding blond hair. Dressed in faded blue jeans and a white T-shirt, he was no more interesting, no more remarkable than any of the dozens of men who rented vehicles on a typical day from Wade, the manager of the busy Budget Rent-A-Car agency. Yet, for some reason, his image lingered in her mind.

When she saw him for the first time, he muttered something about moving and asked if he could rent a truck. Politely she pointed out several available vehicles including a white Ford Econoline Van—the one with the windowless cargo area.

He looked at the van, seemed satisfied and told her, "I'll take it."

She watched as he parked his own car—a big blue older model station wagon—in front of the rental office and came in. "Be careful," Wade warned, "if you leave the car on the street overnight, one of our industrious San Carlos police officers will put a parking citation on it by the time you get back."

"Thanks. I'll move it right now," he said, seeming grateful for the tip.

Wade didn't see where he drove the car but she assumed he parked it on one of the residential sidestreets. Ten minutes later, he returned.

5

"Is this for personal or business use?" Wade asked him as she filled in the blanks on the rental agreement.

"Personal business," he responded without hesitation.

She handed him the agreement (left-handed like me, she thought as he angled the one-page form into position to sign it) and took a lingering look at his California driver's license. Then Wade gave him the keys to the Ford van, license number 2K72291, and he drove away.

Monday Morning 11 A.M.

"Denise, please don't do that." Joan Redlick gently chided her daughter as the younger woman poured a cup of strong, black coffee and lit another cigarette. "That's the worst thing you can do to yourself and you've been trying to quit."

"Sorry, Mom." Denise looked up at her mother, obviously embarrassed, and quickly stubbed out her smoldering cigarette. Her sullen mood that morning was a perfect match for the dismal, gray sky visible through the kitchen window. As she contemplated her plans for the day, Denise wondered aloud if the weather would clear long enough to run her errands without donning a raincoat or jacket.

But watching her daughter, Joan suspected that Denise's gloomy demeanor was more than just a reflection of the damp and cheerless weather. She had heard Denise talking earlier that morning on the private phone in her bedroom. Joan couldn't help but wonder if, like dozens of other times over the past month, the voice on the other end of the line had triggered Denise's silent brooding.

"Come on, honey, have some breakfast," Joan gently prodded her daughter who, over the past few months, had lost nearly twenty-five pounds. For Denise, who fought to keep her weight in line most of her life, her new figure was a startling barometer of the emotional pressure she had been under.

Denise shook her head. "Look at me, I'm losing so much weight I don't have to diet anymore."

"It's not an improvement," her mother said frowning, for it was a change her mother was becoming increasingly more apprehensive about.

6

"I'm having lunch with Lori," Denise replied, trying to justify her lack of interest in food. "Don't worry, I just don't want anything to eat right now."

Bundled in her white terry cloth robe, Denise—her shoulder length, frosted blond hair still unbrushed—seemed in no hurry to get dressed that morning. Usually by this time on Mondays she had already been at work for an hour. But it was Veteran's Day and all the banks, including the Bank of America branch in neighboring San Francisco where she worked as a teller, were closed.

Harry Redlick, who had been upstairs watching television in the den, slipped into the kitchen. Although he was delighted to have his daughter living with them again in the home where she had grown up, his heart ached as he watched her cope with the pain of her shattered wedding plans. He was relieved that Denise and one of her many friends, Chris Morganti, would be 2,000 miles away in New York on Saturday, the day on which Denise had, until a little more than a month ago, planned to marry Craig Anderson.

"I just want to get her on that plane, get past this horrible weekend, and have her come back with a whole new outlook on life," he had optimistically remarked to his wife when they had awakened a few hours earlier.

Harry poured his cold coffee down the kitchen sink, put his mug on the tile counter and glanced at his watch. In less than half an hour, he was due at Kaiser Hospital in South San Francisco for a medical checkup. Harry gave Denise a kiss on the cheek. "We'll talk about your travel plans later," he said.

"Ok, Dad," she muttered without looking up.

"I've never seen her so depressed," Joan whispered to him as she said good-bye in the hall. She returned to the kitchen and watched her daughter sitting quietly, wordlessly, at the maple table. Joan tried another strategy to entice Denise out of her apparent despair.

"Come on, Denise," Joan shrugged. "Why don't you put on your new pants and sweater." The two of them had gone shopping together over the weekend and picked out several new outfits for the trip back East. As Denise listlessly got up from the kitchen table to walk down the hall to her bedroom, her mother had yet another thought.

Remembering how much Denise liked to borrow Joan's clothing, Joan offered Denise her shiny new, gray belt to wear with the grey wool slacks. Forcing a smile, Denise thanked her mother, took the belt, closed the bedroom door behind her and slipped out of her robe.

When Denise's bedroom phone rang, Joan shivered. Denise let it ring twice more before reluctantly lifting the receiver.

"Hello?" Denise briskly answered with none of her usual cheerfulness.

"Gee, you're in a great mood," Lori Voreyer teased, sensing the tension in her cousin's greeting. "What's wrong?"

"Oh, I thought it might be Craig," Denise responded with a sigh. The two women, close friends since childhood, chatted long enough for Lori to learn that Denise had spent most of Saturday afternoon talking with Craig who had surprised her suddenly by showing up at the beauty salon where she was having her hair frosted. Denise promised to tell Lori about it all during lunch. "Let's meet around 12:30 p.m.," she said, and hung up.

Denise also placed a quick call to Charles Nan, another teller at the bank. A small group of bank employees was planning to gather that night at the home of another teller, Rossana Hanak, in Pacifica to watch the San Francisco Forty-Niners battle the Denver Broncos in a critical game for the Bay Area team.

Charles was sleeping late when his mother woke him up to tell him Denise was on the phone. He would later recall that he glanced at his bedroom clock and it was 11:19.

"I talked to Rossana's husband," Denise said. "She's having her wisdom teeth out and he said she's really feeling awful. She's not up to having everyone over. I know how you're feeling down about your dad being in the hospital. Do you want to go someplace and watch the game anyway?"

"Denise, you're always so thoughtful," Charles said. "Thanks."

"I'll call you this afternoon after I get home from the travel agency so we can pick a place to meet," Denise promised.

When Denise finally emerged from her room, her appearance instantly brought a smile to Joan's face. Joan thought, at that very moment, how beautiful her daughter looked in her new grey slacks, a colorful striped sweater and a long black cardigan. And, she was immensely relieved to see Denise's spirits perking up.

"I'm meeting Charles to watch the game tonight," Denise told her mother. "But I should be home early."

Calling a good-bye to her mother, Denise walked out the kitchen door, down to the two-car garage and out to the driveway. Her own car, a Datsun 280Z, was being repaired after being rear-ended in an accident. So Denise was borrowing her father's white 1978 Triumph sports car, the car that had been her own before he helped her buy "the Z." Joan went to the living room window when she heard the screeching of the Triumph's burglar alarm. Denise had forgotten to turn off the security system before opening the driver's side door with her key.

As Joan looked out, she saw Denise had a big smile on her face. Joan would later recall, "She was laughing at herself, running around the back of the car and it looked like she was saying, 'Oh no, I did it again.'"

As far as anyone knows, Denise Redlick drove straight to the Casey Travel Agency at 1633 Bayshore Highway as soon as she left her parents' house on Monday morning.

She arrived at 12:40 p.m., ten minutes later than she and her cousin planned. She was meticulously attired in grey and black right down to her two-toned leather boots. Her blond hair was softly curled and Lori noticed her long, slender nails had been perfectly manicured. Lori even noticed the shade of polish, a deep burgundy. It appeared, Lori thought, that the old Denise, the one who cared about how she looked, had returned.

At first, they talked about the trip to New York and discussed a few ideas about where Denise and Chris might stay. Lori had been surprised at the destination Denise and Chris had finally selected. When Denise first dropped in the office in October to look at travel literature, she had talked about taking a trip to a tropical climate, maybe a Club Med. But a week or so later, Denise announced that she and Chris was going to New York, far from tropical in mid-November.

"Denise, if you want to go somewhere warm, why don't you say so?" Lori suggested with impatience.

"Oh, it's okay," Denise said with a shrug. "I really don't care."

Lori thought it was so typical of her cousin to give in, to let people she cared about have their own ways.

It wasn't long before the conversation turned to a familiar topic, Craig Anderson. Lori didn't like what Denise was telling her.

Anderson, Denise said, had suddenly appeared on Saturday at the hair salon where Denise had gone for an appointment. "I hadn't told Craig I was going so I was startled to see him," she mused. "The two of us drove up to Sawyer Camp Road to talk."

"Denise, why on earth did you get in the car with him?" Lori asked, worried about her cousin.

"Oh, no way," Denise assured her. "I know better than that. We took our own cars. He said he needed to talk so after we got there, we just sat in Craig's Mercedes for more than four hours."

Lori frowned.

"Don't worry," Denise continued, "most of the time I just sat there and listened to Craig talk about why I should give him another chance." She looked up, miserable. "At one point, he even cried. He told me that he loved me and still wanted to marry me." She shook her head and bit down on her lower lip. "I don't know what it is about Craig, but that man can talk anyone into anything."

Lori patted her cousin's shoulder protectively. "You didn't give in, did you? You shouldn't be such a push-over."

Denise, however, convinced Lori that she had been firm, for the first time, in her decision to end her relationship with Craig for good. "I told him, 'I just don't feel the same way about you anymore.'

"That's the first time I've really said it," she added. "Craig was very quiet after that."

After more small talk and a quick lunch the two women walked back to the travel agency where Lori booked hotel reservations for Denise and Chris.

As they parted company, Denise said she was on her way to Mervyn's department store, just across Bayshore Freeway in Millbrae, and mentioned that she was going out with some friends that evening to watch the football game.

Denise promised to call Lori when she got home. Denise's last words were, "Don't worry. I'll talk to you tonight."

Monday 6 P.M.

The second time Kathleen Wade saw him was on Monday evening, a little over twenty-four hours later. The glass door swung open filling the sparsely-furnished rental agency office with a burst of brisk November air. Kathleen looked up and there he was again.

"I guess you're about to close," he said as he approached the counter desk to check in the van on Monday evening.

"No, you've got plenty of time," she answered, giving him a quick business-like smile although she really wanted to wrap up her work and go home. In just fifteen minutes, at 6 p.m., the agency would be closing. Business had been slow, probably because it was Veteran's Day and, for many of the agency's regular clients, it was a holiday. But Wade tried to give good service to her customers. "Renting a car is a real pain," she sympathetically declared.

Wade stamped the "time in" on the rental agreement: Nov 11 17:47.

After Wade told him the charges, he pulled out a few bills from his faded brown leather wallet and shook his head. "I'm paying cash," he said. "I'll have to run home and get the rest. I'll be back in a few minutes."

"No problem. We'll still be open," she assured him. He disappeared and Wade returned to finishing her end-of-the-day paperwork.

As an employee of the agency for three years, Wade was regarded by her supervisors as one of their most efficient staff members. Several times the company had called upon her to testify in court. On one occasion, a customer who had driven off in a brand-new Buick—and never returned—was eventually arrested in Texas after making an illegal U-turn. The suspect was extradited and tried in San Mateo County Superior Court where Wade, in her usual calm and self-assured manner, testified that he was indeed the man who had rented the car from her more than a year ago. The suspect was convicted.

Wade took her job seriously, although she sometimes wondered if all her co-workers did. More than once she had gone home and complained to her husband that some of the agency's workers were lazy, that they weren't as careful in their tasks as they should be.

Just as he had promised, the customer returned fifteen minutes later. He had changed to a navy blue sweatsuit. She took the rest of his money and tore his VISA credit card deposit slip into tiny pieces, routine practice for the 10 percent or so of the agency's customers who wind up paying cash.

Wade handed the man a copy of the completed rental agreement and placed the office copies into a bin with a batch of others that would be sent by messenger to the main office in San Jose on Tuesday.

In the lot outside, Aristotle Jordan swore lightly as he stepped into a puddle walking around the white van emblazoned with the conspicuous orange and black Budget Rent-A-Truck logo across each side. He did a quick inspection for damage. The lot attendant had spent much of that day outdoors and he was tired. The sun had already set and, like most mid-November nights on the San Francisco Peninsula, it was chilly.

"Nothing wrong here," he mumbled as he moved toward the back of the vehicle examining the exterior.

The last customer of the day, the man who rented the van, finished his business in the office and stepped outside where Jordan greeted him with a clipboard containing the vehicle damage and equipment report. The customer scrawled his signature. Jordan glanced at it—a legible name that meant nothing to Jordan at the time—on the line opposite "check in." The customer handed the clipboard back to Jordan wordlessly. Moving at a leisurely pace he walked away.

Jordan drove the white van to the rear of the parking lot, stepped out and locked it.

12

Where is She?

Looking at her watch ten minutes later, Kathleen Wade was glad the long day was finally over. She flipped off the agency lights and locked the office doors. With a fast wave to each other, she and Jordan got in their cars to drive home.

■ CHAPTER TWO ■

The Sunshine Girl

■ **9:30 P.M.**

When the Redlicks came home from dinner at Joan's parents' house in San Francisco, Joan noticed that the two phone messages that she had left that afternoon for Denise from Charles—one on the refrigerator and the other on Denise's pillow in her bedroom—hadn't been touched. Joan was baffled. No matter what plans Denise ever had, she always rushed home to scoop up her phone messages and somehow found the time to call everyone back before rushing off to the next activity.

Joan brushed aside a "funny feeling" about why on this particular day Denise hadn't come home in between running her afternoon errands and meeting her friend to watch the game. It was so unlike her. ■

From the moment she was born, Denise Susan Redlick brought sunshine to her parents' lives.

As soon as she was old enough to realize the difference between giving and receiving, Denise became a giver. She was the rare type of child who never asked for Christmas presents, but spent all her time choosing gifts for others. When her brother, like most older siblings, teased her to the point that she would cry, she would never retaliate but tried to win him over by cook-

14

ing his breakfast or making his favorite lunch. She always worked hard to please the people she loved.

Denise's burning desire to make other people happy was a trait that would last the rest of her life. As one of her closest friends would say, there "wasn't a mean bone in Denise's body."

Harry and Joan Redlick (the former Joan Bellantoni) were San Franciscans who met at Lake Tahoe and were married on August 26, 1956. Like many young couples in San Francisco in the late 1950s, Harry and Joan saw golden opportunities in the booming bedroom communities of California. Lured by avocado green parks with shiny new swingsets and sparkling elementary schools, they looked around San Bruno, and found streets with names like Juniper, Holly and Chestnut, where they could buy a brand new, three-bedroom, two-bathroom, ranch-style house with its own cozy backyard for $19,000 (a mere $4,000 down), a house that would be worth more than fifteen times that just thirty years later. Just a month before their son Michael was born, Joan and Harry bought their house in the hilly Crestmoor section, where living room windows featured sweeping views of the San Francisco Bay, San Francisco International Airport, Mt. Diablo in the East Bay and beyond.

During the years that followed, San Bruno, like other post-quake Peninsula towns, slowly grew westward from the bayside and across the railroad tracks toward the coastal range and into an area where hundreds of dairy cattle once grazed.

As time passed, San Mateo County's population boomed. More than 580,000 people lived in its nineteen cities by 1980. Even more significantly, like Burlingame, San Mateo, Millbrae and the other suburbs, San Bruno was still considered a safe place to live and raise a family compared to many districts of "the City," just a few miles to the north. In 1984, the same year that seventy-three people were murdered in San Francisco, San Bruno police proudly boasted of a murder-free crime record.

People who lived in the Peninsula's communities just didn't expect bad things to happen to their neighbors, their friends or themselves.

■ 11 P.M.

Harry and Joan lounged in bed and watched the Forty-Niners on television. The game in Mile High Stadium was an especially memorable one, and, for San Francisco fans, not happily so. During a field goal attempt by kicker Ray Wershing, with back-up quarterback Matt Cavanaugh holding the ball in place, a Denver fan threw a snowball from the endzone landing just a few feet from Cavanaugh. The distracted quarterback took his eye off the ball just long enough for it to tilt out of alignment. Because of it, the kick was off center, causing his team to lose out on three points. The Broncos won the game 17-16, a loss that kept the Forty-Niners from winning their division.

Joan must have dozed off shortly after the game ended, because she suddenly realized that the 11 p.m. news was over. She also realized, with a start, that she hadn't heard her daughter come in.

"Harry, Denise isn't home and she has to go to work tomorrow," Joan muttered. It wasn't like her daughter to be so casual about staying out late on a work night. She had always been able to trust Denise to do the right thing, Joan thought proudly, though she certainly had high spirits. Joan picked up a paperback book on her nightstand and tried to read. But her thoughts kept returning to her daughter. ■

Even as a young child Denise was never frightened by a new challenge. She took up ice skating, tap dancing, ballet, baton twirling, swimming, skiing and flute lessons. "She wanted to try everything and I let her do it," Joan recalled. That she never really excelled in any of these endeavors didn't discourage her in the least. "She had a lot of nerve," her mother always said. "She tried different sports, like scuba diving, that 'scared me half to death'."

Despite her fun-loving manner, her friends also thought of Denise as the most responsible of the girls, the "one of us with the most common sense," one friend observed.

"She was the one who had us all wearing seat belts long

before it was required," another friend, Michele McKindley, agreed.

Denise compulsively locked her car doors, her friends noticed. One time, Denise was riding with Chris Morganti when they stopped in the driveway of Chris' parents' home just long enough to run in quickly and drop off a package. When Denise locked the passenger's door as she got out of the car, Chris kidded her about it ("You're obsessed!" she said), but Denise just laughed and kept the door locked anyway.

In fact, Denise's girlfriends teasingly called her "mom," which she accepted with her usual good humor.

Denise was also full of good-hearted mischief. "We raised all kinds of heck," Michele, a pretty brunette with high cheekbones and a warm smile, said of their high school days. As leader of the junior varsity cheerleading squad in their sophomore years, Denise organized a clandestine moonlit Halloween mission to the pumpkin farms of Half Moon Bay some fifteen miles away on the Pacific Ocean coast. There, the girls swiped dozens of tiny jack-o-lanterns as secret gifts for the basketball team members.

Another night, she and Michele sneaked onto their rival high school campus, Capuchino, where they chopped down a tree and tossed it into the swimming pool. Word of the caper quickly circulated at Crestmoor but they were relieved that no one ever found out who the culprits were.

During four years on the hilltop campus of Crestmoor High School, Denise, Michele, Julie Medrano and Suzanne Parshooto, an inseparable quartet of best friends, always staked out the same bench in a corner of the Great Court, the gathering place in the center of the campus, and were delighted when they discovered that a picture of the four of them having lunch in their little corner had surfaced in their yearbook.

Denise loved to play harmless jokes on her friends. After high school, she often visited Michele, who had moved to Lodi, a farming town two hours south east of San Bruno on the edge of the San Joaquin Valley. Denise would sit at Michele's window, see a car drive by and wave frantically. "Who's that?" Michele would naively ask. Denise would give her a look that told Michele she had been tricked again. "Who would I know in *Lodi?*" Denise would ask with a giggle.

Denise was the first to admit that she was not a serious student. While she received a few "A"s on her report card (primarily in physical education classes), most academic subjects—like chemistry and math—didn't come easily for her.

"Denise was more into socializing than studying," her cousin, Lori observed. Lori's brother, Johnny, was in Denise's geometry class although he was two years younger. "Poor Denise, she's really struggling," he remarked once to his sister when his older cousin was getting "D"s on her tests.

Denise charmed her classmates—who honored her by giving her the "best laugh" award in their senior yearbook—and her co-workers, with her easy-going, seemingly carefree personality. She acquired dozens of loyal friends at school and at work. She had a habit of making people feel as if their friendship, their interests and their lives, no matter how briefly she had known them, really mattered to her.

"None of us ever had as many friends as Denise was blessed with," one of her friends recalled.

Small gestures of thoughtfulness were commonplace for Denise. No one was surprised when she went out of her way to bring the mother of a friend a box of candy on her birthday or offer a neighbor a ride in her car when it meant driving five miles out of her way. When a friend gave a party, it was Denise who would stay around later to help clean the kitchen.

When, in her senior year, Denise began working as a teller at the Bank of America, she seemed to have found her ideal career, one that utilized her people skills.

"Although Denise had a lot of exterior beauty, I quickly realized that she was a woman with a lot of inner beauty as well," said Charles Nan, who worked with Denise. "It may sound corny," he continued, "but light radiated from her. You could feel the positiveness about her. No matter how she was feeling, what kind of day it was outside or what she had been through in her personal life, Denise always made me think of sunshine."

But it was Denise's family relationships which seemed most important to her. Joan recognized that her bond with Denise was

18

an extraordinary one. "I always took her into my confidence. I was always straight with her and she, in turn, was always straight with me."

As a teenager, Denise filled a dozen photo albums with snapshots of her parents, her brother, his wife and their child, her grandparents and her cousins, writing little captions to describe special events. The Redlicks often got together with Joan's sister, Carolyn, and her husband, John, and their three children—Lori, Karen and Johnny—who also lived in Crestmoor for holidays, birthdays and other celebrations.

In fact, it was more important to Denise than anything else that she never disappoint her parents. When she and Michele enrolled in an evening typing class at Skyline Community College after high school graduation, they knew within a few weeks that college wasn't for them. But Denise dreaded telling her parents that she was dropping out. Before she mustered the courage to break the news, she and Michele had been going out for ice cream sundaes everyday for weeks instead of going to class.

During high school Denise never went steady, though she had dates for important proms and events. Despite her happy exterior she was always unhappy with the way she looked, especially with her weight—which tended to be on the chubby side. One time, tired of her light brown hair, she dyed her hair red and the nickname "Red" stuck with her for years. She accepted it goodnaturedly and laughed when her father bought personalized plates that said "Reds 792" for her Datsun 280Z.

Denise's first serious relationship began just after high school. She was working as a teller at the San Francisco International Airport branch of the Bank of America and Art Thomas was an import-export customs broker who worked at an office nearby. Art thought Denise was pretty and quite friendly and asked her out although, in his words, "she was a little overweight." A muscular blond with soft blue eyes, Art felt that Denise was afraid to get too involved with him because he was three years older and supporting himself while she was just out of high school and still living with her parents. Rather than push himself

19

on someone who wasn't sure if she was ready for a relationship, Art stopped dating her.

But later that year, when Art's mom died, Denise sent him a sympathy card and hinted that she might like to see him again. He called her the day after his mother's funeral and their casual dates quickly turned into a serious commitment. The Denise he fell in love with was warm, outgoing, happy and dependable. Whenever they had a problem, she was willing to talk about it and work things out, he said.

By the summer of 1981, they were engaged, but later the engagement was broken. Art felt it was because Denise had so little experience with men before him and really wasn't ready for a lifelong commitment.

Over the next few years, Denise had several steady dates but was never serious enough about any of them to think about marriage. But, as she watched most of the women close to her, like her cousin Lori and her long-time friend Debi, marry and move into their own cozy homes and have babies, Denise reportedly told her friends that she wanted to settle down.

Debi warned her one day in a lighthearted way. "Denise, now be careful, that's no reason to wind up with just anybody who comes along."

In September 1984, Denise traveled to Europe with her father. She told her girlfriends that she was glad she was unattached during this once-in-a-lifetime trip, but, when she returned, she was especially lonely that she had no one with whom to share her experience. For the first time, Denise felt she should move out of the family home and begin to develop a separate life.

By the end of that year, Denise said she was ready for a serious and permanent relationship.

That's when Craig Anderson entered Denise Redlick's life and swept her off her feet.

■ CHAPTER THREE ■

First Impressions

Joan's anxiety rose. She nudged her husband. "She's still not home," she told Harry.

Harry was a little put out that his daughter hadn't given her parents a call, as she usually did, to keep them from worrying about her.

"I've got a bad feeling about this," Joan said in a worried tone. Harry looked at his wife searchingly and tried to mask his own anxiety, but she rushed on, "And I can't simply call Charles. I've never met him and I don't have his phone number. In fact, I don't even know his last name."

"You don't think she could have been with Craig?" she went on, obviously wanting her husband to deny the idea.

And Harry was about to do just that when he noticed his wife's panicked look and knew that only Denise, herself, would be able to reassure her mother. Wordlessly, he put his arm around Joan and they huddled together in the big bed. ■

It began as a blind date.

A woman who worked with Denise at the Bank of America had been telling her about a very eligible and attractive bachelor whom she knew, the son of one of her closest friends.

From what she said, Craig Anderson was more interesting, and certainly more promising, than anyone Denise had previously dated. He was the owner of his own paint supply store in San Carlos (a spinoff of the paint manufacturing company that his grandfather had founded in San Francisco in the 1940s), owned an attractive home in the White Oaks section of San Carlos, drove a Porsche 924 and was moderately wealthy. He was also tall and blond with magnetic blue eyes.

Denise was definitely intrigued.

One day, after Denise had been hearing about this eligible bachelor for several months, he called her at work and asked her for a date. Immediately, she accepted, although she was worried about the impression she would make. Denise sometimes thought of herself as unattractive because of her weight problem.

But from their initial date, Craig made Denise feel important and, for the first time, beautiful.

Denise asked her mother and several of her girlfriends what she should wear for her date with this special person. She finally settled on a sleek, cream-colored pantsuit and heels, showing off the results of her recent diet. Joan and Harry were going out that night, but they saw Denise before they left the house. Joan couldn't help but think, as she looked at her lovely daughter, that the young man she was about to meet would certainly be impressed.

He arrived a few minutes after 7:00 p.m. Denise opened the door and liked what she saw. Just as her co-worker had told her, he was tall—over six feet, she guessed—and he had straight, sun-bleached hair and bright blue eyes. He certainly wasn't movie-star handsome, but he had the kind of wholesome, athletic looks that had appealed to her in the past. Most of all, his eyes lit up at the sight of her.

"Well, I'm Denise," she nervously giggled as he handed her a bouquet of pink carnations. "I'm ready. I'll just grab my coat."

Craig helped her slip on her jacket and walked beside her down the path from her parents' house to the sidewalk where he had parked his Porsche. Denise commented on the car—about which she had heard—and he was obviously pleased.

"Yeah, it's okay, but I'm thinking about trading it in for a

22

Mercedes," he told her as he opened the passenger's door and she slid inside.

For a few minutes, they sat in front of the house as he told her he had made reservations at three restaurants and asked which one she would prefer. Denise chose Ming's, a popular Cantonese restaurant in the mid-Peninsula, just off Highway 101. As they drove, Denise felt self-conscious as she noticed how self-assured he seemed—a lot different from most of the men she had dated who were closer to her own age—and began to wonder what he could possibly see in her. But he showed no evidence of being bored with her conversation, instead making her feel the center of attention, encouraging her to talk about her job, her recent trip to Europe, and about her newborn nephew, Mathew.

"He's so adorable," Denise said, showing Craig a snapshot she carried in her purse. "You've got to meet him. He's the cutest little baby in the world."

But Denise was not one to dwell on herself. She asked Craig many questions, learning that he had two younger brothers and a sister and that, like herself, he enjoyed a close relationship with his grandparents. As Craig talked about how both of his parents had graduated from Balboa High School in San Francisco, Denise couldn't believe what she was hearing.

"Craig, so did my mom!" Denise exclaimed. As they compared family notes, they discovered that his mother, Shirley, and Denise's aunt, Carolyn, were even in the same class and had a number of mutual friends.

Sharing a platter of *dim sum* in the noisy dining room, they exchanged their own memories of high school. Craig told Denise how, during his senior year at Mills High School in Millbrae, he had been an all-county, tight-end and that his ability had earned him a college football scholarship, although a knee injury had kept him from playing. She laughed as he described the traditional "Toilet Bowl." The annual Thanksgiving weekend football game between Mills and Burlingame alumni had begun in the 1970s as a way for old friends to keep in touch and had grown every year, until, in 1982, it was even featured in a light-hearted story on a San Francisco television program. Denise accepted his invitation to attend and watch him play in the next "Toilet Bowl."

23

By the time Craig asked for a second pot of tea, Denise had decided that Craig was an extremely responsible and sensitive man. He told her that, as the oldest of four children, he had always felt a need to set an example, and had begun working in the family paint business when he was sixteen. When he was twenty-five, he was appointed secretary-treasurer of the corporation and, two years later, opened his own paint supply store in San Carlos. Besides managing the store, he had just launched a companion business—contracting painting jobs on the Peninsula and hiring dozens of subcontractors to do the work.

Obviously, Craig was a man with ambition, Denise surmised. He listened intently as she talked about herself, her friends and her life. He was, in every respect, a perfect gentleman, she told her friends.

Denise's parents didn't meet Craig until a week or so later when he came to their house for Thanksgiving. He wore a handsome blue-grey suit and blue tie that highlighted his eyes. This wasn't an irresponsible kid in blue jeans, Joan thought with relief. Finally, Denise had met a caring, capable man. Harry and Craig hit it off from the start. They spent some time that evening animatedly talking about Craig's plans to buy a Mercedes 500SEL.

There was a secure feeling for the Redlicks in knowing that their daughter's suitor was from a family that had something in common with their own—San Francisco roots. "It was all very wonderful in the beginning," Joan observed.

By Christmas, Denise was exclusively dating Craig. Joan was pleased when Craig asked for her advice about what to buy Denise for a Christmas present. He spent hours shopping at malls and boutiques, looking for something special. The silk blouse, wool pants and sweater he finally chose for her were both beautiful and expensive.

In fact, he bought Denise lots of small presents during those first few months of dating. The cute little knickknacks and stuffed animals that expressed his affection, soon began to dot her bedroom. He seemed eager to make Denise feel special and she liked it. Not coincidentally, he made a very good impression on Joan and Harry.

She's finally met someone who's really meant for her, Joan said.

"How great this will be for Denise," Joan told Harry one day. "She'll never have to worry about a thing. She can stay home if she wants, and never have to work and struggle to make a living."

It appeared that Joan and Harry had every reason to encourage the relationship.

Lynn Redlick, from the beginning, thought her sister-in-law's companion charming and sociable.

Only once in those early months did Lynn find Craig less than friendly. It was during Christmas at a party at Denise's godparents' home in San Mateo. Lynn asked Craig what he thought of Denise, fully expecting him to describe her the way her family thought of her—pretty, fun to be with, generous and kind. "I expected him to say something like, 'Wow, she's a neat lady,' " said Lynn. Instead, Craig sort of brushed the questions aside as if he was bothered by the intrusion. "I figured it was just his personality to be private like that," she said.

Otherwise, he laughed a lot and teased Denise in a good-natured way which led Lynn to think he really enjoyed her company. "Whenever we saw them together, he was really loving toward Denise," Lynn said. "In front of the family he treated her like a queen."

Craig and Denise sometimes babysat for Mike and Lynn's little boy, Matthew, and Craig displayed what Lynn believed was genuine love for the boy as the months went on. "He's wonderful around Matthew," Lynn said.

Denise's friends were impressed with Craig, too.

Chris Morganti met Craig while Denise was housesitting. Denise invited Chris, a vivacious, curly-haired brunette with a husky voice, to drop in that Sunday on the pretense of watching a football game on the big screen television, but actually to meet Craig. She was eager for Chris' approval.

Craig was nervous about meeting Chris. He asked Denise what he should wear, what Chris was like and what they should talk about.

"He really likes me," Denise had told Chris. When Craig finally arrived later than he had promised, he was extremely apologetic and polite, shaking hands very formally with Chris and then, as he sat next to Denise on the couch to watch the football game, making Chris the center of attention as he asked her gentle questions about herself and her life, while stroking Denise's hand tenderly at the same time.

"He appeared to be so caring toward Denise and interested in her," Chris said.

Soon after that, Chris met Denise and Craig one evening at the Hyatt Hotel lounge in Burlingame, a popular place for dancing and drinks. Chris, looking back on that night, remembered how much fun they had and how friendly and outgoing Craig had been. "He obviously was a guy who liked to have a good time, just like Denise. There was nothing about Craig not to like," Chris said.

Denise's other good friend, Michele, hadn't met Craig yet so she was eager to hear Chris' report.

"She said he was a good catch," Michele bragged. "I remember her saying he had a beautiful home. I thought, Well, thank God! At least one of us has finally found a prince charming."

When Craig invited Michele to join him and Denise at his house for dinner, he graciously showed Michele around the immaculate, attractively decorated ranch-style house, stopping to ask her advice about a chair he was thinking about buying, what color and what kind of upholstery would look best. As he leaned forward fastening his blue eyes on her, he seemed genuinely interested in her opinion. Michele gave Denise a wink behind her back as if to say, in a way only two best friends could understand, "He really wants me to like him, doesn't he?"

Toward the end of January, Craig said he wanted to take Denise somewhere special for her twenty-third birthday on February 10th. At first he asked Denise where she would like to go. She suggested Disneyworld in Florida, but Craig smiled at her choice and said he thought Nassau, in the Bahamas, would be more romantic.

On the trip, Denise was captivated by the beautiful sunsets, the candlelit dinners in expensive restaurants and the strolls along pristine beaches. Even though it rained during part of their vacation, they were thoroughly content and, it seemed, very much in love.

Harry and Joan picked the couple up at San Francisco International Airport when they returned. It wasn't until the four of them were seated around the kitchen table, drinking coffee and talking about the trip, that Craig said beaming, "Well, aren't you going to tell them?"

Denise proudly announced, "we're getting married," and showed her parents the matching gold bands that they had purchased at a bazaar in Nassau. In response to the family's request, Craig said he would mount the heirloom diamond that had belonged to Harry's mother on Denise's ring.

Joan and Harry were delighted, and especially by what they perceived as "Craig's feeling for family." They were not really surprised at the news. Denise and Craig seemed perfect for each other.

With Harry scheduled to leave for a six-month sabbatical in Germany, he and Joan decided to host an engagement party. Thirty people, including Craig's parents, two brothers, sister and grandparents, along with Denise's closest relatives, were invited to the catered dinner. It was a happy occasion and the two families got along marvelously.

As she raised her glass to toast the couple, Denise's grandmother—who was always concerned about Denise's happiness—looked especially pleased. "He's too good to be true," she observed to her daughter who nodded happily in agreement.

■ CHAPTER FOUR ■

Dark Hints

■ 2 A.M.

Harry and Joan, who had by now gotten out of bed, were sitting tensely side-by-side. They got up and soon began pacing the living room. Finally, they agreed that they should call Craig Anderson at his house in San Carlos. Harry dialed the seven digits and heard the phone ring several times before Craig answered.

Shaking slightly, Harry asked, "Craig, Denise isn't home and we're worried about her. Have you seen her or is she with you by any chance?"

In an annoyed, sleepy voice Craig said, "She's not here. In fact, I haven't seen her all day."

"She's probably out with her friends someplace," Craig calmly suggested.

Harry recoiled. "Of course, she's not simply out with her friends at two o'clock on a Tuesday morning," he said quickly.

"And you know you woke me up," Craig snapped back.

Alarmed, Harry hung up and repeated Craig's end of the brief conversation. Joan's eyes widened in disbelief. ■

■ **2:10 A.M.**

Harry was on the phone again. This time to the San Carlos Police Department.

"This is Harry Redlick," he quickly explained. "My daughter, Denise, has not come home as expected." He paused to gather his thoughts. "And I have reason to believe she might be at a house in San Carlos. Could you possibly have an officer drive by the house on Kelton Avenue and look for the white Triumph that Denise was driving Monday?"

The dispatcher declined the request.

Exasperated at the lack of cooperation, the Redlicks then called the California Highway Patrol which has jurisdiction over state roadways and freeways.

"Could you tell me if there have been any car accidents in the area involving a white Triumph and if Denise Redlick has been a victim?" Harry solemnly asked.

The police CHP dispatcher seemed to take forever replying. "There have been no reported accidents involving a Denise Redlick or a white Triumph."

"Thank God," Harry murmured. Quickly he relayed the information to his wife, but Joan felt far less reassured.

"I was hoping that there had been an accident, that she was in the hospital and we could go see her," Joan said. "It's far better than other scenarios that are taking shape in my mind." They looked searchingly at each other.

At Joan's urging, Harry agreed to drive the twelve miles to San Carlos, driving twice past Craig's house and up and down his quiet street looking, in vain, for the Triumph. For a moment, he thought about knocking on Craig's door and confronting him, but Harry wasn't sure what he would say or do. So he decided he'd better get back home to Joan as fast as he could.

Meanwhile Joan called her sister, Carolyn, who had been asleep. Carolyn got dressed and drove down the hill to the Redlicks' house in a matter of minutes. She, too, sensed that Denise's failure to come home by then was foreboding. ■

Denise had found a prince charming, her friends believed, and continued to congratulate her as Craig continued to charm them. So they were surprised in June when Denise and Michele planned to drive to San Luis Obispo to see their best friends from high school—Julie and Susanne—graduate from California Poly-Technical University and Craig said Denise absolutely could not go.

"It doesn't seem like it is his right to tell Denise that she couldn't spend a weekend celebrating her best friends' achievement," Michele complained. But she drove down alone.

After the graduation ceremony, Michele joined Julie and Susanne at a party to celebrate. Shocked, Michele saw Denise and Craig walk into the room. From his sullen look, Craig clearly wasn't happy to be there, barely being sociable and keeping a careful eye on anyone with whom Denise mingled.

As the party began to wind down, Denise whispered to Michele, "Craig really wants to take us shopping."

So the three of them drove to a nearby shopping mall. Guiding them to a store he liked, Craig took charge. He walked over to the rack and quickly picked out clothing and jewelry for Denise to try on. Michele wasn't sure she liked the beige jumpsuit and silver earrings he had chosen for her to model. But Denise eventually bought the outfit. She thought it strange that he told Denise what she should wear and Denise didn't object. "If he didn't like it, she didn't try it on," Michele said.

That evening, for the first time, Craig Anderson's temper flared in public. The three friends stopped at a nearby restaurant for dinner. The lanky waitress gave them the menus and disinterestedly recited the specials for the evening. Politely Craig asked Denise and Michele for their orders and conveyed them to the waitress who returned a few minutes later. "I'm sorry," she said quickly, "the filet of sole is no longer available."

"That's okay," Denise replied and looked down at her menu, "I'll have the poached salmon."

A few minutes later, Craig observed the waitress serving sole to a customer at a nearby table. He was furious. Loudly, he called the waitress over. "She wanted the special. Why the hell can't she have it?" Craig demanded.

Denise quietly patted Craig's hand. "Please forget about it. It isn't important," she urged.

"I don't care," Craig responded harshly. "You wanted the special and they can damn well fix it for you."

After his comments, the three of them ate their dinners in awkward silence. When they left the restaurant and went outside, Craig was still fuming. His eyes blazed as he faced Denise and demanded, "Why don't you ever let me handle things? That's my job."

Denise begged, "Craig, it's just a minor problem. Please, don't let it spoil our evening."

But it did.

That summer, other people noticed Craig was letting little things get to him, and Denise had a difficult time living up to her fiance's expectations of her.

One weekend in May, Denise's brother, Mike, and his wife, Lynn, drove down to Svedahl, a hamlet of cabins owned by Scandinavian families in the Santa Cruz Mountains, to join Craig and Denise. Another disturbing incident took place.

Mike had been at the pool alone. Slowly, he walked the quarter mile to the cabin to clean up for dinner. Making his way around a clump of trees, he heard loud voices. Craig's voice boomed. He was chastising Denise—an outburst punctuated with a number of four-letter words—for boiling, rather than frying, the hot dogs. To Mike, the angry outburst seemed unreasonable, but Denise, to her brother's distress, just stood there accepting the abuse.

Later, Craig apologized to Mike for his behavior. "I just blew a fuse," he told Mike. "Everything's okay now."

"You shouldn't lay into Denise over something so trivial," Mike told Craig.

Looking miserable Craig agreed. "It won't happen again," he promised.

Mike felt relieved to hear Craig so contrite. "We've all done stuff like that, lost our tempers over little things." He confided to Lynn later. "I trust Craig. It was an isolated event."

It wasn't, however.

During a twenty-first birthday party for Johnny, Denise's

31

cousin, Craig was helping to tend bar in the upstairs family room. Denise thought Craig, who seldom drank at family parties, was pouring too much alcohol in the mixed drinks and she softly told him so.

Shocking those who stood nearby, Craig yelled out, "Shut up, bitch."

As the summer went on, in front of their friends, Craig began to tease Denise, telling her she was too fat, that she ought to sign up for an exercise class. He always ended by saying, "Of course, I love you anyway, no matter how you look," but his words made everyone uncomfortable except Denise, who insisted that she was too fat and was lucky to have someone like Craig want her.

In June, when Michele, Denise and Craig again drove to Svedahl, Craig seemed to flirt a lot with other women at the pool. Denise made excuses for him. "He's just like that in public," she said, shrugging off the incident, "You don't know how loving and gentle he is when we're alone."

Michele looked lingeringly at her. "You better challenge him, Red," Michele told her best friend when they were having a cup of coffee together. "Tell him, 'Hey mister, you aren't Tom Selleck, you know!'" Later she whispered, "Denise, you have to be more firm. Say 'Knock it off!' when he flirts with other women."

But Denise just couldn't seem to stand up to her fiance. "It just wasn't her nature," Michele said sadly.

However, Craig loudly objected to Denise being noticed by other men.

"What am I doing to make guys look at me?" Denise miserably asked. Her friends tried to help her understand that Craig was laying his problems on her, but it was to no avail. Denise obviously loved him and kept hoping if she changed, then maybe he would too.

Meanwhile Denise's attractiveness to other men seemed to be a growing problem for Craig. "I don't want to lose you to someone else," he said firmly and repeatedly.

"That couldn't happen," Denise insisted.

His attitude became surly when Denise was a bridesmaid at a friend's wedding. The bride had decided to have each bridesmaid escorted down the aisle by one of the ushers. Denise was matched, for the ceremony, with a tall, handsome blond, a friend of the groom. Craig, who sat next to Denise's mother, turned as white as a ghost and began shaking as he stared intensely at Denise on another man's arm.

Later, during the reception at a Burlingame hotel, the wedding party followed the bride and groom onto the dance floor for the traditional "first dance." As is the custom, Denise danced with her wedding partner. When the next song began, Denise made the mistake of dancing with him again. When she rejoined her own group, Craig was livid.

Denise and Craig immediately left the room and disappeared into the foyer. When some pictures needed to be taken, Chris decided to find out what was taking the couple so long. Chris found Craig and Denise sitting together on the stairs. Denise's face was blotchy and red, tears fell down her cheeks.

"Come on, you guys, this is a wedding! It's supposed to be fun," Chris chided her friend. "Come on back to the reception."

Chris left them and a few minutes later, Craig and Denise rejoined the wedding guests. When Chris had a chance to ask Denise what had happened, Denise brushed the question aside. "Craig doesn't like me to dance with other guys," she said softly. "That's just the way he feels." Denise shrugged and walked away.

But Craig's attitude was beginning to visibly affect Denise. She had always been meticulous in the way she dressed and groomed herself. But, by summer, Denise's family noticed that she hardly wore make-up at all and barely combed her hair. Her regular beauty salon appointments stopped. When Joan asked Denise why she made herself look so plain, Denise told her it was because of Craig.

"He says that when I go to work, I'm not dressing for him. I'm dressing for other people and he doesn't want me to do that," she told her mother.

However, Lori, Denise's cousin, couldn't help noticing that Craig liked to flaunt his own body. It often seemed to her he was making a statement—Hey! Check me out!—even though he forbade Denise to attract any attention by her own appearance. When the Redlick and Kristovich families gathered on July 4 at

Karen's house in Pleasanton, Lori said, "He had on the tightest nylon jogging shorts I've ever seen in my life. All the other men who were there were wearing long pants." She was embarrassed to even look at Craig—who was obviously showing off his tan and trim physique—and she couldn't understand why Denise didn't ask him to change clothes.

"Denise was different around Craig than she had been with any other guys," Chris said. She had always been outgoing, outspoken, but now she was reticent, retiring. Whatever Craig wanted, she seemed to accept. Moreover, she continually made excuses about why she couldn't see her friends.

By July, Denise's friends realized that they hadn't spent any time with her in months. Chris started trying to set up a girls' night out to remedy the situation. Several tentative dates were made, but Denise canceled each of them with different excuses. Finally, Denise asked her girlfriends if they could come to Craig's house for an evening instead. "Craig's going to be out playing racquetball," Denise assured them.

Since that seemed to be the only way to get together with Denise, the girls agreed. But when they arrived at his house, Craig was there after all. Denise vaguely explained, "Craig's friends couldn't meet him at the health club so he's staying home."

Craig retreated to a room at the back of the house but it was as if he was sitting in the living room with them.

"Remember that vacation we took to Las Vegas in 1984," Cindy said smiling.

Denise put her fingers to her lips. "Shhhh!"

Glancing toward the hallway, it was clear that Denise was extremely worried that Craig might hear them and find out about the trip even though it had occurred before he and Denise had met. When Cindy Pacini brought out the photo album from her wedding, Denise couldn't go through the pictures and get the album out of the way fast enough. Obviously, the incident that had caused Denise and Craig to argue at the wedding was still a sore subject.

When Denise's friends drove away that night, they agreed that something was wrong with Denise's relationship. They talked about whether they should tell Denise how they felt, but decided not to do it. After all, Denise was old enough to decide how she wanted to live her life and with whom.

In August, Debi Ronzani, who hadn't seen very much of Denise over the past year, finally met Craig Anderson for the first time. She invited Denise and her fiance over to her house for dinner so that Craig could get to know her husband, Randy.

As the four of them sat around the dinner table, Debi innocently asked "Where do you plan to spend your honeymoon?"

"I'd like to go to Hawaii," Denise replied, smiling.

Craig was incredulous. "Why would anyone in their right mind want to go to Hawaii?" he chided Denise. "I know that place like the back of my hand. It's boring." Craig said it would make a lot more sense to honeymoon in Europe since he could speak several languages.

"I didn't know that," Denise interrupted.

Craig did not answer her, but rushed on, "Hawaii's out of the question."

Denise wordlessly nodded, once again giving in.

Clearing the dishes, Denise gave Debi an embarrassed, apologetic look as if to say I'm sorry he's being this way.

Later, in the kitchen, Debi whispered to Randy, "I wish I hadn't even asked."

When Michele, who had gotten to know Craig better than any of Denise's friends, learned that Denise and Craig were going to spend another summer weekend together at the cabin in Svedahl, she suggested that it was a good time for Denise to get everything out into the open, to tell Craig that she had a mind of her own. Michele was hopeful that, this time, Denise might straighten things out.

When Michele and Denise talked on the phone a few days later, Denise thanked her, saying that she and Craig had, in fact, talked about the problems in their relationship and that "everything was going to be fine now."

But Michele wasn't so sure. She felt that there were things that Denise wasn't sharing with her, probably because she knew Michele, in return, would give her advice she wasn't willing to hear.

CHAPTER FIVE

Increasing Tension

■ **6 A.M.**

By the time the sun had risen, Joan had made numerous calls to people she thought might have some idea where Denise could be, including Lori, Michele and Chris, and even her ex-boyfriend, Art Thomas.

None of them knew.

Finally, Joan placed another call to Craig.

"Please," she begged, "do you know where Denise is?"

"She's probably out somewhere with her friends," he insisted again, the annoyance in his voice plain.

"That's highly unlikely at six o'clock in the morning," Joan said, her anxiety now escalating into alarm. ■

As the wedding date drew closer, the tension between Denise and Craig seemed to grow. Denise kept attributing it to wedding jitters. One day in early September, Denise's Aunt Carolyn was watching her grandchildren at Lori's house. Lori emerged from the shower to find Joan and Denise, who obviously had been sobbing, in the living room.

"Craig and Denise broke up," Carolyn filled Lori in. "You've got to talk to her."

Lori and Denise went for a long walk and Denise told her

things about Craig that she never admitted before—that he was excessively jealous, demanding of her time and that he had an unreasonable temper. "He's been flaunting his relationship with his old girlfriend, Lucy, while insisting that I don't even look at another guy. We'll probably never get back together," Denise said miserably.

"Denise, it's probably for the better," Lori said. "You really need a guy who will let you be your own person. And Craig," Lori continued, "needs a girl who is content being in his shadow all the time."

But Denise was worried about Craig.

"There will be no one for him to lean on," she said. "What's going to happen to him if I leave him?" She was worried, too, that she wouldn't be strong enough to stay away from him if she did try to break it off for good.

After their long talk, they went back to Lori's house and told Joan and Carolyn that the engagement was off. Denise seemed relieved, Carolyn recalled.

Not too long after, Craig showed up asking if he could talk to Denise.

That night, Craig and Denise spent three hours talking privately in a bedroom. Lori asked over and over what was going on. "Are they *still* in there?" she asked exasperated.

When they emerged hand in hand, Denise took her aunt aside and told her that they had patched things up and that they were going to get married after all.

"I was very disappointed," Carolyn said. But she kept her feelings to herself. "To me, Denise never really seemed happy when she was with Craig. I told Joan once, she just doesn't glow the way someone in love should glow."

In the fall, Craig booked honeymoon reservations at Las Brisas, the Acapulco resort where each of the expensive suites overlooking the Pacific ocean has its own swimming pool. Meanwhile, Joan began to plan the wedding. She noticed that Denise seemed to shy away from working out the details. Finally, it was Joan and Harry who decided the ceremony would be held at Our Lady of Angels Catholic Church in Burlingame, Craig's family's parish, followed by a reception for three hundred twenty-five

guests with hors-d'oeuvres, champagne, an open bar, a sit-down
dinner and dancing at the Clarion Hotel in Millbrae.

From the beginning, Craig made it clear he preferred to have
the wedding reception at a country club, not a common hotel,
but, since Joan and Harry were paying for the entire celebration,
they settled for the best they could afford. In mid-September, with
the engraved invitations ready to be addressed, Denise was on
pins and needles wondering if Craig was going to marry her at all.

One day, Denise called her sister-in-law, Lynn, and said she
needed to talk to her about Craig. Denise arrived at Lynn's apartment, shaking.

"Sit down and have some dinner with us," Lynn said.

"I'm too upset," Denise replied tensely. "Craig is being so
uncooperative about the wedding plans. He's refused to draw up
his list of people to invite to the wedding. I think maybe he wants
to back out."

"That's strange," Lynn mused. "Why should he act like that?
What's wrong with him?"

Denise shook her head miserably, tears coming into her
eyes.

"Denise," Lynn said quietly, "are you still sure you even want
to marry Craig? You ought to think carefully about what you're
getting into."

But Denise was adamant about going through with the plans.
"I couldn't call it off again," Denise declared, referring to her first
broken engagement to Art. "Besides, when Craig and I are alone
together, everything is perfect. It's just when other people—especially men—are around that he becomes a different person."

Time was running out to get the invitations ready and Joan
had lost her patience with the situation. She called Craig and invited him to dinner, asking him to bring along his guest list. As if
there had never been a problem, Craig said, "oh, sure," and
showed up for dinner that night looking embarrassed but re-
solved, list in hand.

"Everything is fine now," Denise said later to Lynn. "I was
the one who was making a problem out of it, not Craig."

But her mother knew Denise was rationalizing, once again
trying to attain the domestic bliss she wanted so badly. By then,

Denise had revealed to Joan that Craig had threatened several times to cancel the wedding.

"He's so nervous," she said sadly. "Everything will be going along fine then suddenly he tells me, 'You'll see, I'll be history. I'll walk right out of this.'"

One such threat grew out of Craig's claim that he was receiving anonymous calls from a woman who was telling him that Denise had been a tramp before she met Craig and that he ought to find out what kind of sleazy life she had led. Joan didn't learn about these calls until she heard Chris, who was visiting, telling the person on the phone, "You better stop what you're doing."

After Chris left, Joan called Denise into the bedroom. "What on earth is going on?" Then, it all came pouring out.

"Mom, some girl is calling Craig at work and telling him terrible things about me," Denise said. "Everytime he gets one of these calls, he clams up and won't even talk to me. He's really upset and he's even thinking about calling off the wedding." Denise said that she had asked Chris to make an anonymous call to the girl they believed was calling Craig and tell her to back off.

Joan was angry. When Craig came over for dinner, she confronted him. "Craig, this person obviously has problems," she said. "Why don't you just hang up?"

Craig grew oddly silent and stared at her for a long while. Then he stormed out of the house. Denise, crying, ran after him.

Eventually, Craig said that the calls stopped. It was many months later that Joan came to believe that Craig had fabricated the story about the caller.

There were many times that Joan intervened to sort out problems in the relationship. Although Craig acted contrite and sweet with Denise's parents, and professed to love Joan and Harry, he seemed to resent Denise's closeness with her parents, especially her mother. He began to reproach Denise for being immature and unable to make up her own mind without turning to her parents or her friends for help. To one of his old girlfriends, Craig called Denise a "mama's girl."

Joan apprehensively watched as Denise became more and more withdrawn from her family. "But I thought she was just breaking away from us," she said, trying not to let the change in her daughter bother her.

On the day Denise and Joan went to pick up her wedding dress, Denise was strangely quiet. Joan looked intently at her daughter and asked point-blank, "Are you absolutely sure you want to marry Craig? You can back out, Denise. Don't feel as though you have to go through with it."

"Yes, mom, I'm absolutely sure," Denise insisted, not meeting her mother's eyes, "I'm going to marry Craig."

■ CHAPTER SIX ■

The Break Up

■ Tuesday 7:30 A.M.

Joan called the Bank of America to ask for Charles, Denise's friend and co-worker.

"Charles, did you see Denise last night?" Joan asked.

Charles said that, much to his surprise, Denise had never contacted him as she promised.

"Tell her to call me immediately if she comes into work," Joan said.

When she hung up from talking to Charles, there was only one call left to make—to the San Bruno Police Department.

Her husband's name was quite familiar to them. A former city school board trustee and a current planning commissioner, Harry was acquainted with many of the officers as well as the police chief. He knew the police department number by heart, but his hand was shaking so badly that he had to dial the number twice to get it right.

Harry's voice broke when he said to the police dispatcher who answered, "My daughter, Denise Redlick, is apparently missing."

Perhaps it was their knowledge of him or perhaps it was his ominous tone which made them respond instantly.

Officer Thomas Harrington arrived at the Redlick's house twenty minutes later. He asked the Redlicks some basic information on Denise—her age, height, weight, coloring and occupation—

41

and then listened to Harry and Joan describe the assumed disap-
pearance of their daughter.

In his report, Harrington noted that, according to the parents,
the "missing person's" failure to return home without notifying her
parents was "very much out of character." He also wrote that "the
victim" had been planning to be married the coming Saturday but
that she had broken up with her fiance in early October.

"The parents of the victim advise that on at least one occa-
sion, the ex-fiance has struck the victim," Harrington wrote. The
officer noted that Denise Redlick took no extra clothing or personal
items from her home although she had numerous credit cards in
her possession.

Not long after Harrington left, John Kristovich, Carolyn's hus-
band, joined the somber vigil.

Too impatient to wait for the police to call with information,
Harry and John, who had been a San Francisco police officer for
thirty years before quitting to sell real estate, got in Harry's car and
the two men began their own search.

They drove up and down El Camino Real, circling around the
parking lots at Mervyns in Millbrae, the Tanforan Shopping Center
in San Bruno and the Hillsdale Shopping Center in San Mateo
where Denise might have stopped to run errands. One time, years
earlier, John's own car was stolen and by persistently driving
around, he finally found it. Harry figured that his white Triumph
with its black top would be easy to spot. But they did not see a
single car that resembled the missing vehicle. ■

On September 28th, with the wedding only seven weeks away,
Frances Bellantoni hosted a bridal shower for her granddaughter
Denise at the Brentwood Lodge in South San Francisco. Around
forty women, mostly relatives and close family friends, were invited to the luncheon.

Denise arrived with Craig who, most of the women observed,
was charming and friendly, walking around to the tables to say
"Hello" to each of the women and to give those he knew well a
kiss or a hug.

But Carolyn thought that her niece looked terrible. She wore no make-up and the gray shapeless dress she wore made her look frumpy. She sensed that Denise was unhappy, but Denise, as usual, said nothing to suggest that anything was wrong.

After the shower, Craig and Denise drove to San Francisco to attend the wedding of a friend of Craig. At the reception, a Crestmoor graduate who had played football with Michael Redlick approached Denise.

"Aren't you Michael Redlick's sister?" the handsome young man asked her. They chatted briefly and he asked her to dance.

After the music stopped and Denise began to leave the dance floor, she was shocked to hear Craig call out in a loud voice, "So, have you fucked him, too?"

Denise became immediately defensive and angry. "I haven't done anything. Why are you acting like this?" she cried. She ran to the women's restroom where she became sick to her stomach.

Shirley Anderson, Craig's mother, ran in after Denise to console her future daughter-in-law. Within minutes, Craig, who was waiting outside for Denise to emerge, got impatient and barged in.

"I want to leave here now, but not with you, Craig," Denise whispered through her tears. A woman she knew came into the restroom, and Denise asked for a ride.

But Craig stepped in. "I'm your escort and nobody else is going to take you home," he insisted.

Still sobbing, Denise ran outside with Craig at her heels. Catching up with her, he pushed her up against the building. Denise's head hit the side of the building with a thud, knocking off one of the delicate gold earrings given to her by her mother. It was never found. Finally, Denise and Craig got into her car with Craig behind the wheel and he began driving toward Highway 101.

Denise begged Craig, "Please. Either let me out or drive me to my parents' house."

Craig did not answer, but drove toward his home in San Carlos. Denise, now frightened and irrational, began to beat on his shoulder. "Let me out of here!"

"You're out of control, you bitch!" he yelled back.

Suddenly, he reached out with his right hand and lashed Denise across the face. When he drew his arm back, he kept on talking as if nothing out of the ordinary had happened. Cowering in the corner, Denise let him drive her to his house. By morning they had made up again, but Denise was still hurt and confused. Later that day, she went with Craig to a party for his grandmother and soberly accepted congratulations on her forthcoming wedding.

Joan and Harry had returned from a birthday party for their one-year-old grandson when a friend of Shirley Anderson's telephoned. "Is Denise all right?" the caller, the same woman who had set up Craig and Denise's first date, asked.

Joan was perplexed. "I haven't seen her since yesterday. Why do you ask?"

That's when Joan learned that there had been a problem between Craig and Denise at the wedding on Saturday. But the caller wasn't exactly sure what happened, only that she had seen Denise sobbing in the restroom and that Craig looked furious.

Joan hung up and immediately called Shirley Anderson who couldn't shed much more light on the argument. Shirley was obviously upset too. "I love Denise," she said, "like a daughter. She's such a wonderful influence on my son. If he screws this relationship up too, I'll never speak to him again."

Puzzled at her words, Joan made one more call, this time to Denise at Craig's house. "Is everything okay, honey?" Denise insisted that it was, and instantly changed the subject. But when Joan hung up, she told Harry, "Denise doesn't sound right. She's too quiet."

Joan couldn't put her feelings about Denise out of her mind. There was one question she had to ask Denise, but she wanted to make sure Craig wasn't there at the time. First thing the next morning, she called Denise at the bank. When Denise came to the phone, she was crying.

"Denise, did he hit you?" Joan asked dreading the answer.

"He did, mom," Denise reluctantly responded.

"Denise, we've got to talk about this," Joan said quickly.

Denise agreed and both women immediately left their jobs and met at the house in San Bruno where Denise, still sobbing, described what had happened at the wedding and on the drive to San Carlos.

Joan was outraged. "You've got to stay here with us," she pleaded with Denise.

By mid-day, Craig, who had been trying to reach Denise at the bank, called the Redlick's house looking for her. Joan refused to put her daughter on the phone.

"You bastard, you hit my daughter, didn't you?" Joan demanded.

Craig made no attempt to deny it.

"That's it. It's over!" Joan declared. "I won't allow her to talk to you again."

But when Joan hung up, Denise told her mother she felt concerned about Craig, about how he was going to handle the break-up. "You've got to go talk to him, mom," she begged.

So Joan drove to San Carlos and knocked on Craig's door. When he answered, it looked as if he had been crying, too.

Joan was there for more than an hour. She asked Craig what had gone wrong in his relationship with her daughter and how things could have been different. It was obvious he regretted what he had done, but Joan was not convinced that he had the ability to keep himself from letting it happen again.

"Why are you so jealous around her?"

Craig didn't agree with the observation. "I'm really not a jealous person, Joan," he said.

"Oh yes, you are," Joan insisted.

Craig looked away, seeming deep in thought. "There's something about Denise. It's not that she's a flirt, but even when she's just sitting there, there's something about her that attracts other men."

Joan thought that was odd. "What do you mean, Craig?"

But Craig couldn't put it into words. "It's just something that she does," he insisted.

"Craig, there's nothing wrong with men looking at Denise. You should take it as a compliment when someone finds the girl you are going to marry attractive," Joan told him. "Harry is happy when someone finds me attractive. That's part of the way things are in a good relationship."

Craig shook his head and didn't meet her eyes.

He doesn't seem to comprehend what I'm saying, Joan thought. They discussed Craig striking Denise and he said he lost his temper and that it would never happen again.

"Joan, I've never hit a woman before like that. I just don't know what happened."

When Joan left Craig's house that day, she felt sad for Denise that all her plans for the future had been shattered. But she knew that it was better to find out now that Craig Anderson, despite the Mercedes, the elegant home and the successful business, wasn't the man that Denise should marry.

Over the next few weeks, Denise reluctantly began to inform her friends and relatives that the wedding had been canceled. When she first called Lynn and Mike to tell them what had happened and that she had moved back home, they were relieved.

"She sounded very calm and self-assured," Lynn said. "Denise had always valued the opinions of others. She seemed to need someone to take her under their wing and tell her what to do, but in the week after the break-up, she seemed quite confident."

However, that self-confidence began to crumble. Craig was calling Denise at work, the calls leaving Denise shaking and crying. Sometimes her supervisor and friend, Rossana Hanak, would have to send Denise upstairs to the lunch room to compose herself before she could return to her work station.

On one occasion, Denise and Rossana walked outside to talk and Denise told her that she was afraid Craig might kill himself because he was so distraught over their broken engagement.

"She seems more worried about him than about herself," Rossana remarked to Charles Nan.

In mid-October, Joan suggested that Denise see a counselor to help her sort out her feelings. Denise had three appointments with a psychologist at Kaiser Permanente Medical Center. The psychologist said, to her parents' relief, that while Denise was confused about her relationship with her ex-fiance, she was not a self-destructive person and would certainly not take her own life.

Still, Denise continued to be concerned about Craig's own emotional well-being. When he asked her to meet him for counseling with a priest at the church in Burlingame where they had planned to have their wedding, she agreed. "He needs to talk to someone about this," she told her mother. "I'll go. Maybe it will help him."

Joan drove Denise to the church to meet Craig. The priest wasn't there yet so Craig and Denise sat in his car and waited. Reluctant to leave her daughter alone with her former fiance, Joan waited in her own car across the street. When Denise and Craig finally went inside, they were there for more than two hours. When Denise returned, she told Joan the priest had told them they shouldn't marry or get back together.

But Craig was not yet convinced. During October and early November, he sent Denise several cards and letters professing his love for her.

In one three-page letter he referred to "our possible future together." He said he recognized that he had been the cause of many of their problems and begged her to reconsider.

"Over the last eleven months, you have brought me closer to realizing that I honestly need to let someone share all my thoughts," Craig wrote. "I have always been a very private person and I seem to shy away from telling you exactly how I am feeling. I gradually have been trying to overcome this problem."

Craig said he now realized that he needed to let Denise be involved in the day-to-day decisions, both at work and at home. That would start, he said, with the wedding plans. "I am very willing to let you make any future decision regarding dishware, china, crystal, cake, etc., because as long as I have you, those things, I have realized, are not so important. More than anything, I want you to be happy."

That he missed Denise—emotionally and physically—was clear.

"I have never thought as much about starting a family since you and I met and fell in love. My heart has told me so many times that you would be a fantastic mother for our children." Craig said his "heart" and "spirit" had been broken since they had been apart.

Then he promised to "share all my days with you in the future and I will try my best to not hold anything inside. I will love you dearly for all time."

Another time Craig sent Denise a card imprinted, on the outside, "I need to be HELD, long, close and SOON." Inside he wrote, "Denise—I miss you ever so much. Craig."

And, with a bouquet of red roses that arrived at the Redlicks, he attached a card that simply read: "Love you always. Please marry me as we planned. Craig."

Denise was touched by these expressions of affection. She wanted to believe that Craig was the wonderful, caring person she first had thought him to be, and that the violent episode after his friend's wedding was a single mistake that would not happen again. Several times, lonely and sad, she almost gave in to his persistent pleas, but her family and friends begged her not to listen.

"If Craig really cares about you and sincerely wants you back, he has a funny way of showing it," Joan and Harry counseled.

On the Saturday after the break-up, Denise and Joan drove down to San Carlos to collect Denise's clothing and gifts which had to be returned. Denise found most of the things she wanted but when she opened the closet where the engagement gifts had been stored, they were gone. It wasn't until Denise returned home that she realized she hadn't found her rabbit fur coat, which she had worn to the wedding the previous Saturday, or a ring—given to her by her parents for her 21st birthday—which contained several remounted diamonds from Harry's mother's wedding ring.

Over the next few weeks, Joan called Craig several times asking where the ring, the fur coat and the engagement gifts might be. Each time Craig denied that he had them.

Finally, Harry and Joan drove to San Carlos and confronted Craig. When Craig saw them and found out why they had come, he clenched his fists and turned red just as he had when Joan had confronted him about the anonymous caller.

"I don't have either the ring or the fur coat," he insisted. "As for the engagement gifts, I want to keep them for my future. They're at my mother's house."

The Break Up

Despite Craig's unpredictable behavior, Denise continued to worry about him.

One night, she agreed to meet Craig at the Velvet Turtle in Burlingame for dinner. It was the first time she had seen him in weeks and she was relieved to see he was all right. He gave her a greeting card imprinted, "Missing you and the special times we shared." In it he wrote a note inviting her to join him for a trip to Napa Valley to spend the evening in "the most romantic hotel in the wine country."

"This invitation is not to be mistaken as a commitment for our future," the note continued, "but only as some time to spend together sharing our love, which I know in my heart, we feel so deeply for each other." He signed the card, "My love for you is always on my mind. I'll cherish you forever. Craig."

Denise sorrowfully but gently told him they had no future together and declined the invitation.

That fall, Denise had been helping to plan her five-year high school reunion, scheduled for October 25th. She didn't want to go, but Michele, who drove to San Bruno from Lodi the night before, talked her into it. A suite had been rented at the Hyatt Hotel where the reunion was being held, and the members met there for cocktails. Denise tried to be upbeat when she saw friends that night, but her eyes were weary, her smile strained. She was not the old Denise her friends knew.

On Thursday, Michele, back in Lodi, called. Denise talked about her future trip to New York and told Michele that she and her parents had done everything possible to prevent Craig from finding out that she was leaving. "But I have this spooky feeling," Denise said, "that someone is following me. One night last week when I went out to dinner with a friend, I felt it again."

"Denise, you don't think Craig would hire someone, a private investigator or something, to follow you around, do you?" Michele wondered.

Denise was not surprised by the question. "Oh, probably," she responded sadly. "He's been sending me cards and buying flowers and gifts. He even gave me the pearl necklace that he had planned to give me as a wedding gift."

"Denise, I . . ." There was an awkward silence.

"Look," Denise interrupted, "Let's talk again next week and plan a trip to Club Med in Mexico for late November." It was one more step, Denise had felt, toward getting her life back on a different track. "It's absolutely done," she said of her relationship with Craig. "I know now, for sure, that we'll never get back together." Her voice broke.

When Michele hung up the phone that day, she felt badly for Denise, especially since her own life was going well. She had just started dating someone special and she wished that Denise had found someone special, too. But she was happy that Denise, at last, seemed to have put Craig out of her life for good and knew Denise would go on from there.

Before Denise left work on Friday, November 8th, she made plans to meet the other tellers on Monday night at Rossana's house to watch the Forty-Niners game on television.

"She looked happier than I had seen her in a long time," Rossana later reflected. "It was like the old Denise was back."

Saturday, Denise was on time for her beauty salon appointment at the Headquarters, a Millbrae salon. As the stylist, Yvonne Ronzani worked, Denise talked about her upcoming trip to New York. Yvonne had just sat Denise down at a hair dryer in the back of the shop when a tall, thin man walked in, passed Yvonne and sat down next to Denise. As he approached, Denise had just enough time to say to the hairdresser, "Don't discuss anything in front of him," apparently referring, Yvonne thought, to the New York trip.

Yvonne thought the situation was strange since friends, especially men, seldom dropped in to visit with the patrons. Denise talked with her visitor for a few minutes although Yvonne, who was standing just a few feet away, thought she looked uncomfortable.

"How did you know I was here?" Denise asked the tall, blond man, obviously surprised to see him.

Yvonne, however, did not hear the answer. But she did see the man attempt to hold Denise's hand. Later, the two left the salon together.

Afterward, Denise called her friend Debi with whom she was supposed to have lunch. As she apologized for missing their date,

Denise was weeping. Craig, she said, had come by unexpectedly while she was getting her hair done and they had spent the entire afternoon sitting in his car and talking up near a jogging trail along Crystal Springs Reservoir.

"Let's talk," Debi suggested. "I'll come and get you."

"I'd like that," Denise agreed. "I'm so upset."

Debi picked her up and they drove to Crestmoor High School where they parked and talked for several hours.

Craig, Denise said, had begged her to take him back. "He said he would do anything to get me to marry him," Denise recalled. "But I told him I don't want to see him anymore, that we have to put the past behind us and get on with our own separate lives."

■ Tuesday 2:30 P.M.

By the time Harry and John returned to the house two hours later, knowing nothing more than when they had left, Karen, John and Carolyn's oldest daughter had arrived. Karen, aware of the appointment Denise had on the Monday she disappeared, wondered if John and Harry had looked for the missing car at the Casey Travel Agency where Lori worked.

John and Harry were dismayed by their oversight. Within minutes, they and Karen were back in their car to make the six-mile drive to Burlingame. They arrived just in time to see Denise's little Triumph, hooked to the back of a Hughes Shell station tow truck, being towed away.

San Bruno Police Sergeant Robert Metcalfe had found the car parked about ninety feet from the east entrance to the building. Already at the scene to take the report for the city of Burlingame was Officer James Potter who found no indication that anyone had broken into or tampered with the vehicle. Even the Blaupunkt stereo tape deck and a half dozen cassette tapes were intact.

What immediately struck Harry as odd, knowing Denise's propensity for locking car doors, was Potter's observation that the door on the driver's side was left unlocked.

"Denise never, absolutely never, left her car without locking all the doors," Harry soberly insisted. *"My daughter has met with foul play,"* he declared. *He looked sadly at John. "I know we're never going to see Denise again."* ∎

PART TWO

The Investigation

■ CHAPTER SEVEN ■

Alibis

Tom Chase, Commander of the Burlingame police department's detective bureau, had just returned from lunch on Tuesday afternoon to find that a missing person investigation that had begun in San Bruno that morning had, with the discovery of a car, wound up in his jurisdiction. Chase, a tall, square-jawed man with a no-nonsense manner, had a message to contact Sergeant Robert Metcalfe at the San Bruno department to provide him with the background. Metcalfe, who had just returned to his station from the office building where the Triumph had been located, filled him in.

"Okay, so this one is ours," Chase said. Metcalfe quickly agreed. Just a month earlier, that might not have been the case. Up until then, each of the nineteen municipal police departments in San Mateo County was responsible for missing person reports for people who lived in their jurisdiction. San Bruno police would have proceeded with the search for Denise Redlick. But the chiefs of the departments, at their fall meeting, had agreed that, from that point on, missing person investigations would be handled by the police department in the city in which the apparently suspicious circumstances had occurred.

"There had always been so much confusion in the past in these cases, especially when they involved children," Chase said. In some instances parents might be separated, with the child living off and on in two different homes which, under the old way of doing it, made it difficult to decide which agency was in charge. The new policy was intended to eliminate those uncertainties.

At 3:30 p.m., Harry, John and Karen, still in shock over the realization that they had no idea where Denise might be, were ushered into the detective bureau by Sergeant Jack Van Etten where they were introduced to Commander Chase and Inspector Tom Marriscolo who was slightly pudgy with a friendly, boyish face. As they all solemnly sat at a large table surrounded by detectives' desks, they patiently answered Chase's questions about Denise's credit cards, travel habits, friends and relatives out of the area that she might have gone to visit, and clothing that she was wearing when last seen. But Harry was growing agitated. He was thinking, as relatives of missing persons often do when deluged with seemingly monotonous questions by investigators, "Let's just get this over with and go find my daughter."

As they continued to talk, Van Etten joined in, asking more questions about personal problems that Denise might be having that might cause her to runaway. Harry sighed heavily and told them, as he had told Officer Harrington earlier in the day, about the broken engagement.

"But she was getting over that," he stressed. "She was looking forward to her trip to New York on Thursday."

Karen, an outspoken and opinionated woman, finally couldn't take anymore. She was tired of these officers implying that her cousin, whom she had grown up with and knew as well as her own sister, might simply walk out without leaving a trace. Suddenly she leaned forward, her face reddening and pointed her finger accusingly at Chase.

"Listen," Karen declared, "my cousin did not just disappear. Denise would never have just left like that of her own free will."

Chase quickly shot back, "How can you be sure of that?"

"Because I KNOW my cousin," Karen replied, her finger still wagging in the air. "I've known her all my life. Denise would absolutely, positively not do that!"

Karen's persuasive affirmation would stand out in Marriscolo's mind for years to come.

As the interview wound down, Marriscolo told the family that he would have the Triumph "processed"—examined for fingerprints—that afternoon. But Officer Potter had already told the detectives that he had looked around and under the sports car and had found nothing unusual, only that the driver's door was unlocked and the passenger's door was locked. Potter had then followed in his own patrol car as the Triumph was towed to the basement garage of the Burlingame Police Department.

Chase said, "Mr. Redlick, please provide us as soon as possible with a photograph of Denise that can be distributed to the local news media right away."

Harry grimly agreed.

After Harry, John and Karen had left, Chase sat down with Van Etten and Marriscolo to consider the strange case of the missing San Bruno woman. Where many missing person reports might not generate much activity by a police department until after the person had been gone for several days, something made Chase feel that this case deserved a more prompt response.

"A lot of people disappear because they just want to be by themselves," said Chase who has been involved in hundreds of missing person reports during his law enforcement career. "Ninety-nine percent of the time, the so-called missing person turns up in a day or so. A lot of these people just go away on their own for a short time."

Van Etten and Marriscolo nodded.

"But what we've heard about Denise Redlick is different," he mused. "I suspect that this is not a typical missing person case at all."

Marriscolo leaned forward. "I agree."

"The family felt it was extremely unusual for her to have gone away like this," Chase continued. "I'm impressed by the parents' insistence that Denise always kept them informed about where she went, who she would be with and when she would be home."

"And, when she wasn't able to be home on time, she would call her parents and let them know she was running late," Marriscolo added.

"If you're twenty-three years of age and you have a reputation for being that punctual, still calling your mom to say you'll be late for dinner, then it seems real strange that you would be gone for an entire night without a word." Chase scratched his head and looked off in the distance. "Twenty-seven years of experience in this business has got me thinking that we should move on this right now."

Realizing that the detective who usually investigated missing persons was on vacation, Chase assigned the case to Marriscolo. Then the officers considered the lack of evidence and quickly agreed there was one logical place to begin looking for clues.

From his experience, Chase knew that if something had happened to Denise Redlick, the most likely candidate would be an individual who was close to her. In fact, eighty-five percent of murder victims are killed by someone they know, he reflected. Not that the Burlingame police were, at that point, assuming Denise had been murdered. But Chase decided to "work with the worst possible premise" from the start.

"Let's get the boyfriend out of the picture right away," Chase told Marriscolo. "One of the first things we should do is pin down his activities, have him account for where he was yesterday afternoon."

He looked down at the report. "He's the owner of a shop called Anderson Paint Company in San Carlos." He read on and raised an eyebrow. "I think I know his parents," he murmured." The Andersons lived near me in Burlingame for years. Ron was involved in coaching Little League at the same time that I was active in Burlingame youth sports. And his wife, Shirley, I vaguely remember, was active in the PTA when her children were enrolled in the town's elementary schools." Although he hadn't seen them in years, Chase remarked that the Andersons had seemed nothing short of an "all American family."

Chase phoned Craig Anderson at his shop in San Carlos. Craig seemed neither surprised nor alarmed by the call. The commander explained that Denise Redlick's parents had filed a missing person report.

"We're wondering if you could come by the station tonight to talk about her disappearance," Chase asked Anderson. "You're not a suspect or anything like that, but we think you might know some things about Denise—where she likes to go, what she likes to do—that might help us out."

"Sure," Anderson responded without hesitation. "I was planning to go work out at the gym tonight, but I guess I could come by when I close the shop."

"I'll be there," said Chase, who usually left the office by five o'clock. But he had a feeling that he shouldn't put off the interview a day.

Dressed in a blue jogging suit that zipped up to his neck, Anderson appeared at the station at a little after six p.m. The two men—both more than six feet tall—shook hands as Craig sat down on the other side of Chase's desk.

As Marriscolo and Van Etten secretly observed the interview from behind a two-way mirror in the wall of the commander's office, Chase introduced himself to Denise Redlick's former fiancee.

"Let's talk about this whole thing right now," Chase said, kicking off the interview. Much to his surprise, Anderson responded with a rambling reflection of his recent meetings with Denise, his impressions of her relationship with her family, and his thoughts on their broken engagement.

"When Harry Redlick called me at two in the morning, he woke me up with questions about where Denise might be," Craig said bluntly. "I didn't think that much about it, you know, because I haven't even been with her that much for, I guess, about six weeks."

He recalled having dinner with her the previous Tuesday and parking with her in Millbrae on Saturday when they had, as he remembered it, a nice conversation about their future and "whether we wanted to continue on with this thing."

"It's always been difficult with Denise because she's really indecisive sometimes," he said. "I think, in some ways, the reason the thing blew up is I wasn't patient enough with her. She's, as far as I'm concerned, a lot more immature than someone I'd like to be involved with."

Anderson, easing back in his chair, went on to say that he had sent her flowers and written her letters over the past few weeks but had decided not to put any more pressure on her. He said he had gone to the hair salon on Saturday after calling Denise's house and being told by Joan that Denise was getting her hair done.

"Her parents are the nicest people you'd ever want to meet but the umbilical cord between her parents and her is very strong and, um, I don't really think they influence her that much. They give her a lot of space, but there's a certain amount of pressure there," he declared, adding, "I feel like an outsider." Which was the reason, he said, he thought it would be best if he met Denise somewhere other than her parents' house.

According to Craig, he and Denise left the beauty salon in her mother's car and drove up to Interstate 280, where they parked at the end of Hillcrest Boulevard where it meets Sawyer Camp Trail, and talked for four or five hours.

As they parted, he recalled, Denise said, "I'm almost waiting for someone to tell me the right thing to do 'cause I really don't know what to do. I know that I love you, but I don't think I'm in love with you."

"I held myself back from saying what I wanted to, that 'you know, Denise, you can't turn to mommy and daddy everytime something happens'."

Changing the subject, Anderson explained that they had gotten engaged in February when they traveled to the Bahamas, ten days in "crappy weather" although they never argued and had a wonderful time. He described how well their families hit it off. "Our grandparents love each other to death, and our parents love each other to death." And when he and Denise split up, he felt sorry for Denise's parents, Harry and Joan, because of all the money that had been spent on the wedding. But if their relationship is right, "It's gonna be there a month or two months from now, I felt very positive that she would come around, to be honest with you, and it was just going to be up to me to be patient." He added that he had no animosity or negative feelings toward Denise.

Chase, who had purposefully let Anderson ramble on, finally cut in and asked pointedly, "What do you think, then, happened to her? Got any feelings?"

Anderson did not directly answer the question, instead continuing to talk about Denise's indecisiveness and how her immaturity often made their living together difficult. "Denise," he said, "is used to having her father come home and hug her and say 'well, hi honey, how are you?' and her mother having dinner ready on the table. But, when Denise was staying with him in San Carlos, he had just started a second business—managing a painting crew—and didn't always have time to be affectionate and attentive toward Denise when he came home from work. As a result, she frequently called her parents and shared her personal problems.

"I love the family and they are all the nicest people you ever want to meet, but I think you need a certain amount of privacy, I really started wondering if I wanted that kind of relationship for the future."

At their recent meeting, Anderson claimed Denise had said, "I just wish everyone would leave me alone."

"Maybe she just went away somewhere to try and get her head together," he declared. Craig added that Denise was always very secretive about where she was going, even if she was going out with a girlfriend. It seemed as if he wasn't supposed to know —which really irritated him.

Chase looked at him appraisingly and then casually suggested several possible scenarios for Denise's disappearance—including that she just walked away or "that you took her."

Anderson shook his head. "No," he said calmly, "I'm not at all despondent over the break up. I had, in fact, begun to wonder if I ever really wanted to marry Denise."

Chase, impatient to hear Anderson's explanation for where he had been around the time Denise vanished, turned the conversation in that direction. "I'm wondering if we can hear this a helluva lot quicker if I could find out where you were yesterday."

"Uh-huh. Sure."

"Did you have the paint store open?"

"Um, yeah, I was . . . I'm normally the only one there. I arrived at the shop around 7:45 a.m. and stayed until around 4:30 or 5 p.m. Then I went home to work on remodeling my bathroom until around 6 p.m. Then I went to Long's and bought some soap. Then I came home," he said matter of factly, "took a shower and watched some of the Forty-Niner game. A friend called and we talked for a while. I was there the rest of the night," he added.

"Between noon and when you closed the shop, did anyone

come in and make any purchases?" Chase asked keeping his voice calm and easy.

Craig recalled making three sales that day but noted that, with the "shitty weather" that day, most painters weren't working. He said they were all cash sales and that he only had handwritten receipts. "But someone might have seen me," he said shrugging, "at the Jack-in-the-Box next door or the gas station across the street."

"What about the phone calls?" Chase asked.

Craig said he didn't recall any toll calls ("I'm really tight when it comes to that") and said he spent most of the night doing bookwork and sitting around "like a bump on a log."

Chase leaned toward him, keeping his tone level. "Would you submit to something similar to a lie detector test? It's called a voice stress analysis." He passed a sheet of paper to Anderson. "Here's a list of questions I'll ask." He paused. "The test is a means of eliminating people. To get them the hell out of the way so the investigators can focus elsewhere."

Craig looked at him thoughtfully and nodded.

"The results can't be used in court," Chase added. "All I'm trying to do is clean up a missing person report. We're on the same side, you know." Again Craig nodded as Chase went on. "With the stress test results in hand, I can report to the missing woman's family and to my own boss, Chief Fred Palmer, that you're in the clear."

Craig hesitated. "I haven't even consulted with an attorney," he said appraisingly. "I'm a bit nervous about being the target of so many questions."

"Don't worry," Chase assured him, "being nervous won't alter the test results."

The commander stepped out of the office for a few minutes so that Craig could call his father for advice. Ron Anderson apparently told his son that he should proceed with the test. Chase led Anderson to an interview room where he began to set up the equipment.

The Burlingame Police Department, in 1985, was one of only a few in the Bay Area, and the only one in San Mateo County, using voice stress analysis on a regular basis to interview criminal suspects as well as candidates for jobs. The polygraph (what most people think of as a "lie detector") uses electronic sensors to simultaneously measure automatic changes in cardiovascular rate, respiration and galvanic skin response. For the person being interviewed, the machinery can seem intimidating, even frightening.

Voice stress analysis, however, requires no sensors and can be conducted anywhere a tape recorder can be used. An officer can even tape record a subject in the field and return to the department to run the tape through the analyzer to come up with a stress profile.

The voice exam is based on the belief that miniscule muscle impulses zip through the body, prompting changes in physiological activity. The theory is that the muscle tremors are suppressed or even eliminated in proportion to the degree of stress perceived by the subject and those changes are directly reflected in voice frequencies. The examiner looks for a dozen different types of patterns in graphs of those frequencies. The symmetry of the graphs, called blocking, increases with the amount of stress. However, every individual's pattern is unique and one person's graphs can't be compared to another person's.

"One person's baseline is another person's guilt," according to Sergeant James Eldredge who conducts many of Burlingame's voice stress exams. The department has, in fact, successfully used voice stress to eliminate suspects. In investigating the theft of $1000 at a Burlingame company, all employees with access to company cash were subjected to the voice stress test. Commander Gary Missel, who also is a trained voice stress analyzer, concluded that none of them had taken the money. The employer was skeptical, but had egg on his face when, a few weeks later, the cash was found misplaced in a drawer.

Interspersed throughout the test are several "control" questions (Is today Tuesday? Are you sitting? Is your name Craig?), irrelevant to the investigation at hand, to determine what the interviewee's graph looks like when he is telling the truth. It also includes a question to which the subject is asked to deliberately not tell the truth (In the last six months, have you ever exceeded the speed limit?) so that the examiner can see what kind of pattern is created when the individual tells a known lie.

The responses to these innocuous questions help the examiner analyze the responses to more pointed, meaningful questions.

With a microphone propped on the table in front of him, Craig Anderson was asked several miscellaneous questions and mingled in were straightforward questions about the disappearance of his former fiance.

The questions included:

Do you know how Denise Redlick disappeared?

Did you have anything to do with Denise Redlick's disappearance?

Did you take Denise yesterday?

And, do you know for sure who took Denise?

Craig seemed relaxed and self-assured as the commander read the twenty-eight questions and watched the computer etch the jagged lines that formed a series of graphs. When it was over, Chase thanked Craig for being so cooperative.

"Oh, by the way, it would be helpful, if you could give me the names of some people who saw you at work on Monday," Chase said.

"I'll give you a call tomorrow," Anderson promised as the two men shook hands and parted.

The results of Anderson's voice stress test were, over the next few days, the subject of considerable debate amongst the department's three trained examiners—Chase, Missel and Eldredge— and a fourth examiner from outside the department, a consultant in Los Angeles. Chase reported he didn't see the distinctive blocking that he would expect if Anderson were involved in Denise's disappearance. What confused the issue, he said, was that the graphs displayed some blocking, with patterns on the top or bottom line of each chart, to some degree on irrelevant questions. On the other hand, he also knew that pathological liars, who believe they are telling the truth even when they are lying, may not reveal any stress.

Chase wrote in his report that the voice stress examiners' opinions ranged from Anderson having some knowledge of where Denise might be to his actually spiriting Denise away, directly causing her disappearance.

What seemed far more important than the voice stress interpretations, Chase thought, was the fact that Craig wanted to take the test and seemed to have no apprehensions about it.

Anderson had made a mostly favorable impression on Chase that night. "He sounded as if his scout master and his local priest would come to his aid if he were accused of anything," Chase told Marriscolo the next morning. "He sounded very good. He wasn't the least bit nervous."

Despite this positive impression, when Anderson left the station and slid into the driver's seat of his Mercedes, he was followed. With Tom Marriscolo and Inspector Kevin Collopy in one car and Jan Van Etten in another, a careful block or so behind, Anderson drove east on Millbrae Avenue to Highway 101. Five miles south, he took the Hillsdale Boulevard exit and drove east toward Foster City where he stopped at an Alpha Beta grocery store. Marriscolo, who followed Craig into the store, was intrigued as he watched Anderson compare prices on brands of detergent, toilet paper and canned food. "It took nearly an hour," the officer observed to his partner, "for him to buy two medium-sized bags of groceries. And this guy's got money to burn," the inspector muttered in amazement.

On leaving, the officers tailed Anderson back onto the freeway and south to the Holly Avenue exit from which he drove directly to his home in San Carlos. They sat outside in the cold for an hour or so until Anderson got back in his car and drove to another house a short distance away. The investigators later learned that it was the home of a woman that Craig had been friends with since childhood. After a short visit, Craig drove back home and turned the lights off. Knowing little more about Craig Anderson than they had before leaving the police station, the officers departed.

But when Marriscolo went home that evening, he told his wife, Nancy, about the case and his uneasy feeling that Denise Redlick had met with foul play.

"There was no doubt in my mind that her parents were telling the truth when they said that Denise would let them know where she was every minute of the day," Marriscolo said of the missing woman's family. "I looked at them sitting there at the table and thought that these were not the typical skittish relatives of a kid who simply just takes off and disappears. They were so completely convincing."

And, he admitted, the long rambling conversation between Chase and Anderson had caused him to further wonder about Anderson's sincerity. He felt Anderson had shown far too little emotion about the woman he had supposedly loved enough to marry and that he had never given Chase a straight answer to any single question.

"I just don't see the genuine concern about Denise that should be there," he observed.

Moreover from what he had heard, Denise Redlick wouldn't simply "go off somewhere" as Craig suggested.

"This isn't San Francisco," Marriscolo told his wife. "We just don't have people snatched off the street at random in broad daylight."

Despite Marriscolo's insecurity about him, further information provided by Anderson the following Wednesday morning tended to temper any suspicions that he might be a valid suspect in Denise Redlick's sudden disappearance.

As promised, Anderson called Chase with the names of three men, John Sollor, a painting foreman; Frank Roberts, a painting spray equipment salesman; and Mike Shea, a licensed contractor, who he claimed had seen him at Anderson Paint Company on Monday.

Over the next day, Collopy and Chase would contact all three men; each of them confirmed the information provided by Anderson.

Shea said he had picked up supplies at Anderson's shop at around 9:10 a.m. and returned for more paint, which Anderson mixed, at noon. Sollor, who was painting a house in San Carlos when the officers found him, said he saw Craig Anderson at the store between 3:45 and 4:15 p.m. Roberts said he found Anderson alone at the shop around 4:30 p.m.

His alibis seemed perfect. Furthermore, Anderson invited Chase to search his house before Chase could even ask.

"The circumstances, you know, might make somebody think I wanted to do something to her," Anderson told Chase on the phone. "If you want to take a look inside, be my guest."

"I'd like to do that," Chase said. "I'll just wait around until you close up the shop and meet you there, say around 5:50 p.m."

"No, no, Tom," Anderson said. "You can go on up there ahead of me. Stop by here and pick up the key. Just promise to be careful and not to "mess things up."

Chase accepted the offer and went to the brick-covered, ranch-style house alone. He opened the door to find it immaculate although spartanly furnished. Slowly he walked from room to room and then into the garage and out to the patio in the yard. He noticed that, as Craig had indicated during their talk the night before, the bathroom was being remodeled. A wall had obviously been partially stripped down to the plaster and removed.

Chase later wrote in his report, "I did search Anderson's house, garage and grounds, specifically for a body, with negative results."

With three witnesses to vouch for Anderson's activities on Monday and with nothing out of the ordinary found at his home, Craig Anderson—up until then, the only logical suspect in Denise Redlick's disappearance—no longer appeared to be a suspect.

■ CHAPTER EIGHT ■

Dead Ends

Within twenty-four hours of the Triumph being found on Old Bayshore Highway, the search for Denise Redlick had evolved into the most comprehensive missing person investigation in which the Burlingame Police Department had ever been involved.

"I'm taking you off everything else," Chase told Inspector Marriscolo. "I want you on this case full time." The commander began doling out daily assignments to all five detectives in the bureau. This was a search in which no stone would be left unturned.

On Wednesday morning, Burlingame police officers began knocking on doors and thumbing through stacks of phone directories to contact any individual, agency or business that might have had some contact with Denise Susan Redlick, dead or alive, since 1:40 p.m. on Monday.

Her name was immediately entered into every computer system available that helps law enforcement agencies track down missing persons. Among them was the Police Information Network subject file which covers nine San Francisco Bay Area counties. If Denise Redlick came in contact with a police officer and her identification was entered into the PIN subject file, the officer would be instructed to contact Inspector Tom Marriscolo at the Burlingame Police Department before letting her go. The subject file is a means of finding anyone from a reluctant witness to a crime suspect. Denise's name was also logged into the National

Crime Information Center, a system primarily used to notify police departments across the country when a warrant has been issued for an individual's arrest and extradition is desired. But the system can also be used to locate missing persons.

However, if Denise Redlick were alive and simply "out there somewhere," finding her through either method would not be guaranteed, Chase realized. The police officer who detains someone must take the initiative to ask for a check with either system. Furthermore, Denise would have to make a mistake, running a red light, for example, that would attract the attention of a police officer. A very law-abiding person—and Denise appeared to be just that—is not likely to turn up through such methods. Filing her name, Chase sadly realized, was probably nothing more than a formality.

Gently, Marriscolo approached Harry Redlick on Wednesday afternoon and asked him to sign a release so that Denise's dental records—used to make positive identification of deceased crime victims—would be immediately available if they might be needed.

One of Jack Van Etten's first assignments was to contact people who occupy offices overlooking the eastern or front parking lot in the three-story complex on Bayshore Highway. Van Etten visited seventeen suites including the coffee shop on the first floor where Denise and Lori had lunch on Monday.

In one suite, John Vorese, looking at a flyer with Denise's picture, told Van Etten that he had seen the missing woman between 11:30 a.m. and 12:30 p.m. on Monday in the lunch room. More interestingly, he said he thought he might have passed her as he walked out of the main entrance of the building heading toward the eastside parking lot at around 1:00 p.m. He remembered her long, black, coat-like sweater. But Vorese was unable to provide any other useful information.

In another suite, Carol Omar told Van Etten she had stopped by her office around 9:15 a.m. on Sunday, November 10th, and had noticed a man, perhaps thirty to forty years old, average height and weight, with brown, medium length hair and, "bug eyes," wearing a light tan overcoat, lurking inside the building near the door. Omar said the unfamiliar man acted strangely by staring at her and she found it unusual for anyone to be standing at that location at the time. Furthermore, she had noticed no delivery trucks in the lot that he might have arrived in. The man, she told the sergeant, was still there when she left the building a few minutes later.

But Van Etten was unable to gather any further information about the suspicious man in the tan overcoat and the lead was soon abandoned.

Officer Potter, assigned to question passersby at the Bayshore building, came across a delivery man who had been at the same location around 1:15 p.m. Monday. The delivery man recalled that there was only one other vehicle, a black van, possibly a Ford or Chevy, moving through the lot at the time he arrived, forcing him to move his own delivery van to let the driver by. It was an older model with a flat rather than protruding front end, and it was plain, with no distinctive markings or painted designs or windows. The delivery man also remembered the driver—a man with dark hair and a moustache wearing a white T-shirt. Potter wrote down the name, address and phone number of the possible witness although the investigative team would later dismiss the information as another of many false leads.

Based on the assumption that Denise might have simply gone away somewhere to think about things, Van Etten also went to nine hotels and inns in Burlingame, which has more rooms for tourists and visitors than any other city in the county, and neighboring Millbrae. He distributed fliers and checked for room rentals under Redlick's name. The results, he wrote in his report, were negative.

It was also Van Etten's task to contact taxi companies that provide service in Burlingame. Did a woman fitting Denise's description take a taxi from the Bayshore building, leaving her car behind? Logs were checked for Checker Cab, Yellow Cab, Luxor Cab and Town Taxi, none of which had any pickups on Monday at the office building. Van Etten left a batch of fliers at each company office to be distributed to the taxi cab drivers.

In another long-shot effort to come up with a clue, the sergeant contacted the operations director for SamTrans, the country wide bus system on California Drive in Burlingame. Van Etten had an official identify the bus routes that would have had stops on Bayshore Highway on Veterans Day. He learned that route 78 travels north and south past the office building while route 3B has a stop just a quarter mile away at the intersection of Millbrae Avenue and Old Bayshore. But the drivers of the buses had not seen any woman resembling Denise. Van Etten again deposited a stack of fliers.

Meanwhile, Inspector Collopy had been contacting local hospitals, including their psychiatric units, for admissions under the name Denise Susan Redlick. There were none.

Chase also began checking credit card companies to determine if any of Denise Redlick's accounts had been used since Monday afternoon. All eight companies reported that her accounts had been inactive.

When Joan Redlick went to the Bank of America to take care of some business, she was greeted by several tellers who knew Denise and had been following the tragic news.

"Mrs. Redlick, we're all hoping and praying that there will be a big withdrawal from Denise's account," said one of the tellers.

"I'll be celebrating if that happens," Joan responded with a smile of gratitude. But, as the days passed, the balance on Denise's savings account never changed.

Three weeks later when the commander checked the same list, all of the accounts were still dormant. By then it had become more and more apparent that the missing young woman had lost complete contact with the world she had known.

With the extensive publicity concerning Denise's disappearance, the police department dispatchers began keeping track of their unsolicited leads on "tip sheets." Each sheet indicated the caller's name and address, date and time called, description of the "suspect" and "suspect vehicle," and a brief comment on the suspicious circumstances. In the first few weeks, calls came in every day. While some were so vague that there was little the officers could do to investigate further, many provided enough information to make a return call and that call often led to others.

Many of the "tips" were from women in the Burlingame area who had become, as a result of stories about Denise, exceptionally suspicious of men who approached them under unusual circumstances. In fact, it was shocking to discover just how many such incidents occurred. One such call came from an attractive, thirty-ish Burlingame woman who, on November 5th, had been driving her car on Highway 101 near San Bruno Avenue when a man in a Cadillac El Dorado pulled alongside her, flashed a badge through the window and signaled for her to pull over to the side of the freeway.

There, he told her he was a narcotics officer for the "State Police." He engaged her in conversation for nearly an hour, bragging that he had a machine gun in his trunk and had kept some of the dope he had confiscated in the raids. By the time he drove away, he had convinced her to give him her business card so that he could call her to arrange a date in the near future.

The woman said she thought the officer's behavior was odd and unprofessional, but she kept it to herself out of fear he might lose his job if she reported him to the authorities. When she saw a flyer about Denise and realized the stranger had stopped her only a short distance from where the missing woman's car was found, she decided to call the police.

Officer Potter interviewed the woman on November 14th. She was able to provide a good description of the man who had approached her, including the type of glasses and jewelry that he had been wearing that day.

The tip was mentioned in a television news update about the search for Denise. That prompted a second tip from a San Mateo businesswoman who said that one of her clients could very well be the man impersonating a "State Police" officer and that the client had, one recent day, followed one of her female employees to her home. That time, he claimed to be a Burlingame cop and had given her his address.

Within a few hours, Marriscolo identified a guard who fit the description provided by both women. The guard, on leave at the time, adamantly denied using his badge to pick up women and agreed to take a voice stress exam given by Chase. Chase concluded that the guard had nothing to do with Denise Redlick's disappearance at the end of their interview.

That the stories about Denise spooked other women in the

area was apparent to Marriscolo. Another call came from a woman who worked in a building on Airport Boulevard on the Bay front. She was returning to work after her lunch hour when a man walked up to her window in the parking lot and said, in a matter of fact manner, "Get in my car." The woman snatched a quick glance at the man's license plate number and sped away. Two days later, Collopy tracked down the registered owner of the vehicle who said he might have talked to the woman who filed the report, but denied that he had ordered her to get in his car. Collopy snapped a Polaroid picture of the suspect and later showed it to the frightened woman who was positive that he was the man who had approached her.

Collopy warned him about his threatening action. But he concluded that, like the state prison guard, the man had nothing to do with Denise.

Amid the many tips the officers investigated were tips that bordered on the bizarre or completely unbelievable. There were many who said they had seen a woman resembling Denise, sometimes driving a car and sometimes as a passenger in a car. One caller was certain he saw Denise in San Francisco. Another man was certain that the woman who waited on him at a restaurant in Lafayette, a city across the Bay just east of Oakland, was Denise. Marriscolo asked the Contra County Sheriff's Department to check out the report and concluded it had no merit. A man called from the Russian River resort town of Guernville, eighty miles north of San Francisco, claiming that he had seen Denise with two black men. Marriscolo sent out a teletype to the area, but the tip proved to be just another dead end.

A San Francisco security guard called about a blonde woman he saw sitting on a box in the back of a white Chevy van in which two white men occupied the front seat. The scene aroused his suspicions because she appeared to be very uncomfortable, he said.

Another tip came from a Hillsborough man who had been at the airport to see his sister off and had noticed a young couple who boarded the same place at the last minute. The man had a tight grip on the woman's arm. She looked like Denise Redlick and she had quite obviously been crying.

Another caller said he picked up a "dazed" female hitchhiker in San Jose and he was certain that she was the missing San Bruno woman.

One caller said he had grown up with Craig Anderson and that he had heard Anderson was pouring concrete for a backyard patio on the day after Denise disappeared. The possibility that the patio was a cover-up for a murder wasn't as far-fetched as it might sound. Just a few years before, a man had been convicted of burying his victim under a freshly poured backyard patio. Marriscolo and Collopy drove to San Carlos and while Craig was at work, quickly ascertained that his patio had been there long before Denise's disappearance.

The officers investigated as many tips as they could. Most were useless. There were times that Marriscolo could only scratch his head in disbelief at the wild stories that came his way like the woman who called, in total seriousness, about her dream.

"I dreamed that the person who took Denise ate the body and buried the bones," she told the dispatcher who dutifully scribbled the message.

The grimmest task facing both the professionals and volunteers in the struggle to learn the fate of Denise Redlick was the search for a body.

Chase directed one of his detectives, Sergeant Buzz Kruttschnitt, to conduct the first of the foot searches that Thursday. For three hours, Kruttschnitt led four officers and an intern in a search around the area where Denise was believed to have disappeared. The crew walked along the rocky bayfront shoreline, paying special attention to inlets and storm runoff pipes adjacent to Old Bayshore Highway from the north city limit southward to where the highway joins Airport Boulevard and juts eastward at an angle on bayfill. They also scanned drainage ditches, dumpsters, storage areas behind buildings, and the dense foliage in several bayside parks. They returned to the police station with no items of evidence and no new leads.

Pat Chavez, with Community Outreach, had worked with the Contra Costa County Sheriff's Department's Search and Rescue unit in the past since she was from that side of the bay. Chavez arranged to have the unit send its bloodhound team to San Mateo County to assist in the search for Denise.

Stephen Andrews, a Contra Costa sheriff's reserve, and members of his all-volunteer search team met Marriscolo at the Redlick's house on Friday afternoon. Andrews explained to Joan and Harry that they would begin by searching the "point last seen," the office building from which Denise had vanished. But the bloodhounds needed to become familiar with the highly specific scent of the missing person. The handlers would need several items of Denise's clothing.

Joan didn't hesitate. She quickly went to Denise's room and returned to the living room with two of her daughter's sweaters. She and Harry declined, however, to observe the search. Instead, several of Denise's friends piled into their cars and followed Andrews and his crew to Old Bayshore Highway.

The two black and brown bloodhounds enlisted for the search, Emma and Solo, resembled basset hounds, with the same sagging jowls, but weigh more than one hundred pounds each. Each breed of search dog has a particular proficiency. The breed used by Contra Costa is particularly capable of city work, while other dogs are at their best in mountainous terrain. Each bloodhound has its own characteristic way of indicating that it is hot on the trail. Some will hold their heads up while some drop their heads. In others, the tail will stand up straight like an antenna. Some, Andrews said, will work slowly and methodically, while others will take off at a brisk clip.

"When they do, you better have your tennis shoes on because it's hard to keep up," Andrews explained.

The important advantage of using bloodhounds, rather than German shepherds and some other dogs favored by search and rescue teams, is that their ability to discriminate a scent comes naturally.

At the Bayshore building, handler Bev Mestressat, standing at the front door, held a sweater in front of Emma's big, black nose. The dog sniffed it several times and then wandered off with Bev, holding the ten foot leash to which the hound was harnessed, close behind.

Emma walked in a slow but deliberate line from the doorway to the parking lot, roughly to the location where the Triumph sports car had been parked, where she seemed to lose interest in the scent. While her pattern didn't tell the investigators anything new, it did help confirm what had been suspected—that Denise did get as far as her father's car.

Then, the searchers drove up the hill to Skyline Boulevard, the old north-south route through the county that was supplemented by the adjacent eight-lane Interstate 280 in the 1960s, and gathered under the shadow of the Doran Bridge, a spectacular freeway crossing over San Mateo Creek where it enters Crystal Springs Reservoir. The location had been selected for the search because it was believed to be near where Denise and Craig had parked for four hours the previous Saturday to talk about their relationship. With a small group of searchers joining Bev and Emma and a second group accompanying handler Judy Robb and her bloodhound, Solo, the search—linked by radio transmitters—got underway.

After again familiarizing themselves with Denise's scent, the dogs began silently "working a scent" north along Skyline Boulevard until reaching a freeway onramp. On the return trip back to the command post, both dogs began showing a great deal of interest, by arching their heads and maneuvering their handlers toward the west side of the road, closer to the reservoir which is surrounded by dense manzanitas and other shrubs. When the dogs reached an aquaduct about one-quarter mile west of Skyline, their level of interest seemed most intense.

After the dogs had returned to the command post, Andrews led six search and rescue volunteers back to the aquaduct to conduct a "grid search" of the area without the dogs. But they were unable to find anything relevant to the search for Denise Redlick.

On Saturday, San Mateo County's own volunteer team got its chance to conduct a major search. Marriscolo contacted Dave Hayes, a detective with the San Mateo County Sheriff's Office, to request the team's assistance.

The county S & R unit relies heavily on trained volunteers, both teenage Explorer Scouts and adults, many of whom are graduates of the Explorer team, to conduct around a dozen or so searches every year at the request of various law enforcement agencies. In most cases, the target of the search is a crucial piece of evidence, like a bloody knife tossed out of a car window on Highway 101. But the unit had, over the years, also scored several successful body searches.

Hayes and Larry Boss, another Sheriff's detective involved in S & R, contacted the volunteers who were briefed by Marriscolo at Burlingame Police Department at 9 a.m. on Saturday. Then, the search party traveled in a convoy of sheriff's department trucks to the Burlingame landfill site about a mile south of the building where Denise was last seen. As they entered the gate, they were confronted by gigantic hills of smelly, decaying garbage accumulated over many years. It was the unit's first extensive search through a dump and it was not a particularly pleasant task.

Armed with shovels and racks to sift through the top layer of garbage, the seven Explorer Scouts and two adult volunteers were stationed around the perimeter of the site and instructed to work their way to the center.

Meanwhile, Marriscolo was directing another group of searchers that was scanning an area along the bayside south of the dump. Using Explorers and police reserves, they traversed selected areas of Sawyer Camp Trail. The Explorers, retracing an area covered by the Contra Costa dog team on Friday, found a coyote jawbone which, Marriscolo noted, was completely consistent with what the dog team's leaders had expected to find.

That day alone more than one hundred volunteer hours were spent in the search for Denise Redlick. Yet, they were no closer to finding the missing woman.

Although Tom Marriscolo had never met Denise Redlick, he began to feel that he had known her all his life.

A consummate investigator with an exceptional interest in technical details, he is also a compassionate person who believes that, in a case as serious as this one, the detectives couldn't know too much about the apparent victim.

"I strongly believe that you've got to get to know that person, really get inside his or her mind," Marriscolo said. With the cooperation of Denise Redlick's parents and friends, he was doing just that. "Some of the things I did made some of the guys I work with think I was a little goofy," he added. But what he learned about Denise Redlick strengthened his conviction that Denise had not just simply disappeared.

On Saturday afternoon, Marriscolo asked Joan and Harry to leave the house so he could spend a few hours privately in Denise's room. Once alone inside, he thumbed through her high school yearbooks, reading thoughtful and flattering notes that had been written to her by both male and female friends. He read the details of her diary which he found filled with upbeat reflections on outings with her relatives and girlfriends. Surprisingly, little was written about Craig Anderson. He turned the pages of her photo albums and noticed how she had just as many pictures of her relatives, including her parents, as she did of her close friends.

Another night, Marriscolo spent nearly four hours chatting with Michele, Chris and Debi. With Marriscolo's encouragement, the girls talked about Denise's personal life, about the men she dated, about the crazy things she and her girlfriends had done over the years, and about her goals in life. He left the room that night feeling that Denise was an extremely responsible and cautious person.

On Sunday, Marriscolo drove his car to 1633 Bayshore Highway where he slowly walked around and inside the building, trying to sense how Denise might have felt and what she might have encountered as she walked away from the travel agency on November 11th. When he left there and returned to the police station to write up reports, he glanced at the photograph of Denise on his desk and suddenly felt sad and depressed. Before he left the office he made one last call, as had become his nightly custom, to Joan Redlick.

When he got home at 10 o'clock that night, he told Nancy, "Denise Redlick is dead. I'd stake my life on it."

If Craig Anderson was trying to hide anything from the Burlingame police, he was doing a masterful job of it. But despite his voluntary submittal to the voice stress analysis and his verified list of alibi witnesses, Chase felt that Craig might know more about Denise's disappearance than was apparent. Throughout the first week after Denise vanished, Commander Chase ordered his detectives to continue their surveillance of Craig's activities.

The location of his house, on a corner in a quiet neighborhood, made it difficult to observe it for any length of time without being noticed. After a few days, the officers suspected that Anderson knew he was being watched. One night, he drove to a friend's house, went inside, came out, got in another car and drove home as if he were trying to confuse anyone who might be watching him. On another night, he stepped outside onto his walkway, looked up and down the street for no apparent reason, and then wandered back inside, behavior which the officer observing him that night regarded as strange.

But most nights, Craig simply stayed home by himself. Chase eventually decided his officers' time would be better spent in other ways and the day-to-day surveillance was canceled.

On Thursday November 14th, Pat Chavez and David Carter from Community Outreach suggested that it might be helpful for them to meet with Craig. Carter explained to Joan that it was part of their routine procedure to interview everyone with close ties to the missing person.

Joan and Harry felt uneasy about inviting Craig to their home. But their suspicions of him were tempered by their desperation to find Denise.

Joan retreated to the bedroom for privacy and called Craig that afternoon to ask him if he would come by their house. He seemed not at all reluctant. Joan explained that two representatives from a missing children's outreach program had some questions that only Craig might be able to answer "because you had such a close relationship."

"They feel it's important to talk to you and I would like to see you, too," Joan told Craig.

Craig said his own phone had been ringing off the hook. His relatives, friends and business associates began calling him after seeing the news reports about Denise.

"My mom, my dad, my friends, you know, everyone is just

sick about it because they all love her just as much as I did," Craig declared.

"I know, I know," Joan said. "We have to hope that she's alive some place."

Craig said he felt "really positive because I just can't believe that anything can happen to her."

"I know. That's the way we feel too," Joan said. "I thought that maybe if we can get together, maybe there's something, something that we've missed, Craig. You know, we need you. So, please."

Craig told her she didn't have to say please, that it was no problem. "I'll do anything," he promised.

"I know you will," Joan said. "That's why I'm calling you, okay?"

"Okay," Craig said.

As promised, Craig, wearing a beige mock turtleneck ski-style brown sweater and parka, arrived at 9 p.m. Only a few people other than Joan, Harry, David and Pat were there. Carolyn Kristovich, who had never trusted Craig, met him at the door and awkwardly embraced him. John Kristovich was in the dining room working on flyers. Michele went out for a while but came back later to find Craig sitting at the kitchen table with Chavez and Carter.

"I'm sorry to be seeing you under these circumstances," Michele said, giving Craig, who stood up to greet her, a stiff hug. Then, she retreated to Denise's bedroom hoping he might wander in later to talk. She was disappointed when he did not.

At first Craig went upstairs to the den where he, Joan and Harry talked for a while about what had gone wrong in his relationship with Denise. Craig explained that he thought Denise was just not ready for marriage, that she hadn't been able to break away from her family. Joan and Harry told him that he hadn't been patient enough with their daughter and that he had failed to communicate his feelings to her.

"You demanded too much control over her life, Craig," Joan said, upset. "You didn't even let her see her friends. And that was important to Denise."

"Denise is so darn spoiled," Craig countered. "She's used to having everything done for her and sometimes, when I would get home from work, I would just be too tired to cater to her." Besides, he said, he was always picking up after Denise around the house. She had a habit of throwing her belongings anywhere and although he liked things to be neat, he tried to be patient with her.

Joan looked over at Harry. She couldn't understand why he wasn't being direct and demanding with Craig as they had planned. It seemed like she was doing all the talking.

At 10 o'clock, the three of them watched the news on KTVU. The second story that night was a somber update on the search for Denise. The report showed several of Denise's friends tucking flyers under the windshield wipers of cars at the building where she was last seen. Craig watched in silence.

At around 10:15 p.m., Craig went back downstairs to the kitchen where he was introduced to Pat and David. The three of them sat at the table as the two outreach workers asked him a pre-planned series of simple questions about Denise—what friends she had been seeing the most, where she liked to go in her free time, what plans she had for travel and about her career plans.

Craig said he had seen Denise on Saturday before she disappeared and that she seemed happy at times and depressed at times. But he also said she expressed a desire to be by herself for a while and get everyone off her back.

"She talked about meeting new people, men and women," Craig declared. "It seemed like she was really confused about where her life was headed. She said she really wanted someone to tell her what to do."

When the interview was over, Craig hugged Joan and shook Harry's hand before he closed the front door behind him. He was barely out the door, however, when Pat Chavez shrieked, "Oh my God, did you see his hands?"

Joan looked puzzled. But Harry knew exactly what Chavez meant. "The scratches," he said hoarsely. "His hands were all scratched up."

"What?" Joan asked in disbelief. "Harry, why on earth didn't you say something? I can't believe you didn't say something."

But Harry had felt as if he were in a trance. Sitting to Craig's left, he had seen a scratch on his neck, his ear and his nose. And he thought he had seen scratches on the tops of both of Craig's hands.

Chavez concurred. Both of Craig's hands were covered with groove-like scratches, she said, and she also noticed a scratch about three inches long on the right side of his neck and a smaller one on his left ear lobe.

"We've got to tell the police," Joan said, understanding the implications of what she was hearing.

Early Friday morning, Harry was on the phone to Commander Chase to describe to him the suspicious wounds etched on Craig's hands.

But Chase was not at all surprised. "I noticed them on Tuesday night," he told Harry who was startled to hear Chase reply so calmly. "We can't jump to any conclusions. First, we've got to find out what explanation he has for those scratches."

When Harry hung up, he told Joan that Chase had seemed only mildly interested in the scratches. But as Denise's father, he couldn't get the picture of them, and the horrible image of how they might have been caused, out of his mind.

More depressed than ever, Joan felt their meeting with Craig had been an utter failure. They had hoped that they could encourage Craig to talk about Denise, to say something, intentionally or otherwise, that might provide them with a clue as to where their daughter might be. But Harry had become so infuriated after seeing Craig's wounds that he could barely speak. And she felt certain that if the marks on Craig's arms had any significance at all, he must have felt Harry's eyes focusing on them during the strained visit.

Chris Morganti, who had been planning to go to New York with Denise, instead spent her two week vacation helping full time in the search. Like many others who had been participating in the grim vigil at the Redlick's house, Chris had left the house the night of Craig's visit around 6:30 p.m. Joan and Harry had decided it would be best if only a few people were present when Craig dropped in. Chris and her sister, Cindy, had gone back to Chris' apartment in Millbrae where they spent the evening thinking and talking about Denise.

At around 11 p.m. the phone rang. It was Craig. Chris didn't even know that he knew her phone number. They had talked on the phone only once before and that was strictly a business call, to arrange for Chris to purchase several gallons of surplus paint for the day care center.

Craig was in the mood to talk, and, as he chatted away, Chris jotted notes on a scratchpad. Cindy looked over Chris' shoulder as her sister prodded Craig along with leading questions.

Craig said he was worried that the publicity about Denise's disappearance was going to be bad for business. When he went to the bank in San Carlos, the teller asked him, "Wasn't that you I saw on television last night?" referring to the engagement photography that one station included in its report.

"I really don't like people I don't know asking me about my personal life," he explained. But he joked that, "maybe it'll make me popular." He said he was trying to pull his life back together and that he had signed up for an aerobics class with an instructor who "works the shit out of us."

"I haven't even been hurting," he said. "I guess I'm in pretty good shape from running."

Changing the subject, Craig asked Chris if she had seen the report on KTVU that night. Chris said that she had.

"Who were the people passing out the flyers?" Craig inquired.

"Which ones?" Chris asked.

"Those two guys, the tall one and then that other shorter guy?"

Chris said they were Mark Gooch, who Denise used to date and a friend of Mark's.

"You know, if she doesn't come home soon, I'm going to go find her," Craig declared.

Chris wasn't the only friend of Denise's who was caught off guard by a phone call from Craig that night.

About an hour after Craig left the house in San Bruno, Denise's bedroom phone rang. Michele picked it up expecting to hear one of Denise's friends privately checking to see how Harry and Joan were holding up.

She wasn't prepared to hear Craig's voice on the other end.

"I wanted to tell you why I'm not helping everyone look for

Denise," Craig said to Michele. In fact, Michele and many of Denise's relatives and friends who were gathering at the house everyday were wondering just that.

"For someone who says he loves her as much as you say you do, I am curious to know why you haven't been here," Michele said.

"It's just too hard for me," said Craig. "I just get too emotional. Besides, I just know she's out there somewhere with some of her friends."

"I know that's not true, Craig," Michele responded. "Red's always told me when she leaves town. She's never kept anything like that a secret from me."

Craig quickly changed the subject, asking Michele about her boyfriend. He also asked her, as he had with Chris, the names of the two men who appeared in the television report earlier that evening. Annoyed with his seeming indifference to Denise's plight, Michele abruptly brought Craig back to the only subject that mattered at that very moment.

"Craig, where on earth is Denise?"

"She's out there somewhere, Michele. I just know she's out there somewhere."

Michele hung up feeling angry and confused. For three days she had been encouraging everyone at Denise's house to keep an open mind. While there were a number of her friends who wanted to "get Craig," and who talked about going to his house and confronting him with their suspicions that he had done something to her, Michele was the voice of reason. "What if it's not him?" she warned. "What if we put all our energy into accusing Craig and, every day, we're just getting farther and farther away from Denise and whoever it is that really took her?"

That evening was a turning point for her. When she talked to Craig and heard his strange answers, she made up her mind he knew more than he had told anyone and that the implications were ominous.

"I realized that very night that Denise was never coming back," she said.

Commander Chase's original perceptions of Craig Anderson were changing also. On Friday morning, after talking to Harry and hearing about Craig's visit to the Redlicks' house and his subsequent calls to Chris and Michele, the commander dialed the number of Anderson Paint Company in San Carlos. Chase and Marriscolo had talked about the possibility of asking Craig to submit to a polygraph, a traditional lie detector test, conducted by an examiner from outside of the police department and having his car turned over to the county crime lab technicians for forensic testing. But Chase quickly sensed that Craig was less enthusiastic about talking to him than he had been on Tuesday night when he had taken the voice stress test. Rather than risk further alienating Anderson so early in the investigation, Chase didn't bring up the subject of an independent polygraph.

Anderson said he wasn't happy with the way he had been treated at the Redlicks'. He told Chase he was offended that two strangers, Pat Chavez and David Carter, had interrogated him, distorting his purpose in driving to San Bruno as a favor to Joan and Harry. Chase agreed with Anderson there. He was becoming increasingly annoyed with Community Outreach and what he regarded as its interference in serious aspects of the police investigation. He thought the volunteers ought to stick to handing out flyers and not doing things that would, in fact, alienate people like Craig.

Craig was also upset that KTVU had broadcast his picture during the story about Denise. He feared that his customers and clients might feel he was being implicated in his ex-fiance's disappearance which could hurt his business.

"There's a couple of things I need to ask you," Chase said. "I'm wondering first of all how you got all those scratches on your hands. You had some on your neck and ears, too."

"Oh, Tom, I hope nobody's going to make something out of that. I've been fixing up the house, trying to keep my mind off everything that happened with Denise. I got cut up over the weekend when I was doing some work in the bathroom and cleaning up some trash in the yard. That's all there is to that."

"And why were you asking Chris and Michele about the guys that you saw on television?"

Craig said he had only called Michele because he knew she was a good friend of Denise and he wanted to talk to her privately, without Joan and Harry and everyone else eavesdropping. When he asked about the people passing out the flyers, he was only curious because they weren't people he recognized from the year that he and Denise were together. "I was just trying to make conversation," Craig said. "It really wasn't any big thing."

Then Craig let out a deep sigh, and when he spoke next, he sounded frustrated and miserable.

"Look, Tom, her parents asked me to come over there and help so I did. But I'm really tired of people trying to turn the positive things I do into negative ones. I don't want to look like I'm uncooperative, but I just can't handle it anymore. I've got to get on with my life. I've got a business to run."

Chase hung up and took a look at the notes he had jotted down as he and Craig talked. It was the third time he had talked to Craig, once at the station and now twice on the phone. Again, Craig had said nothing to suggest that he was concealing a thing from the police. But the scratches, Chase thought, were rather curious. Still, the three customers who could vouch for Anderson's whereabouts on Monday afternoon were definitely significant. Craig could not have been in two places at the same time. Perhaps, Chase thought tiredly, they should look elsewhere for a suspect.

But Marriscolo was not convinced.

"Something's just not right about that guy," he declared. By then Marriscolo had talked to more than a dozen people who knew Denise or Craig. Despite favorable first impressions of the man and complimentary surface comments about him, Marriscolo had the uneasy feeling that there was more to Craig Anderson than his cooperative manner suggested.

■ CHAPTER NINE ■

Some Ends,
Some Leads

In the weeks after the missing person report was filed with San Bruno police, the once peaceful Redlick home was transformed into a bustling command post. From sunup to long past sundown, the desperate need to find Denise dominated the household.

As Joan watched the frenzy of activity, she grew increasingly cynical and pessimistic about Denise being found alive. "It is," she said to Harry, "as if I am watching a horrible movie plot unfold around me." What was most difficult to believe was that her close-knit family had taken center stage. And yet, she couldn't help but hope in the back of her mind that her daughter might just burst through the door with her characteristic giggle at any minute wondering, "what's everyone doing here?"

As information about Denise Redlick's disappearance began to appear on television, radio and in the newspapers, dozens of friends, relatives and even virtual strangers began calling and coming to the house to offer support and to participate in what would become a massive search for the young woman.

Joan and Harry were stunned by the numbers of people who dropped by the house to pick up flyers to distribute in assigned sections of the Bay Area. People whom Denise had known in high school but hadn't seen since graduation offered their help. Even several of Denise's old boyfriends showed up. "People are coming out of the woodwork," Karen commented aloud.

However, a few of those friends were irritated by Marriscolo's merciless questioning. Art Thomas, who had become a police officer, had come by the house and was talking to one of Denise's girlfriends in the living room when he heard Marriscolo say to another person, "Just because he's a cop doesn't mean he wouldn't kill someone."

Art's ears perked up and he was offended at the implication that he might harm Denise. "But I guess since I'm a cop too, I understand what he had to do," Art said later. He patiently answered the Burlingame officer's questions about Denise, saying he had last run into her a week before when he made a deposit at the bank.

Charles Nan also felt that Marriscolo came on too strong during their initial contact. The inspector had called Nan at the bank just after Denise's car was located, and began grilling him.

"You were supposed to be with Denise last night," Tom abruptly began in a harsh tone of voice. "Where were you?"

Nan, taken back feeling like he was being treated as a suspect, said he had stayed home—his mom could vouch for that—to watch the football game because Denise failed to call him. He had gone to bed after the game. Then they talked about Denise and how she had been handling her recent broken engagement.

"If I had been him, I would have been grasping at straws, too," Nan declared.

From the first, Harry and Joan realized that it was to their advantage to cooperate with the news media. Each day, there were phone calls from reporters wanting to interview them and update the story that was prompting thousands of other young Peninsula women to wonder if the streets of their own communities were safe even in broad daylight. Each time the television reporters arrived to set up their bright lights in the Redlick's living room, Harry and Joan sat in front of the video cameras and answered the same, painful questions.

KGO-TV reporter Chuck Coppola focused on the fears that Denise's disappearance had aroused in the Burlingame area. Coppola went to Prime Time, an athletic club just across the freeway from where Denise was last seen, where the management had organized a "buddy system" , providing female members with escorts to and from their cars.

One woman who has used the service told Coppola, "Burlingame always seemed to me like a step back in time, more 1950s, where you could go for a walk in the evening and not necessarily lock your doors."

Two days after Denise had last been seen, KPIX reporter Nancy Herr asked Harry and Joan to talk about their daughter's disappearance.

"I fear for her safety," Harry said. "I just hope that wherever she is, she's still alive and she's safe and we can get her back."

Joan was asked to describe her daughter. She took a deep breath and managed a slight smile. "She's delightful, loving, sweet, caring, good, very involved with people. She's the most wonderful daughter anyone could ever have."

Herr's report, like those of so many other television stations over the next few weeks, included a photograph taken at the engagement party in March showing the Redlicks, Harry and Michael seated on either side of Craig, their wives standing behind them and Denise standing in the center with her hands resting on Craig's shoulders.

It was Herr's story that first promoted the involvement of Pat Chavez and David Carter of Community Outreach who had recently spent time talking with Craig Anderson. Just a year earlier, in November 1984, the organization had coordinated the heavily-publicized search for a missing University of California at Berkeley student, Roberta Lee. Among the most active searchers was the victim's boyfriend, Bradley Page. But when her brutally beaten body was found in an East Bay recreation area five weeks after her disappearance, Page became a suspect in her slaying. He was convicted of her voluntary manslaughter in 1988.

Carter spoke from experience when he warned Joan and Harry what they were up against. "The first seventy-two hours are crucial in finding someone alive. After that, you are usually looking for a body."

Carter had turned the Redlick's dining room table into the base station for the exhaustive campaign to alert the public by distributing a series of flyers with photographs of Denise and the Triumph. Using stacks of maps obtained from the American Automobile Association, Carter devised a color-coded system of identifying areas that needed to be covered, areas that had been covered, and areas that needed to be covered again. Over the next few months, more than one hundred thousand flyers would be distributed throughout the Bay Area and selected areas of California. A few would even wind up as far away as Australia and Hawaii as searchers scheduled to travel to those areas remembered to bring a few flyers with them. But more important, nearly every major business in San Mateo County, including supermarkets, dry cleaners, bookstores, service stations and restaurants, would have a poster taped to its window. Denise's smiling face, her left hand showing off a sparkling diamond engagement ring poised near her cheek, would be ingrained in the minds of thousands of people who had never met her or even seen her before.

Chavez encouraged the Redlicks to stay in touch with the news media, to be as accessible as possible. The more publicity, the better, she said. Harry agreed. "We couldn't help but think that someone might notice Denise's picture and say, 'I remember seeing her!'" Harry declared.

In their determination to do as much as they could to draw attention to their daughter's disappearance, Harry and Joan often permitted reporters to document painfully intimate glimpses of their devastated lives. On one occasion, Joan allowed a television reporter to display on camera the elegant satin gown that Denise would have worn if her wedding had not been cancelled. At Thanksgiving, the Redlicks invited television reporters into their home to film their joyless dinner.

One reporter asked Joan about the outpouring of love and support that they had received from the community. "It makes you realize you had it all the time," Joan said. "You don't really appreciate it or think about it, but it was always there."

Aid and comfort to Joan, Harry, Michael and his wife, Lynn, and others who were close to Denise came in many forms. Roma's Delicatessen donated platters of food, nuns from Saint Robert's gathered to pray, Lynn's Print Shop duplicated thousands of posters and scores of people showed up to take a batch of flyers, offer words of sympathy and help alert the community.

All the attention left little room for privacy, which, at times, Tom Marriscolo found exceedingly frustrating. When he wanted to talk confidentially with Joan and Harry, there were always a half dozen people walking in and out of the room. At times he became annoyed with Chavez and Carter who seemed to feel they had the right to be in on every development in the investigation. In his firm and authoritarian manner, the inspector reminded them that they were volunteers, not police officers.

Joan didn't mind that there were a dozen people or more for dinner every night. "I knew that once everybody left, when the excitement died down, I was going to have to face Denise's absence on my own," she said. "I really didn't want all these people to leave."

Harry and Joan abandoned any thought of going to work and their employers told them to take as much time as they needed. One night Joan finally slept from the sheer exhaustion of having been up for days. For months afterward, she took two tranquilizers every night to help her block out the living nightmare so she could get some rest. But with each sunrise, the ordeal would begin again.

Throughout each long, exhausting day of searching, waiting and praying, there was speculation. Had Denise simply gone away to think things through because she was troubled over the broken engagement and the uncertainty of her future as Craig Anderson had suggested? It was a possibility that few who knew Denise and were aware of her unusually close relationship with her family found logical or probable. Had Denise been abducted by a crazed stranger who was now holding her as a sex slave? The scenario was more plausible than it might sound considering that San Mateo County Superior Court had just served as the venue for a strange and notorious case out of Red Bluff, California in which a man had been accused and ultimately convicted of kidnapping a twenty-year-old woman and holding her captive to use in acts of bondage for seven years, much of that time in a box under his bed. Many of those who gathered at the Redlicks' envisioned a different, but perhaps equally bizarre plot.

Some of Denise's friends had begun to discuss the possibility that Craig kidnapped Denise and was holding her hostage until he would drag her to the church and force her to marry him. In Michele's scenario, Denise would be dressed in her satin wedding gown and Craig would be holding a gun to her head, forcing her to recite her vows. Michele and two of Denise's friends even drove to Our Lady of Angel's Church on Sunday and sat in the car hoping to catch a glimpse of Craig and Denise. Instead, all they got was a reprimand from Marriscolo who had also driven to the church that day and had noticed the car. He had asked them earlier not to go off on their own investigation.

But as far as Michele and Cindy Pacini were concerned, no one else, not even the police, could do anything fast enough in the search for Denise. The two women spent an entire day driving up and down the coastline, covering more than one hundred miles, peering into gullies, caves and canyons, not really knowing what to look for but feeling as though they had to try. They left flyers at roadside cafes, and they found a home in Aptos, a seaside town south of Santa Cruz that, according to the phone directory, was occupied by a Craig Anderson.

The girls walked around the house, peeking into windows and, sure enough, Craig Anderson emerged. Only this Craig Anderson was sixty years old and wondered what they were doing on his property. When Michele stammered an explanation, he listened and ultimately offered to distribute flyers in his neighborhood.

Later, while trying to find Svedahl so that they could snoop around Anderson's cabin, they became lost on the winding country roads and never did make it to the cabin. For a long time afterward, Michele was convinced that if Denise were indeed dead, she was buried there at the cabin. For all their sleuthing, Michele and Cindy earned the nicknames "Cagney and Lacey."

Marriscolo finally accepted that these were people who could not be convinced that they should not be involved. They simply cared too much. "It didn't matter what you told them," he said, "they would still do what they thought was right. If I had to do it all over again, I would send them places to do things for us."

For a brief time a few observers, mostly reporters who were covering the case, wondered if there might be a link between Denise's fate and that of another missing San Brunan, Daniel Johnson. Reporters had even begun combining stories of the two missing person reports, emphasizing striking similarities in the cases.

Danny, who like Denise was twenty-three, disappeared four days after Denise on Friday, November 15th. He was last seen at 10:30 a.m. when a friend dropped him off at the corner of Ocean and Phelan Avenues next to San Francisco City College.

His mother, Mary, the director of two nursery schools told reporters that, like Denise, her son would not simply just go away for a few days without telling anyone. "It's just not within his character," she told one reporter for The San Mateo Times. "It's not like him."

Danny also lived with his parents just a mile away from the Redlicks and the two families belonged to the same church, Saint Robert's. Danny was a student at Skyline College, a two year community college located in northwest San Bruno. He was wearing a red nylon jacket, gray pants and tennis shoes when he reportedly walked down Ocean Avenue to retrieve his fiance's car which was parked about a half-mile away and was not seen again.

"He's such a happy person," his fiance was quoted as saying. "He doesn't have any problems. He just wouldn't get up and leave."

But, beyond the coincidental similarities, there was no apparent reason to tie the cases together. Investigators were quick to note that Denise and Danny apparently did not know each other and attended different high schools.

Yet, the two families found some comfort in their contact with each other. Joan and Mary Johnson often talked, sharing thoughts on the misery of having a child vanish and wondering how their separate but similar ordeals might end.

"It compounds the sadness to know it is happening twice," Harry Redlick told a reporter for the San Francisco Examiner.

"You can say you're sorry but until you feel what its like to have an empty house in the morning, it's incomprehensible."

San Bruno City Council established two separate $10,000 reward funds to encourage tips in the searches for Denise and Danny. Chavez and Carter began to distribute flyers for Denise and Danny together. That, Carter later said, proved to be a mistake since it might have mislead some recipients into thinking the two cases were related.

But the search for Danny Johnson would end much sooner. His body was found in a rural, unincorporated area of Sonoma County north of San Francisco on December 3. He had been shot in the chest. Investigators believed that his body had been dumped there after he had been killed somewhere else.

As Harry and Joan Redlick sat in a pew at Saint Robert's Catholic Church during the Mass of Christian Burial for Danny, they could not help but say their own special prayers for Denise's safe return.

For every missing person who attracts the attention of the media, there are dozens of psychics and, Chase said, "wannabe psychics," who step forward to offer their "inspired" guidance. The case of Denise Redlick seemed to draw more than the usual amount of seers.

Clearly, the psychics' subculture is an offbeat, eccentric one. Joan and Carolyn, who fielded most of the calls, were admittedly skeptical but desperate. With each psychic's promise that Denise was alive their spirits would lift. With each vision of Denise as a murder victim, their hopes would plummet. At times they could barely believe that they had gotten mixed up with people who made important decisions based on such things as astrological signs, but they were grasping at any offer that came their way.

"I couldn't help but think, 'suppose one of these psychics is right?'" said Joan. "Of course, thousands of places fit some of the descriptions. But we weren't about to leave a single stone unturned."

One especially persistent psychic called the first week and told Joan that, as of the last "signal" she had received from Denise, she was still alive. The psychic offered a vivid and chilling description of Denise's situation.

"Her hands are bound and she's being held by four to five men who are wearing ski masks," the woman said. She could see, she said, rows of greenhouses, artichokes blossoming and a vast body of water, possibly the ocean, nearby. She also recommended that Joan contact another psychic in the local network, a woman in Oakland, who was especially insightful with this kind of problem although, she warned, the woman was just getting over the flu which is an inhibitor, and also has a problem with her gift when the moon is in Scorpio which happened to be occurring at that time.

Many of the unsolicited visions sent Denise's relatives scurrying on wild goose chases. One psychic provided this unusually specific vision: Denise was whisked away by someone in an older model, gold and beige car, possibly with Nebraska license plates, and was being held in a closet with her hands and feet tied, in a small, shack-like house fifteen to twenty minutes south of San Bruno, in a run-down neighborhood in the 400 block, five houses from the corner of a street with a "tgy" in the street name. This person even went as far as to say that the house on the adjacent property was painted a rust color.

Michele and a group of Denise's friends spent hours driving around until they found a house in a neighborhood that they felt fit the psychic's description. They kept an eye on the house for several hours until they sadly admitted to themselves that there was nothing going on in the bungalow that had anything to do with Denise Redlick.

When a psychic told Joan that she could see Denise near a body of water and something that looked like a cross, several of Denise's friends went exploring at Skylawn Memorial Park, a cemetery west of San Mateo that overlooks the Pacific Ocean. "I don't really know what we were looking for," said Debi Ronzani. "I was hoping maybe we could find a purse or a shoe or some sign of a struggle. I really didn't want to find Denise." In fact, they spent several hours prowling the vast cemetery grounds and found nothing.

Joan and Carolyn went to see a psychic in Daly City who had

called Joan and said she could provide them with some information if they provided her with some articles of Denise's clothing.
Carolyn took with her a pair of Denise's shoes and a sweatsuit
and left them at the pyschic's house. Despite numerous follow-up
phone calls to the seer, Carolyn never heard from the woman
again and never got the clothing back.

Another psychic called the Redlicks and said he had a feeling
he could provide them with a reading if they would provide him
with some of Denise's gold, silver or platinum jewelry. With some
apprehensions, Harry and John met the psychic, who refused to
give them his name, and spent several hours driving around the
Bay Area with him before they realized that they were getting
nowhere. They took back the jewelry, thanked the psychic, who
seemed confused but sincere, and departed.

One day, a Burlingame man arrived at the police station to
report his vision to Marriscolo. The self-proclaimed psychic was
certain that the boyfriend did it.

"When she came out of the building, she was put into the
trunk of a car," he told Marriscolo. Three men were involved in
the abduction, one of them dressed in green hospital garb and
another in coveralls, he said. They chained her to a bed and se-
dated her in a house in the East Bay on a street with a name like
Athens or Athenia. The self-proclaimed psychic had even found
such a street in Oakland but when he drove there, he couldn't find
a house similar to the one he had pictured in his vision. The person who lives in the house is named Rick, he said. "They are
trying to brainwash her into marrying him," he also declared.

For the most part, the psychics' tips were misguided. Yet, the
Redlick family followed what leads they could, desperately hoping that the advice might lead them to Denise.

Of the more than a dozen psychics who offered readings,
Denise's family hired only one, a woman in Maryland whom they
paid $250. In her first of several readings provided over a period
of months, the psychic said that Denise's body might be near Coyote Point, a bayside recreation area in San Mateo, possibly near
the Castaways Restaurant. "Her death was more accidental than
it was deliberate," she declared. "Whoever did this to Denise had
to stop the car afterward to regain control of himself."

Based on her description, Marriscolo, Collopy and Denise's friends scoured Coyote Point, including the entire park and the area to the west of the San Mateo municipal golf course. Again, their search turned up nothing.

Marriscolo, who had never worked with psychics before, was concerned that the Redlicks might be tempted to pay psychics who were saying things that anyone could have said. It was a safe bet to suggest that there was "something like a cross" in the vicinity since even a utility pole could fit that vague description. "I wasn't impressed with the ones that said her body was alongside a roadway," he noted. "Obviously, it's not going to be on top of a mountain."

Yet, he listened and occasionally followed up on a tip not wanting to leave any avenue untraveled in the search for Denise Redlick.

It had seemed like a good idea at the time. Lori's husband had a friend who was a priest in San Francisco. He asked Father William McCain if he could perform a special ceremony to help the desperate Redlick family. The priest eagerly agreed.

One Wednesday night, Father Bill arrived at the San Bruno home carrying a large votive candle that had been blessed on his church's altar. Harry and Joan clasped hands as the priest lit the candle and said a prayer for Denise Redlick.

The candle flickered and glowed each day as determined searchers left the house with armfuls of flyers. Amid the flurry of activity throughout the week, the candle was barely noticed by most of those who visited although Joan would glance toward it occasionally during the day and feel a twinge of hope.

As the weekend passed and the candle began to fade, no one dared mention aloud that seven days were almost gone. On Sunday night, the Redlicks gathered at Saint Robert's Church for a special prayer service for Denise. As Joan entered the vestibule, she felt as though she was walking into a terrifying dream. To be sitting in the same church where she and Denise had attended services just one week before—but this time to be praying for Denise's safe return—seemed absurd. While she was restless to go back home to wait for Denise, her stomach churned with the realization that for every day Denise was gone, the likelihood of ever seeing her alive again was waning.

Two evenings later the candle had sputtered to darkness. The melted remains sat on the table for several days until someone pushed them aside. Soon after, they were quietly moved out of sight and the candle was never mentioned again.

■ CHAPTER TEN ■

Memories and Feelings

On November 16th, the day Craig and Denise would have been married if their engagement had not been called off, Joan and Harry half expected to receive a call from Craig. When they hadn't heard from him by early evening, Joan decided to call him.

When he answered, Craig talked at length about how much he loved Denise and how he's "never going to let that go."

"Joan, I almost couldn't believe it when I met her because I loved her almost from the beginning. I was walking above the ground for like three months," Craig said. "I remember those days so vividly, you know, that it was just unbelievable. It just seemed like every day that went by, it got better. I guess if you need people, sometimes you give a little piece of your heart, you know, and the little shithead took the biggest piece of mine so far," Craig said.

"Well, someday you'll meet someone and you'll be okay," Joan responded, seeming sympathetic. "But you know we'll never have another daughter so . . ."

Craig cut her off before she could finish. "I can't even think about that right now," he said. "I can't even relate to it. She sure as shit better come home, I'll tell you that."

Joan explained that by this time the police had begun to take a public position that Denise had been abducted and was not just simply a runaway.

"Joan, I'm a positive person and I just don't think I don't know why, I may be wrong, but I just think that she's still alive," Craig insisted.

"Do you?" Joan asked.

"I just, I don't know, I mean, I don't know where in the hell that little shit would go or what she would do. But I can't help but think there must be someone, somewhere, that she's with. I don't know, a friend something, I don't know."

That made Joan angry. "I cannot think of one person I haven't contacted. That's the whole damn thing."

"Yeah, so you know what I did?" Craig asked. He went on to explain that, after watching the news on Thursday night with Joan and Harry, he called Chris and Michele and asked them about the people he had seen on television circulating flyers. He was surprised and impressed, he said, to see all of these people whom he had never even met before involved in the search for Denise.

Joan explained that they were all friends of Denise or Mike. "I've had more than fifty people who really care about Denise here and more coming all the time," she said without directly asking Craig why he hadn't volunteered.

Craig avoided the unasked, but implied question.

Craig went on to mention that he was trying to pull his life back together, to want to be around other people after splitting up with Denise, but it was taking longer than he expected. "You know I loved that girl to death," he said. He then asked if Harry was okay and Joan put him on the phone. "I wanted to tell you that I love you a lot and I really miss you," Craig offered.

Harry thanked him for his words. "It's really needed at this time."

When Harry said it had been a "horrible day," that he had been watching the clock and thinking about the schedule of events that had been planned to celebrate the wedding, Craig said he couldn't escape the wedding images either.

"I told myself I wasn't going to watch the clock, but every ten minutes, I'd walk in the other room and look at it," Craig said.

After Thanksgiving, Joan called Craig again. By then, any hope of finding Denise alive had truly vanished. Joan was deeply depressed and, at the same time, angry with Craig. His distance was adding fuel to her growing conviction that he had done something to Denise. She had decided to be more direct in her conversations with Craig. She asked him why he didn't want to be with Denise's family during this traumatic time.

He didn't dodge the question. "Joan, I would like nothing better, but I tell you the truth, a detective came yesterday and everything I say or do is scrutinized and I just, I just have to stay away. It's just that simple. You know everything I say or do people keep track of." Nevertheless he was deeply distraught over Denise's disappearance, he said. One day he started crying and couldn't stop.

He didn't seem alarmed about her vanishing at first, he said because she had just told him a few days before that she needed to get away for a while. Besides, he said, he had spent six weeks trying to detach himself from her and trying to get strong again.

"I was a broken man for about four weeks, you know, and I'll admit, the first two weeks, I was a wreck. I mean a wreck," he said.

Still, Craig seemed neither secretive or evasive. He talked about Denise as if he really cared and even seemed to break down and cry a few times.

"Where do you think she is, Craig?" Joan asked.

"Oh, God, if I knew. I wish I knew."

"I don't think she's alive Craig."

"God, don't say that."

"I don't know how I'm going to live."

"Damn her," Craig said sharply.

On two occasions, within three weeks of Denise's disappearance, Craig claimed that he had received anonymous threats.

One threat, he told the police on November 20th, came in the form of a phone call at 1 o'clock in the morning. The caller, a man with a garbled voice said, "You're going to die." When Craig asked who was calling, the voice said, "Fuck you," and hung up. The call was extremely unnerving, Craig said. He told Joan that

101

his own attorney advised him to let the police know about the call, that it might help in the search for Denise. The voice, Craig said, "was like ice."

"At first, I guess I thought it was a joke or something. And then all of a sudden it hit me, you know, that this man was a nut or something," Craig said. "I'll tell you one thing, if he calls tonight, I'm going to say 'Okay, buddy, why don't you tell me the time and the place and I'll be there because I won't be intimidated.'" Craig said it seemed like the caller was someone close to what was going on.

He prevented any further threats by having his phone changed to an unlisted number a few days later.

On December 7th, Craig turned over to the police an envelope that he claimed had contained an anonymous handwritten threat. The author had written, "You're being watched and you're going to pay."

Marriscolo turned the envelope over to the county crime lab along with a sample of Craig's handwriting from a letter that he had written to Denise in October. Paul Dougherty, the criminologist who examined both items said he was unable to determine if Anderson had sent the threat to himself because the sample of handwriting was too small. "But whoever addressed the envelope spent a lot of time disguising his handwriting," Dougherty said.

Regardless of who had written the letter, Craig seemed genuinely concerned about his own safety. On December 9th, he ordered a security system installed in his San Carlos home.

That Craig was the target of anonymous threats was not at all unlikely. Marriscolo had heard a rumor that one of Denise's more militant friends had vowed to take matters into his own hands. The inspector heard that the friend had sought out a soldier of fortune who would take care of the situation as it pertained to Craig Anderson—for a price. Marriscolo cornered the alleged culprit one night and warned him to back off.

While officially Anderson had been rejected as a suspect in Denise's disappearance, the Burlingame police continued to focus attention on him.

On November 22nd, Marriscolo and Collopy drove to Svedahl to search the area around the Anderson cabin. They encountered the Swedish community's winter caretakers who said that no one had been near the Anderson's house in recent weeks except for one person building a new deck. The two detectives were looking for some tools, a mound of dirt, or anything that might suggest a buried body, but the area was covered with trees and dense brush making them quickly realize that if someone buried a body there, it might never be found.

Van Etten and Collopy also spent several hours contacting all of the self-storage facilities in San Mateo County, asking if there were any current rentals for Craig Anderson, Roy Anderson, Roy Anderson Paint Company or Image Investments. Again, they came up empty.

Harry Redlick had given Marriscolo a video tape of Denise and Craig's engagement party. Over the coming months, the inspector would rerun that tape dozens of times. Anyone else might have seen two families celebrating friendship and love, but the inspector was only interested in Craig. What he saw, he said, was a man who just didn't fit in, who looked uncomfortable with his role and who never seemed to convey the warmth that one would expect under the supposedly happy circumstances.

Marriscolo often burned the midnight oil in the detective bureau writing up reports and contemplating his next step in the case. One of the swing shift patrol officers who often dropped in to see how the investigation was going, had taken to calling Tom "bulldog" in recognition of his ferocious persistence. Tom strongly felt that, in delving deeper and deeper into Craig Anderson's world, he was on the right track.

But, as the weeks passed, he routinely worked twelve or more hours a day, but still couldn't connect Craig Anderson to Denise Redlick's disappearance.

Nancy Marriscolo realized that her husband had become obsessed with solving this case. Many nights, he would come home from work, give his daughter a hug and then pick up the phone to call Joan or Carolyn. He was relentless.

"It may sound strange, but I think he became very close to Denise," Nancy said. "I think he became very fond of her." Perhaps, she said, he was so intimately drawn to the case because he has a daughter, too. But it might also have been because the Red-licks were wonderful, loving people who appreciated everything that the police did for them.

"In all fairness, a lot of that couldn't be considered productive time," Marriscolo admitted of the long hours. "A lot of times, it was a matter of going up to the Redlick's house in the evening to have a drink and talk things over."

"I remember thinking that maybe he was getting a little too close to the family," Nancy said. But she knew that her husband was an exceptionally caring police officer and accepted that the nights and weekends spent on the case were just something he had to do.

Even though Chase had deliberately taken Marriscolo off all his other cases so that he could devote all his energy to the high-priority, high-profile Redlick investigation, the commander eventually became concerned that Marriscolo had lost all sense of objectivity.

One day, when Commander Chase called Marriscolo into his office and told him to shut the door, the inspector had a feeling he knew what was coming.

"Tom, I think we've got a problem here," Chase diplomatically began. "I'm getting the feeling you're spending too much time on this case. You're spending too much time with Denise's parents and getting too emotionally involved."

Then Chase warned Marriscolo that he might be forced to remove him as chief investigator.

"If you don't back off, I'll have to put someone else on this who can look at things differently," he said.

Marriscolo, fuming, stared at his supervisor in disbelief. He hadn't thought Chase would go so far as to take him off the case. But Chase's threat, he felt, amounted to "pissing in the wind" and he told him so.

"I've put too much time into this for you to take me off now," Marriscolo blurted out. "This isn't an ordinary case. I'm not even putting in for all the overtime I'm racking up."

Both officers calmed down and when Marriscolo left the room, he knew that his role as chief investigator wasn't really in jeopardy.

But when he told his wife what had happened, he said disappointedly that Chase wasn't yet completely convinced that the ex-fiance had harmed, perhaps even killed Denise. Chase's chief discordant concern was his favorable interpretation of the voice stress analysis taken by Anderson. Moreover the commander, Marriscolo felt, was upset that the investigation was going nowhere.

"There's got to be an answer to this thing," Marriscolo told her. "Every other lead we've looked at turns out to be no good. But when I look at this guy Craig Anderson, I get this funny feeling that something's not right."

Nancy regarded her husband's "sixth sense" about things as very perceptive. "He'll fight for what he believes in to the bitter end," she said.

Marriscolo had intentionally kept his distance from Craig, but on November 25th, he and Collopy went to Craig's business ostensibly to collect further information about Denise Redlick's personality. The detectives were also hoping to learn more about Craig.

The interview, which was not recorded, lasted about twenty minutes. For the most part, Craig reiterated what he had told Chase—that Denise, on November 9th, had told him she was under a lot of pressure and needed to get away from it all. He talked freely about the argument at the wedding that ended in his slapping her, and claimed that Denise had hit him in the past. Despite his seeming cooperation, the two detectives felt that Anderson was hiding something. During the interview Collopy had to leave the shop for around ten minutes. When he returned, he thought that Craig seemed extremely upset. He looked pale and shaky. Kevin suspected that Marriscolo had gotten fed up with Anderson and told him so.

"What did you say to him?" Kevin asked as soon as he and Marriscolo left the store.

Marriscolo said he warned Craig that he would be back someday and "when I am, Craig, it's going to be a real bad day for you."

"Did you see how he couldn't even look at me?" Marriscolo asked Collopy. Craig kept looking down at the ground until Marriscolo, determined to make eye contact, was forced to sit on a paint can in order to stare straight into his eyes.

The officers agreed that they hadn't yet gotten to the bottom of what made Craig Anderson tick. That he might have several skeletons in his closet was also a definite possibility. Marriscolo had been receiving vague tips from the people he was interviewing as to Craig's relationship with women before Denise.

By the end of November, Marriscolo had tracked down three women who had dated Anderson over the past decade. The women didn't know each other. At first they were reluctant to say anything but complementary things about Craig, but gradually, as they began to trust Marriscolo as he confided his own fears about the disappearance of Denise Redlick, he began to hear collaborating tales about Craig's mercurial jealousy, possessiveness, and even occasional moments of violence.

Yet, no matter how badly Craig had allegedly treated his former girlfriends, Marriscolo knew he still had very little to tie Craig to the disappearance of his former fiance. But, at the same time that the detective was compiling a disturbing profile of Craig Anderson's dating history, one of Craig's painting subcontractors provided the investigators with a shocking tip.

The contractor, Richard Weeks, dropped in at the station one day in late November and told Marriscolo that Craig had once solicited him to kill someone. According to Weeks, Craig told him one day in 1984, at the paint store, "I want a guy knocked off," and indicated the intended target was a boyfriend of Lucy Larson, a woman Craig was dating at the time. Weeks claimed Craig drove him down to Mountain View—halfway to San Jose—to show him the apartment where he thought the boyfriend (whom Marriscolo later discovered was actually Lucy's ex-husband, Michael Brunicon) lived. Craig had described him, with disdain, as a "biker type," with long hair and a beard, who always dressed in faded blue jeans.

Weeks claimed that Anderson took him to his house and gave him cash for the murder contract. In the initial report, Weeks told Marriscolo the amount was $1,000, although he later said it was $1,000 down with the understanding that the total cost of the contract would be $2,500.

About a week later, Weeks indicated, Anderson became angry because the contract had not been carried out. By then, Weeks had talked to an attorney friend who had told him to keep the money for awhile, so Anderson wouldn't be able to give it to someone else who would carry out the request. "He is probably just going through an emotional time with his girlfriend," Weeks recalled the attorney saying.

Marriscolo, stunned by what he had just heard, knew he had to locate Lucy Larson, the woman with whom Craig had been going out before he became engaged to Denise.

■ CHAPTER ELEVEN ■

A Haunting Past

The last thing on Lucy Larson's mind when she returned from her restful vacation in Cancun, Mexico on Friday, November 29th was Craig Anderson. As she walked to the baggage pick-up area at San Francisco International Airport, she noticed numerous flyers concerning a missing woman taped to walkway walls and restroom doors. But her mind was on retrieving her luggage and the significance of the missing woman's name didn't strike her.

On Monday morning when Lucy arrived at work, she was surprised to find a dozen phone messages—all from an Inspector Tom Marriscolo at the Burlingame Police Department.

"What the heck is this all about?" she asked a co-worker who had taken some of the messages.

"He didn't say," the other employee told her.

All she could think about was that her ex-husband had gotten into some sort of trouble.

When Lucy got in touch with Marriscolo he told her he needed to talk to her about Craig Anderson. Within a half hour, Marriscolo, who had been desperate to reach Lucy, was interviewing her in her company lobby.

After hearing about the murder solicitation allegation, Lucy poured out the details of her turbulent relationship with Craig.

It had been a beautiful, warm night, perfect for romance, back in July 1983. When Lucy joined her friends at a Sunnyvale nightclub after her swingshift in the security department of an electronics corporation, romance was exactly what she encountered.

A tall and slender brunette with a winsome smile and an easy-going manner, Lucy was in a good mood, enjoying a rare night out when a tall, blond man sat down on the stool next to her and asked if he could buy her a drink. She looked at him, grinned and said, "sure, thanks." His name, he told her, was Craig Anderson.

For the next hour or so, the two strangers became better acquainted. Lucy was impressed with what he said and how he said it. He was extremely polite, nice, and attentive. He also impressed her because he was so clean-cut, unlike her estranged husband whose lifestyle had changed for the worse. When they had moved to California from Nevada, Lucy's husband, Michael Brunicon, had bought a 1200CC Harley-Davidson motorcycle and grown his hair long, tying it back in a ponytail. While Lucy was launching a new career and acquiring friends with goals similar to her own, Michael was hooking up with a group of guys who Lucy considered unseemly and undesirable. "We just drifted apart," she confided to her friends.

In contrast, Craig was neatly dressed in clean blue jeans and a striped T-shirt. His hair and moustache were both carefully trimmed. Craig and Lucy talked about their jobs and he told her that he worked for his family's paint supply company in San Francisco although he planned to start his own business someday soon. He also added that he owned a home in a nice area of San Jose along with a duplex in Daly City. During their conversation, he also casually mentioned that his Porsche was parked outside.

Craig gave Lucy the impression that he was a very self-assured person who knew what he wanted out of life and was willing to go after it. But she made a mental note when he told her that one of the problems he had with a girl that he had recently been dating was that she used to talk about her old boyfriends all the time. Lucy knew that if she saw this man again, she wasn't going to make the same mistake.

When they parted that night, Lucy gave Craig her number, so she wasn't surprised the next day when he called and invited her to lunch. That date led to another and another until, in October, Lucy moved into Craig's house in San Jose.

The first six months of their relationship went smoothly, Lucy said. Craig was very generous to both Lucy and her daughter, paying all the expenses for the household when the three of them lived together. And life with Craig was exciting. He was always planning somewhere to go or something to do on weekends. "We never stayed home," she said. They often drove up to the wine country, down to his family cabin in Svedahl, or just went out for nice dinners. "It seemed like he was a guy who had a lot on the ball," she observed. She could not help but be drawn to his magnetic personality.

"He had a way of making women feel special, like he really cared about them," Lucy said. "A lot of people in life take you for granted, but Craig would always tell me how nice I looked and how much he cared for me."

It wasn't until they went to a Christmas party together that she saw a side of Craig that alarmed her.

Craig spent most of the evening talking to people he knew, leaving Lucy with his brother and sister-in-law. She didn't mind because she knew there were many people at the party he hadn't seen for a while. Suddenly, however, Craig rejoined Lucy yanking her arm and yelling at her, "Come on, we're getting out of here. I'm sick of your shit."

She had no idea what she had done to anger him. But they left the party and Craig drove recklessly to a friend's house where another party was going on. He left Lucy sitting in the car in an unfamiliar neighborhood for hours. When he finally took her home, Lucy said she was going to leave him but he apologized for his behavior and begged her to stay. With some apprehension, she agreed.

In early 1985, Lucy began to realize that Craig was "insanely jealous" of any male who came into contact with his girlfriend. He would ask her intimate questions about her relationships with men before she met him and then start an argument when she honestly answered his inquiries. He forbade her to be friendly with the men in her office and even objected to her being with her brother. If she even looked at another man in a car while they

110

were driving down the highway he would angrily challenge her. "What do you want to do? Sleep with him?" or "Does he look like someone you would want to sleep with?" he would shout.

In January, Lucy decided that she'd had enough of Craig's jealousy. So she and her daughter moved out of Craig's house and rented their own apartment. Lucy explained to Craig that it wasn't right for him to be subsidizing her and her little girl. "The truth of the matter is that I'm afraid of him," she told her friends.

But soon after they moved out, Lucy came home to find Craig sitting on her doorstep.

"Lucy, I love you," he convincingly pleaded. "Please let's get back together." After a while she agreed, although years later she couldn't understand why.

"Sometimes when you're in the middle of something, you really can't see how strange it is," she said.

This time Craig, who had opened his new store, moved in with Lucy and her daughter.

In May, Craig offered to take Lucy to Hawaii on a vacation. But the Hawaiian vacation was far from idyllic, Lucy said. As they were sipping cocktails during a happy hour in a bar in Maui, Lucy innocently mentioned that she had worked as a cocktail waitress when her daughter was younger and her husband had been laid off from his job.

Craig was incredulous.

"You did what?" he asked sharply. "I can't believe you'd go to work in a bar. Who took care of your daughter?"

"Craig, I left her with my mother," Lucy said in her own defense.

"Oh great," Craig said. "You worked in a bar and left your own daughter with somebody else. That's a really slutty thing to do and her father isn't worth a damn either. I can't stand the sight of him."

"But Craig, I didn't have a choice," Lucy insisted. "We needed the money."

The argument escalated and Craig began to curse Lucy's ex-husband. He even made a few disparaging remarks about her little girl and spoiled the evening. By the time they returned to their room, they weren't even speaking. The next morning, when she got up to go jogging, Craig forbade her to leave the room. When she went into the bathroom to take a shower, he came after her and slapped her across the face. Lucy immediately made up her mind to leave Craig as soon as they got home.

Since they returned to the Bay Area late at night, Lucy stayed at Craig's in San Carlos. In the morning she discovered that her car keys were missing so she called a locksmith. Lucy gave this account of what happened next:

As she attempted to take back her belongings, Craig "hit me behind the legs and threw me down on the floor and knocked the wind out of me. When I came to, of course I was hysterical."

Lucy claimed that Craig then punched her in the eye and in the ear while she was trying to scratch him. When she broke loose, she ran out the door to her car where the locksmith was finishing his job. She handed him $40, grabbed the newly made car keys and began to insert them in the driver's door lock. But Craig ran out of his house, she said, and tried to yank the new key out of her hand. While she was screaming at him to "get away" , one of Craig's neighbors stepped out onto his lawn. Craig backed off and Lucy sped away.

Her first stop was Craig's store where she encountered Doug Rees, Craig's partner, who was working that day. Lucy told Doug what had happened. "What should I do?" she wailed.

"I think you better tell the police," he advised.

She left the paint shop and drove immediately to the San Carlos Police Department, less than a mile away, where she filed an incident report alleging that she had been the victim of assault and battery.

According to the report filed at 1:30 p.m. on June 2, 1984, Lucy complained that an hour earlier, Craig A. Anderson had struck her on the face twice and bitten her right wrist once during a fight at his home. She told the officer who took the report that she and Anderson had just returned from a vacation in Hawaii and she was leaving his home when he assaulted her. The officer observed that the victim's upper lip was slightly swollen from one blow and her left cheek was slightly discolored from another blow. In addition, he noted that she had a swollen laceration on her right wrist where she claimed Anderson had bitten her.

Lucy, however, had calmed down by the time she related the entire story. She told the officer she did not wish to prosecute and asked for no additional help from the police regarding the incident.

That night, Lucy returned to her own apartment in Mountain View and, for a few days, her ex-husband moved in hoping to patch things up. But, despite the alleged violence, Lucy still didn't cut off her ties with Craig. As he had many times in the past when they argued, he called and sweetly apologized for his irrational behavior.

"I just lost my temper," he told her. "I promise it won't happen again." When her daughter had finished the school year in Mountain View, Lucy packed their things and moved in with Craig in San Carlos. But she finally moved out for good in November 1984. "We remained friends after that," she said.

Even when they weren't living together, Craig still tried to manage her private life, Lucy said. One night he called her and asked her out to dinner. She said she couldn't go because she was meeting a girlfriend at a bar in Menlo Park. Craig insisted that she was only going there to look for guys.

"I'm coming over right now," he said. Sure enough, he showed up a few minutes later. Lucy later claimed that Craig treated her like a prisoner, cornering her in her bedroom so she couldn't leave. Instead of fighting it, she let him take her out, she said. He stayed with her until 2 a.m. when he knew all the bars were closed.

By then, Lucy already suspected that Craig was dating someone else. Her suspicions were confirmed one night in early 1985 when she and her daughter stopped by Craig's house to bring him a little gift for his birthday. Lucy noticed a blue 280Z parked in front but didn't think much of it.

"I've got somebody here," Craig said to her when he opened the door, "You've got to go."

Lucy was furious. "He could always do what he wanted, but I couldn't."

Even then he couldn't seem to admit to Lucy that he had become seriously involved with someone else.

Sometime around May, Craig called Lucy at work and asked

her to ride her bike alongside him while he went jogging, a thing they often did together in the past.

"Ask the other girl," Lucy indignantly suggested.

"Oh come on, Lucy, we can still get together," he convinced her.

After their outing, they returned to his house and were standing in the front yard when the "other woman," who Lucy later came to know as Denise Redlick, drove up in her car. Denise, obviously angry, stomped right past the couple without saying a word and walked in the front door, "like she owned the place," Lucy observed.

"Oops, I guess I got caught," Craig meekly admitted.

Sometime in the late summer of 1985, Craig called Lucy at work and told her he had some of her mail. He asked her to meet him for dinner so he could give it to her. They had a pleasant evening and later, in the parking lot, he snuggled up to Lucy and attempted to kiss her.

Lucy—who had another boyfriend by then—shooed him away. "I'll always care about you, Craig," she told him, "but you have a girlfriend now. Be faithful to her."

In early October, Craig called her and said that he and Denise were no longer together. As he had told many other people, he described the argument at the wedding reception and said that Denise refused to see him anymore because he struck her. He said he was trying to set up meetings so they could work out their differences but she was living with her parents and she would only agree to meet him there.

Lucy thought he seemed depressed, kind of mopey, "like he felt as if he did something wrong and wanted to try to mend his ways."

But later in the month when she talked to Craig again, his demeanor had changed to one of bitterness, Lucy observed. "He wanted to just forget her and go his own way." He talked about joining a health club so he could meet new people and start his life over.

"That girl is just a heartless bitch," Craig told Lucy. "She is willing to throw away everything we built up together. She's not worth the trouble."

Lucy denied any knowledge of Craig putting a contract out on her ex-husband, but Marriscolo didn't think she seemed the least bit surprised by the accusation.

"He was very jealous of my ex-husband," Lucy told him. "Craig regarded Michael as a lowlife. He told me he hated to look at my daughter because it reminded him of the fact that I had been married before and reminded him of her father." In fact, the big fight that she and Craig had the day after they returned from Hawaii stemmed from the fact that she was going to pick up her daughter at her ex-husband's house and Craig thought it was just an ulterior motive to go see Michael.

When Marriscolo left, Lucy remembered that she had promised Craig that she could call him when she returned from her trip to tell him about Cancun. Now she had another reason to call.

After chatting about Mexico, Lucy asked Craig if he and Denise had gotten back together yet. She didn't give him any inkling that she had been contacted by the police or that she knew about Denise's disappearance.

"It's over between us," Craig said. "we're going our separate ways."

Lucy slowly put the receiver back in place. She was stunned that Craig had not even mentioned Denise having disappeared.

Marriscolo also learned that on August 1st, 1984, Craig had gone to the San Carlos City Hall, two months after Lucy Larson filed her allegations of assault and battery, and filed a report of his own. In it, he claimed that Weeks owed Craig's company more than $5000; $4000 for equipment, $800 for a cash loan and $350 to reimburse a bad check. The report also stated that Weeks had threatened to "put the company out of business." Anderson said he had made a friendly effort to no avail to obtain at least partial payment and was planning to take legal action as a last resort.

Anderson claimed that on the day he filed the report with the San Carlos Police Department, Weeks had turned up at the paint store and requested another $900 in cash as a loan to help him recover from a badly underbid job. Craig said he refused to help. At that, Weeks made "veiled threats" about the paint store, Craig alleged. Weeks left the store but called later to say that he was going to cause trouble for Anderson's business through routine inspections.

Anderson said that his business had been inspected by South County Fire Department officials just two months before, in June, and three minor infractions of the city's fire code had been found. All of them were corrected. A fire department inspector had returned to check the work that had been done and given the business a clean bill of health. But on the day that Craig went to City Hall, Anderson Paint had been reinspected on a reported complaint by Richard Weeks. The new inspection had cost him $80 for additional permits that had not been needed in June.

"Anderson is very afraid that his attempt to get the owed money will result in Weeks' doing damage to Anderson's home and business," the San Carlos officer wrote. At the time Craig said he only wanted the police to be aware of the alleged threats in case anything else should happen.

Could Weeks be believed or did he have a vendetta against Craig? Did Craig Anderson, a man with no criminal record, really attempt to arrange a murder contract?

These were the questions that Marriscolo had to consider and he knew he needed more than just Weeks' statement to even consider taking the case to the district attorney. But Weeks said there were others who could give the police information about the transaction. One of them, he claimed, was Doug Rees, Craig's former business partner who now lived in Sacramento. Marriscolo located Rees and made the two hour drive to California's state capital for an interview.

Rees recalled that in 1984, a week or so after Lucy and Craig returned from Hawaii, Richard Weeks came into the store to conduct some business. Doug said he was in the warehouse portion of the shop when he heard Craig ask Weeks if he would "do away" with Lucy's ex-husband. Doug wasn't terribly surprised by the request since a few days earlier, Craig had asked him if he knew somebody who could kill Michael Brunicon. Doug said he had assumed it was a joke and just let it go. "I thought it was only anger speaking," Doug said.

However, Doug had referred Craig to a friend, Emad Musa, who owned a liquor store in San Francisco. But before Craig could even contact Musa, Doug called and told him to "laugh it off" if Anderson should call and ask for help in arranging a killing.

Doug said he had also spoken to Weeks who had said he didn't intend to carry out Anderson's request.

Doug Rees arrived at work on December 11th to find two phone messages, both from Craig Anderson. On the second call, Craig had told the secretary to relay this message: "We've got a problem and we need to talk."

As he had been advised, Rees called the Burlingame Police Department. Chase contacted a homicide detective with the Sacramento County Sheriff's Office who arrived at Doug's office and attached a tape recorder to the phone, Doug finally returned Craig's call at 11:17 a.m.

The two former business partners talked for about fifteen minutes.

Anderson told Rees he was thinking about taking a vacation, maybe to a Club Med in Mexico or Maui for a week or two in early January, and asked Rees if he would like to go along. Craig said he "split over that chick a while ago" and he had been wanting to get away.

"It's been an unusual situation 'cause she evidently took off somewhere," Anderson declared, adding that no one knew where she went.

He also said he was fed up with the way the police had been browbeating him about Denise's disappearance. He said one cop, apparently referring to Marriscolo, came into the shop and "just about turned me upside down." In fact, he heard that the police had been trying to track down a video tape of the wedding where Craig had, by his own admission, gotten into a fight with Denise and wound up slapping her.

"They're digging, you know, for anything and everything," Anderson said to Rees who mumbled his agreement. Then he asked for Rees' help. "You know, I couldn't see anyone even talking to you but, if they do, don't mention anything about any of my old girlfriends or anything like that," Craig said. "You know what I mean?"

"Yeah," Doug said uncomfortably since he had already talked to the police about Lucy.

"You know, you don't know anyone," Craig stressed.

"Yeah, well, just don't worry about it," Rees responded. The two men chatted a while longer about possible vacation destinations. Before they hung up, Rees encouraged Craig to call again. "You know where I am if you need to talk," he said.

The Sacramento homicide detective who had sat in during the call detached the tape recorder and handed the tape to Doug, as he had been instructed to do by Burlingame police. When the detective was gone, Doug went over the conversation in his mind. Craig was his friend, a nice guy, and the Anderson family had always treated him well. Even though they had some disagreements as business partners, their split was amicable. He had no reason, no desire, to contribute to any trouble that Craig might have found himself in with the police.

But Doug was alarmed by the comment about old girlfriends. If he's innocent, Doug thought, what's he trying to hide? Doug had seen how Craig treated Lucy and he had once remarked to Craig's sister, "One day your brother is going to do something that he's really going to regret." The more Doug got to thinking about Denise Redlick, the more he got a sickening feeling that his prophecy may have come true.

That afternoon, Doug placed the cassette tape in a box, went to the post office and sent it to Tom Marriscolo by certified mail.

That same evening, Richard Weeks returned to the Burlingame police station where Marriscolo and Collopy taped a transmitter smaller than a cigarette pack and a wire connected to a tiny microphone on his torso. The radio device was completely concealed by his clothes. Weeks then drove to Craig Anderson's house. The two officers, in a narcotics unit surveillance van, sat outside.

As Collopy and Marriscolo listened to the conversation between Anderson and Weeks, they looked at each other, shaking their heads in disbelief. Weeks had turned into an inventive actor. Numerous times he had strayed way beyond the dialogue that they had planned for him. In exasperation Collopy finally looked at Marriscolo and said, "Why doesn't he just shut the fuck up and get on with it?"

Weeks informed Craig that the police had been asking him questions about Denise Redlick and that they were on to him about "this Mike dude."

"What happened is, somehow they got that piece of paper that you wrote that shit down on," Weeks said, reminding Anderson of the written description of Brunicon. In truth, the piece of paper, if it had ever existed had either been thrown out or lost.

"Dick, get out of here," Anderson said.

"I'm serious, man. I think my partner stole it out of my fucking files," Weeks said.

Weeks inventively claimed that he was going to be subpoenaed to testify before the grand jury (San Mateo County doesn't even have a grand jury to hear criminal charges) and that the cops were "threatening to put me in jail." Continuing his imaginative ranting, Weeks told Anderson that investigators had been harassing him for six days in a row.

"The cops can't subpoena anyone because they don't have anything to go on," Anderson interrupted. "Dick, just live your life like you normally do," he calmly advised.

Over and over, Weeks insisted that he had "to get out of Dodge," maybe to Florida or Las Vegas, or the police were going to get him. But, he told Craig, he didn't have the money to leave.

"Can you cover me to get out of the state?" Weeks asked.

"I don't have any money at the moment," Anderson said.

"All I'm asking is for a plane ticket out of the state, man," Weeks tried again. "Or maybe a couple of hundred dollars to get me started."

Finally, Anderson gave Weeks $300 saying, "that's all I have right now." And then, seeming to sense that something didn't smell right added, "Are you setting me up or anything?" just before handing over the cash.

Weeks brushed the question aside. Thanking Craig for the money, he said as far as he was concerned, "nothing happened."

"Okay, nothing happened," Craig repeated, seeming happy to get the jittery Weeks out of his house.

As prearranged, Weeks drove immediately to Lyon's Restau-

rant a short distance away and met the two officers in the restroom where they removed the concealed radio transmitter containing two mini cassette tapes of the conversation, and took the
three $100 bills into evidence.

■ CHAPTER TWELVE ■

Clues

Mark Gooch had spent almost everyday for a month searching for Denise Redlick. After he and Denise had dated in 1983 and 1984, they had remained good friends. Only this past November they had gone out to dinner and discussed old times.

Now, with Denise missing for more than a month, he was exhausted from thinking about the way things could have been and deeply depressed that the search for her had turned up nothing. Mark, a tall, fair-haired painting contractor with a gruff voice, had gone to high school with Denise and knew many of her best friends. Besides joining the search parties at Coyote Point and on the bayfront, Mark had gotten in his car one day and spent hours driving up and down the coast and around the Crystal Springs Reservoir area hoping to stumble upon a clue.

Gooch called up a friend on December 17th and suggested that they meet at TGI Friday's, a popular San Bruno restaurant, that night for drinks. "I've really got to just unwind and talk to someone," he told her. She said she would try to meet him around 7:00 p.m.

Mark arrived quite early, found an empty stool at the noisy bar and ordered a beer. With his friend nowhere in sight, he began to listen to the conversation of four men occupying the stools to his left and realized that by coincidence, they were painters, too. Gooch, a friendly person, joined in, mentioning to the man closest to him that he was in the same line of work.

"No kidding," said the long-haired blond man seated on the stool next to Mark who introduced himself as Ted Burns. "We've been working on a new Tudor house over on Easton in Burlingame. It's a big job, expected to last a few weeks."

Mark was interested. "Oh really," he said. "I put in a bid for that job but I guess they got somebody who would do it for less. Who got the contract anyway?"

"A guy by the name of Craig Anderson," the painter answered.

Gooch nearly choked on a swig of beer. Quickly glancing up, he realized that Ted hadn't sensed his alarmed reaction. Mark instantly decided to stay cool and find out whatever he could.

For a few minutes, they engaged in job talk. Ted said he had been working as a job site foreman for Anderson for over the past year, that he had done about fifteen jobs for him, and that business had been good. As the other painters left the bar, Mark bought Ted another Long Island Iced Tea and encouraged him to stay.

"Yeah, I've heard of this Anderson guy." Mark said. "What do you think of him?"

Ted shrugged. "He's a boss, not much different than any other, I guess," he said, brushing off the question.

"Isn't he the one whose girlfriend is missing?" asked Mark.

"Yeah, that's the guy," Ted replied and abruptly changed the subject to talk about another painting job that he had recently worked on in San Carlos.

But Mark deftly steered Ted back to the subject of Denise Redlick and the extensive publicity about her disappearance. For a while, they discussed the possibility that the woman, whose pretty face was on posters taped to the lobby doors of the very restaurant in which they were sitting, had been murdered.

Ted, who was well into his third or fourth Long Island Iced Tea, a potent mixture of several types of liquor, was feeling increasingly comfortable with his affable bar companion. "You know, I can't say if Anderson did it or not, but it wouldn't surprise me if he did," Ted suddenly declared. "He could be capable of it. He's pretty weird."

Mark was startled by the candid remark. But Ted was jumping to another subject again. As they talked about growing up in the Bay Area and where each of them had lived, they discovered that one of Ted's friends in high school was Mark's first cousin.

"I can't believe it," Ted laughed. "I feel a lot closer to you now knowing that Joe is your cousin. It's really a small world."

To celebrate the unexpected link, Mark bought Ted another drink.

"What if I were to tell you that I know a little more about this guy Anderson than most people do?" Ted asked.

"Well go ahead. Tell me. We're close now and you can consider me a friend."

"It's like this. I told the cops a lie. I told them I went to Craig's store and that I saw him there the day that girl disappeared. But I really didn't see him there at all."

Mark shivered. He hesitated a little, weighing whether it was the right time to tell Ted that his interest in the case was personal. He took a deep breath and looked Ted in his glassy eyes.

"What if I were to tell you that Denise Redlick is a former girlfriend of mine and I miss her very much and have been helping to look for her for a month?"

This time it was Ted's turn to choke.

"Hey you aren't some kind of cop are you?" Ted asked with a panicked look. " 'Cause if you are, I'm out of here." He started to get up from his bar stool but Mark grabbed him by the arm.

"Oh no you don't. You aren't leaving now. If you try to walk out of here after what you told me, you can be sure that you aren't going to walk out of here in one piece!"

Ted turned and realized that Mark, who was a few inches taller and about twenty pounds heavier than himself, was serious.

"Please, you might know something that could save this girl's life!" Mark pleaded. "She could be out there somewhere right now, alive. We don't know where she is or what condition she's in. We need all the help we can get."

Ted sat back down.

"Craig paid me to tell the cops that I saw him at the store on Veteran's Day. I went to the store that afternoon to get him to pay me for a job but it was closed. I think he might have paid some other people, too."

"You've got to tell the police what you are telling me," Mark urged him.

"No way. I've got my own problems and I don't want to get into any more trouble for lying."

"The cops don't care about you. They care about what happened to Denise," Mark insisted. He told Ted about how her disappearance had devastated her family and friends and that many of them were suspicious of Craig.

"You could be letting a guy who is guilty of kidnapping, maybe even murder, go free," Mark said.

Finally, Ted agreed that he would talk to the police again. But that it would have to be the next morning, not that night. He gave Mark his address and Mark said he would pick him up at 10:00 a.m. Mark thought Ted seemed sincere about setting the record straight, but as they shook hands and walked outside the parking lot, Mark wondered if Ted might get cold feet by the morning. Just to be on the safe side, he discreetly followed Ted to his apartment in South San Francisco just to be sure he hadn't been given a phony address. After calling the bar to alert his friend that he wouldn't be there, he drove home and called Marriscolo. Mark was up most of the night, waiting impatiently for the next day.

To Mark's relief, Ted was waiting at his apartment for a ride on Wednesday morning as planned. They said little as they drove to the Burlingame police station. Van Etten and Collopy were waiting for them. As the four men sat at a table in the detective bureau, Burns poured out his story.

Ted said that on November 12th, he, his two brothers and his father went to Anderson's store between 8:00 a.m. and 9:00 a.m. to talk to Craig about some money he believed Craig owed him. Craig led Ted into his office in the warehouse area and asked him if he would tell the police that he had seen Craig at the store around 1:00 p.m. on Monday. Craig had held up five fingers and said, "it's worth this," Ted claimed, understanding the gesture to mean $500. Ted said that although he was initially reluctant, he finally agreed to do it. He recalled that Craig gave him $200 or $300 that day.

Burns also said he noticed scratches on Anderson's neck and hands at that time.

When Ted was gone, Collopy and Van Etten considered what they had heard.

"Maybe he's just trying to collect the reward," Collopy skeptically suggested.

It was clear, however, what the next step should be. The officers needed to track down the other men who had provided alibis for Anderson to make sure that they, too, hadn't misled the investigation.

One by one, the alibis began to collapse.

Mike Shea, the general contractor who originally told Commander Chase that he had picked up supplies at Anderson's store around noon on November 11th, told the officers that he could no longer be so sure of the date. Anderson had asked him to tell police that he had been there at that time, and since he wasn't certain if he had, he just went along with the seemingly harmless request. Shea conceded that if it really got down to court, he couldn't swear that he had seen Anderson in the shop that day.

Frank Roberts, the paint spray equipment salesman also told them he might have been confused. While he originally thought he had gone to Anderson Paint Company at around 4:30 p.m. on November 11th, he later realized he had been there on Friday, November 8th instead. Roberts discussed being an avid 49er fan with season tickets and confided that when he thought about that memorable game with Denver, he realized he hadn't just come home from Anderson's shop when he sat down to watch the game on his television set at home.

Roberts also remembered giving Craig a ride to work on the morning of November 13th. During their short ride, Craig had said his girlfriend was missing and that if Roberts was questioned by the police, it would "mean a lot to him" if he would tell the cops he was in the store on November 11th.

The new statements by the so-called alibi witnesses made Ted Burns' story seem believable afterall.

Inspector Marriscolo carried a fat file of reports as he strode into the Municipal Court Building in San Mateo. His mission was to obtain a warrant for the arrest of Craig Anderson on two counts of soliciting a murder, one count relating to Richard Weeks and one count relating to Emad Musa.

At the door to Municipal Court Judge Gregory Jensen's chambers, Marriscolo met Chief Deputy District Attorney Bob Bishop, an introspective and quiet man who flies his own plane, to attend convicted murderers' parole hearings around the state. Bishop, who takes an interest in technical legal details, had assisted the detective in preparing the documents. Included in the official papers was a fifteen-page affidavit that summarized every important interview that the Burlingame police had conducted in their investigation of Denise Redlick and Craig Anderson. Included were the shocking interviews with Craig's former girlfriends portraying him as an allegedly possessive, jealous and sometimes irrational lover who has resorted to physical violence to keeping his women in line. Marriscolo had provided several eye-opening examples of the women's allegations.

As Marriscolo and Bishop entered the judge's chambers and sat down, Marriscolo laid the file on Jensen's mahogany desk. In most cases the amount of bail in an arrest warrant is a matter of mutual agreement between the judge and the detective. But Marriscolo knew that it was imperative to keep Anderson in jail so that the police could search for further evidence about Denise Redlick's disappearance. Marriscolo also believed that Craig and his parents were well off. For the detective's objectives to be met, bail would have to be astronomically high. He took a deep breath and made what he hoped was a convincing plea.

"Here's what we've got," he said to Jensen, flipping open the file with a flourish. Quickly he went over the basic details of the case from Denise's disappearance through the murder solicitation allegation and, just that morning, the retracted alibi.

"This man is a danger to the community and a considerable flight risk," Marriscolo fervently argued. He noted that Craig, in one conversation with Joan Redlick, had made threatening remarks even about the police, particularly himself.

"What do you think would be reasonable?" Jensen asked already beginning to thumb through the papers before him. "The bail schedule for a murder solicitation is only $5000."

Tom was ready. "I'm asking for a half million," the detective responded without missing a beat.

The judge raised his eyebrow and locked glances with Marriscolo. Bishop, sitting alongside Marriscolo smiled. He'll never get it, the prosecutor thought to himself. Then the judge dropped his head and began to look slowly over the rest of the file before him, pausing every once in a while to ask a question. Marriscolo saw him hold up the letter drafted by Commander Chase asking for a bail significantly higher than the current bail schedule based on the likelihood that Craig Anderson would flee the jurisdiction if given the chance.

The letter went on to state: "Craig Anderson is so preoccupied with his image in the community and so confident that it is not and cannot be sullied, that his arrest in this matter will cause him to suffer a greater degree of humiliation than can be tolerated by his image of his own personage.

"Anderson has nothing of significant worth in this geographic area to preclude his ego's need fulfillment by fleeing and starting anew in some other area and, thusly, avoiding total embarrassment in this area," Chase further claimed backing Marriscolo's request.

After asking a few more questions, the judge looked off in the distance for a few minutes. Silence permeated the room. Beads of sweat broke out on Marriscolo's upper lip. Then quietly the judge announced his decision. He signed his name and dated the arrest warrant and the search warrants.

When Marriscolo left the judge's chambers that afternoon, he had two very good reasons for the big grin on his face. That day was his thirty-ninth birthday and he was going to be celebrating it with an astounding $500,000 warrant for Craig Anderson's arrest.

For three weeks after Denise had disappeared, Joan and Harry couldn't even think about work. But during the first week of December, they both realized that staying home every day wasn't going to bring Denise back. Even though Joan was constantly crying and Harry was filled with rage, they agreed that they had to get out of the house and reluctantly returned to their jobs.

Lynn Redlick was making dinner on the Wednesday night before Christmas when the phone rang yet again. Since Denise's disappearance, the calls had been constant. Some people felt more comfortable calling Mike and Lynn for updates than they did calling Joan and Harry. Lynn, who was extremely fond of her missing sister-in-law and was as deeply distraught over her disappearance as any of Denise's blood relatives, patiently answered the same questions over and over.

However, she was unprepared to hear Craig on the other end of the line this time.

"I really feel lousy about everything that has been going on," Craig said to her. He added that he knew the police were watching him and that they considered him a suspect. If he was trying to get information out of Lynn about the investigation, he didn't succeed. Lynn listened and volunteered nothing.

Craig went on to say he felt very badly for Joan and Harry and that he loved them as much as anyone could love his own parents.

"I couldn't do anything to hurt Denise," he insisted as Lynn, who had not yet made up her own mind about Craig's possible role in Denise's disappearance, listened. But knowing that suspicions within her family were strong, she was momentarily speechless when Craig asked her if he could bring a Christmas present on Thursday for her son, Matthew. Lynn said she wasn't sure she would be home and suggested that he give her a call first.

Craig had no way of knowing that he would not get the chance.

Chase was sound asleep when the phone alongside his bed jarred him awake at 11:00 p.m. He recognized the voice of a dispatcher who had roused him from his sleep on many other nights.

"You've got a call from a Shirley Anderson," the dispatcher told him. "She wants to talk to you right now."

Chase, who lived only a few blocks from the Andersons' house, was out the door in a matter of minutes. "I would have gone in my bathrobe if I had to," he later said. Concealed under his sweater was a voice-activated tape recorder. With Craig's arrest scheduled to occur in less than twelve hours, Chase was hopeful that the suspect's mother might confide something that would aid in the investigation.

Mrs. Anderson had apparently asked him to her house, he said later, to vent her frustrations with the way that the police had targeted her son. Over a cup of tea, she dutifully defended Craig and insisted that her son could not harm anyone. She was offended and hurt that the investigators could be suspicious of Craig.

Throughout the conversation, Chase tried to encourage her to talk freely about Craig and any problems he may have had in the past that would enlighten the police in their probing of his background. Instead, she denied ever hearing that her son had abused other women and reminded Chase that Craig had never had any trouble before with the police.

When the commander returned home an hour later, he was tired and disappointed. He also felt badly for deceiving Craig Anderson's mother, for not giving her any clue that, in just a few hours, her oldest son would be behind bars.

■ CHAPTER THIRTEEN ■

Under Arrest

When Craig Anderson arrived for work at 9 a.m. on Thursday, December 19th, Burlingame police officers were discreetly watching him from two cars parked outside. Before Craig could even sit down, Commander Chase opened the door to the immaculate shop filled with neatly stacked cans of paint.

"Craig, I've said all along that you can talk to me," Chase began. "Is there anything you want to tell me now?"

Craig looked dumbfounded. "Tom, I've already told you everything there is to say," he declared, "I told you I have no idea where Denise is."

"I'm not here about that," Chase abruptly answered. "I'm here about Richard Weeks and Michael Brunicon."

"What are you talking about?" he asked in a perplexed tone.

"Dick says you asked him to have Brunicon killed. Is that true?" Chase asked.

"That's crazy," Anderson responded. "I don't know what you're talking about."

Chase went on to reiterate the information that had been given to the police about Lucy and Michael and about interviews with Doug Rees, Emad Musa and other sources that had reinforced the allegations of solicitation for murder. He told Craig about the interviews with his old girlfriends and how they had all described him as jealous and violent. Chase tried to determine Craig's reaction but detected no response at all. Craig simply stood there, looking absolutely blank.

"Well then," Chase continued, "I have in my hand a warrant for your arrest, and search warrants for your house, your business and your cars."

Craig turned pale and stood there silently as Chase explained, "You're under arrest for soliciting the murder of Michael Brunicon."

The commander had positioned himself so that Marriscolo, Collopy and Van Etten, seated outside in the unmarked police car, could see him. Although Chase was bugged so that the other officers could hear the conversation over the SK9 line, the quality of reception that morning was poor. But they knew when they heard through the static the word "warrant," it was their cue to join Tom in the paint store. They were at his side in a matter of seconds.

Walking to either side of Anderson, Collopy and Marriscolo placed handcuffs around his wrists and read him his Miranda rights. When asked, Craig meekly gave them his key ring to expedite the court-ordered search. Then they led him outside to Chase's car and sat him in the front passenger's seat. Still hoping to win the suspect's confidence, Chase removed Craig's handcuffs before sliding into his own seat.

Craig turned toward Chase and said tonelessly, "Is my arrest going to be made public for the media and that kind of thing? Are her parents going to be told about this right now?"

Chase nodded. "Of course, the arrest will be a matter of public record." He also reminded Craig of his Miranda rights, that he didn't have to answer any questions if he didn't want to and that he could have an attorney anytime he wanted.

"Yes, I understand," Craig murmured.

Chase said quietly, firmly, "Frankly, the evidence does look a little bleak. You have to help yourself," he added, "you did the most damage to your credibility when you paid Terry to get out of town. I don't want to see you dig a hole any deeper than what you're already in. I just hope you'll level with me."

"Look," Craig interrupted, "I have an explanation. Dick owed me some money and I felt that he was also the type who could keep an eye on Brunicon, nothing more, because I feared that some of the negative things I said about Lucy's ex-husband might get back to him. I was afraid of my house, of getting my windows kicked in or whatever, and of my business. Besides, when Dick said he needed some money that night, he seemed like he was high on something and the idea was to get him out of my house."

Craig waited for Chase to reply and, when he didn't, rambled on further, "I feared for my safety. Period. Bottom line. I hadn't seen him in I don't know how long. He comes driving up to my door and I didn't even want to let him in the house."

The older man's features stiffened. "Maybe, but they'll testify that you wanted Brunicon killed."

"They can testify whatever they want, but that never entered into it," Craig said. "At some point in time I might have said something off the cuff to Doug like, 'Man, I wish the guy was dead', but at no time did I enter into any kind of agreement to rub a guy out. I would never even think of anything like that," he insisted.

Chase steered the rambling dialogue toward the allegations made by Craig's ex-girlfriends.

Craig looked away.

"Well, Craig, the interviews with your old girlfriends paint a picture that is not very flattering," Chase said thoughtfully. "What stands out among other things is the fact that you would be talking about things with these women and all of a sudden you would become real angry. And for a short time you would become very abusive to them. Then, a few minutes later, you would calm right back down."

Again, Chase waited for a reaction from Craig and when Craig said nothing, he went on, "I feel you're not the kind of guy who intended to hurt anyone, that you just lost control for a few minutes or so." He tapped his forehead with his finger.

Craig watched him closely as he spoke. "But that has nothing to do with Denise."

"I know, but it sure helps us put together the whole history of violence."

"I know it does but . . ." Craig protested.

"And there's Lucy who's going to say you kicked the shit out of her in Hawaii," Chase said forcefully. "That's what she and her ex-husband are willing to testify." He pointed a finger at Craig.

"Don't you see? That's what I'm telling you. I mean, you can kid some of the people part of the time, but Jesus Christ . . ."

"I'm not kidding anyone," Craig said showing a touch of anger for the first time. "I don't know how any of this is relevant. I don't feel guilty and I don't feel any remorse because I haven't done anything. I had nothing to do with Denise's disappearance or her abduction or whatever," he bit his lip.

The car pulled into the garage of the station and Chase led his prisoner upstairs for booking. After Craig had been fingerprinted, photographed and allowed to call his mother, Chase, rather than locking Craig in a holding cell, walked the prisoner down the hall to the detective bureau. He sat Craig down in an interview room furnished with a matching couch, armchair, subdued lighting and soft, classical music playing in the background. The room was designed to help the victim of a traumatic crime—a sexual assault for example—feel comfortable enough to talk freely. Chase was hoping the atmosphere might encourage Craig Anderson to make some startling revelation. Once inside, the commander reminded Anderson, who was now officially under arrest, of his legal rights.

The two men, seated across from each other, chatted amiably. Craig continued to deny that he ever arranged to have Brunicon murdered, complaining that the whole affair had been blown way out of proportion.

As they talked, Chase kept guiding Anderson back toward the allegations of his past violence against women. Craig acknowledged that he knew what happened between him and his other girlfriends "wouldn't be a very palatable thing for the authorities." But Anderson protested that "none of those things has anything to do with Denise Redlick."

"For the first time in my life I was able to simply walk away from my problems with Denise and not become unstable about it. I felt very good about that, very confident about that," Craig declared.

But Chase warned him, "A jury will listen to these stories and find the ultimate—where you have been rejected at the last minute, the worst rejection you have had so far."

"I didn't feel rejected though, Tom," Craig insisted. "The

break-up," he said slowly with subtle emphasis on the last word, "was something that was inevitable. Denise and I just hadn't sat down and talked about various issues the way we should have."

"A psychiatrist might see things differently," Chase interrupted. "That might be the 'frosting on the cake' in a circumstantial case. People have, in fact, gone to prison on circumstantial evidence alone," he carefully added.

Then Chase hammered away at Craig's "image," saying forcefully, "it might be to your benefit to admit, right now, that you're not a perfect human afterall, that there's a chink in the armour. Otherwise, in court, you're going to feel like there's a whole army charging with spears and you're standing out there fuckin'-ass naked on a hill."

As they sat silently for a few minutes, Craig passed a hand over his forehead. Then he began slowly, "I haven't leveled with you before about my trouble with girlfriends because I didn't like all the double-talk that was being thrown in my direction." Then he began to digress again.

Listening to him, Chase decided the interview had run its course. Anderson was still beating around the bush and to talk to him any longer would simply be a waste of time.

Rising, Chase locked the handcuffs around his suspect's wrists and led him through the detective bureau to the holding cell. "Look," Chase said slowly, "First, we'll make a thorough search of your house, business and cars. Maybe that will clear you." He tried to make his voice sound sympathetic and responsive. Although by this time Chase had become convinced that Anderson, in fact, had killed Denise and was, in Chase's opinion, a pathological liar.

He knew the real problem was going to be proving it with no body, no weapon, no witnesses, and no tangible evidence of death.

■ CHAPTER FOURTEEN ■

Search Warrant

Contrary to what most people believe, a search warrant is not an open-ended hunting license. Inspector Marriscolo, in an affidavit given to Judge Jensen and later filed with the municipal court clerk, had listed those things that he and other officers would be seeking as they searched Craig's business, house, Mercedes and station wagon. Specifically mentioned were the clothing and jewelry that Denise was wearing on November 11th, the credit cards, bank accounts and checking account books that were believed to be in her purse, and any "human hair and body fluids and blood belonging to Denise Redlick."

In addition, Judge Jensen gave the Burlingame police permission to seize records of bank accounts held by Craig Anderson, Image Investment or Roy Anderson Paint Company, to probe for any possible financial transactions between Richard Weeks and Craig, and telephone records to look for calls made in connection with the alleged solicitation of Brunicon's murder or the disappearance of Denise Redlick. By law, a list of the materials seized at any of the locations must be returned to the court clerk in ten days.

As soon as Chase had left the Anderson Paint Company with his prisoner seated next to him, Marriscolo, Collopy and Van Etten set about their task.

The officers worked their way from the front to the back of Craig's store, finding very little of interest until they began sifting through files in Craig's office in the warehouse area. Looking through a file box containing records for sales over the past months, Marriscolo immediately flipped to Monday, November 11th. There, he found what appeared to be three receipts for sales. Marriscolo recognized the printing on the invoices as Craig's. The three transactions, for $21.26, $15.16, $26.99 plus tax, each indicated the amount and type of paint purchased. On each invoice, Craig had filled in the space for the date: 11-11-85. Sitting with the three invoices was a print out from an adding machine. Again, the date 11-11-85 was printed at the top with net sales totaling $63.41 for the day.

While looking through the warehouse area, Van Etten called the detectives' attention to several ten-foot wide rolls of black plastic, the kind of material used as a ground cover by painters. The officers thought it might have another use.

"You could roll up a body and bury it in that stuff," Van Etten said.

Besides the sales receipts, saving and checking account books and bank statements, the search netted phone records for August, September, October and November, one pair of silver scissors "with unknown matter on them" , and a torn white shirt that the officers envisioned might have been involved in some kind of struggle.

Outside, the detectives used one key on the ring that Craig had given them to enter Craig's station wagon. Under the storage area in the rear of the vehicle, they found numerous packages containing wedding gifts addressed to Craig and Denise. Marriscolo made arrangements for both the station wagon and the Mercedes, which Craig had said was parked in the driveway at his house, to be towed to the police station for a detailed forensic examination.

At 1:00 p.m., the three detectives drove to the house. Marriscolo went through the motions of a proper search, vigorously knocking on the door and yelling "Police! We have a search warrant! Open up!," even though he was absolutely certain no one was home.

Again the officers sifted through Craig's drawers and looked under and on top of furniture and through closets.

In the search warrant affidavit, Marriscolo had told the judge he would be looking for large amounts of cash which several witnesses had told him Craig kept in his house. Specific permission was granted to search Anderson's safe. Although Craig had provided the officers with the key, Marriscolo temporarily misplaced it and, in a rush, decided to break the safe open. He found out that his sources hadn't exaggerated. The safe contained $17,900 in cash which was confiscated and turned over to Craig's attorney a few days later.

The officers also had permission to search the yard area. Along the side of the house, under a stack of wood, were two additional unopened packages in brown postal-style wrappers addressed to Denise Redlick. Reading the return address on the label, Marriscolo realized that, like the boxes found in the station wagon, they were two of the wedding gifts that Craig had adamantly refused were in is possession when confronted about them by Joan Redlick.

The detectives had collected a few items of interest: Denise's passport from under Craig's waterbed, three gold chains that they thought might include one Denise had been wearing, and a woman's gold wedding ring that they later learned was to have been Denise's. When Van Etten opened the drawer of a desk in the dining room, he found four picture frames, all turned face down. The detective flipped them over and felt a chill. Three of the pictures were of Denise with either Craig or members of his family.

All three of the detectives were stricken with what they felt was an intentional, not accidental, action on Craig's part.

"If Anderson is telling the truth and he had nothing to do with Denise's disappearance, this sure seems strange," Van Etten said. "When you're engaged to marry someone, you've got very strong feelings about that person." Jack felt that if Craig still loved Denise, he would have displayed the photographs. If he simply hated her for rejecting him, he would have thrown them out.

"But he had quite deliberately turned them over," Jack said. Any good detective knows that, in homicides, a killer often keeps something to remind him of his victim. The turned over pictures, he thought, meant that in his mind, Craig still had a connection with Denise. "And that connection was murder."

In his twenty-five years in law enforcement, Chase had never before held a press conference. Like most cops, he had found many occasions for criticizing reporters—for being inaccurate, for being judgemental, for sensationalizing cases in which officers came off looking bad.

On the other hand, Chase was astute enough to know that police departments could sometimes use the media to their own advantage. He saw that potential advantage in briefing them about Craig Anderson.

"Someone out there has got to know something but just hasn't put it all together yet," Chase told Chief Fred Palmer after Anderson had been locked away in holding cell number two. "The press could go crazy over this story. I'm thinking maybe we ought to help them along."

Palmer agreed and in less than an hour, Commander John Parkin, the department's media liaison, had notified every newspaper and every television and radio news department in the area that a press conference would be held at the Burlingame Police Station at 3:00 p.m. to announce a development related to the Redlick case. The timing guaranteed coverage on the evening news programs and in the San Francisco Chronicle, the paper with the largest circulation in the Bay Area, the next morning.

Four television stations, three radio stations and six newspapers were represented at the press conference. Photographers and cameramen positioned themselves around the room as Chase and Marriscolo sat at a bare formica table in front of the meeting room.

"Today, Burlingame Police Department investigators arrested Craig Alan Anderson on charges of soliciting a crime of murder," Chase began at 3:10 p.m. "Mr. Anderson came to our attention while we were investigating the disappearance of Denise Redlick. Anderson is Miss Redlick's ex-fiance."

The room stirred. Reporters had repeatedly been told over the past month that Anderson had been cleared in the Redlick case and was not a suspect in her possible kidnapping or murder. Chase was now essentially telling reporters that they hadn't been told the truth. That, in fact, Anderson had been the focus of their efforts from day one.

"In tracing Craig Anderson's love affairs back more than ten years to his high school days, our department came in contact with an individual who said that Anderson paid him $1000 in 1984 to have the former husband of a woman Anderson was dating at that time killed," Chase explained. "Three other individuals have corroborated the story.

As startled reporters scribbled notes, Chase continued, "We learned that Anderson blamed the former husband for his own break-up with the girlfriend." He paused meaningfully and then went on to say that Anderson had described to the would-be murderer the appearance of the man he wanted killed and had even driven his hired client-in-crime to Mountain View in the southern Peninsula to see where the unsuspecting assassination target was living at the time.

"The killing was never carried out," Chase emphasized. "And over the past year, Anderson has been trying to get his money back." Chase looked around him searchingly at the sea of faces. Astute reporters were bound to decide the solicitation for murder charge was partly a department ploy to get what they really wanted—information on Denise Redlick's disappearance. He had to decide how much to tell them.

Chase stopped speaking as reporters, baffled by this bizarre turn of events in the case, began firing questions.

"Was the person who allegedly accepted the murder-for-hire contract, experienced in this sort of thing?"

"He had a criminal background," Chase said, "although none of the earlier charges against him involved murder."

"Would charges be filed against anyone else?"

"No other arrest is anticipated," Chase said, stressing the word anticipated. "It is an example of a situation in which, we would say, there is no honor among thieves. The individual who had been 'hired' took the money without ever intending to kill or arrange the killing of anyone."

Changing the subject, the reporters began to shout questions, eager to take back to their offices new details concerning the page one, five-week old Redlick case. More specifically, they wanted to know if the police had uncovered any evidence pinning Denise's disappearance on Craig.

Marriscolo slowly but firmly gave his answer.

"We are now considering Craig Anderson the prime suspect in Denise Redlick's disappearance," he said, giving the reporters an even stronger lead for their stories. It was the first time that the police officers had acknowledged in public that Craig Anderson, a successful San Carlos businessman who came from an affluent and well thought-of family and was once considered "quite a catch", could be a cold-blooded killer.

"We found that at least two of Anderson's alibi witnesses for the day Miss Redlick disappeared have changed their stories," Marriscolo said, carefully choosing his words. "They no longer are certain of Anderson's whereabouts on November 11. Why they changed their stories, we aren't exactly sure. We certainly didn't provoke them to do so." He stared into the room of reporters hoping he had stirred their interest.

A dark haired television reporter immediately piped up. "Give us information about Anderson and his story, specifically what he was saying about Miss Redlick's disappearance."

Chase paused. "He is an individual who is very imageconscious, who holds himself in high regard and portrays himself as a suitable individual."

"However," he went on, almost letting the remark slip out, "the detectives had interviewed several people who spoke of Craig's 'off-and-on' temper. And our suspicions of Anderson were aroused by his seemingly disinterested attitude toward his former fiance's vanishing act."

Chase shook his head emphatically. "Of course," he admitted, "Anderson says he knows nothing about her disappearance and is saddened by the whole thing. According to him, he hopes she turns up or is found."

As the press conference wound down, the officers went on to say that Anderson was arrested at his paint supply store without resistance and that he was being held in lieu of an astoundingly hefty $500,000 bail in a temporary cell just down the hall from the press conference. Most of the reporters then left the press conference, snatching up copies of Anderson's mug shot. But at 5:00 p.m., when the handcuffed Anderson was led to a police car for the trip to county jail, several television cameramen were still on hand.

By 8:00 a.m. on Friday, his photograph would be seen by more than a million Bay Area residents.

■ CHAPTER FIFTEEN ■

Hard Evidence

The first big break came sooner than anyone expected.

Kevin Seedlock had been watching the late night news on Thursday when a familiar face, that of Craig Anderson who had been subcontracting painting jobs to Kevin over the past year, flashed on the screen. Kevin's eyes popped open wide as he heard the commentator describe Anderson's arrest and as film rolled of the handcuffed murder solicitation suspect being led to a police car.

He thought about the news release all night. Early the next morning, he walked into the kitchen where his parents were having breakfast.

"Mom, we've got to call the police."

"Kevin, what are you talking about?"

"It's Craig Anderson. He's been arrested by the Burlingame police. I saw it on television last night. Something about hiring someone to commit murder."

Walter and Frances Seedlock exchanged shocked glances.

"Sounds like Anderson," Kevin continued, "is also a suspect in the possible murder of his ex-girlfriend, the one who vanished in November. You remember, I told you he was supposed to get married to her but they broke up."

Frances Seedlock was out of her chair before her son finished. She quickly grabbed a phone directory and looked up the number for the Burlingame police. Walter Seedlock, his hand shaking slightly, dialed as she read him the number.

"I think I've got something important to tell you about Craig Anderson," Seedlock said.

Marriscolo was hunched over some paperwork when he picked up the phone. The word "Anderson" caused him to sit upright and grab a pencil. As he did, he signaled to Chase who was sitting in his office.

"What's this all about?" Marriscolo asked the caller.

"Well, Anderson was here at our house one day last month. He was washing out a van and he left a pair of tennis shoes and a shovel."

Marriscolo quickly jotted down directions to the Seedlocks' address, just off the Bayshore Highway in Palo Alto, and told them to stay put. "We'll be down there as fast as we can."

The inspector relayed the information to Chase.

"Jesus Christ," Chase yelled. "You and Collopy get down there right now before these people forget anything!"

Driving as quickly as they could, the two detectives pulled up in front of the modest, one-story house. They were greeted at the door by Walter Seedlock who introduced them to his wife and son. By then, the Seedlocks had read the morning paper detailing Craig's arrest, and they had a good idea that they were in the middle of something very strange. The five of them sat in the living room as the Seedlocks recalled what had transpired on the day that Craig Anderson unexpectedly came to their house.

"It was about 4:00 p.m.," Mrs. Seedlock said hoarsely. "I was watching television and heard a knock at our front door. When I opened it, there was Craig Anderson standing there. He asked me if Kevin was home and I told him, no, he hadn't gotten back from work yet."

"I just killed a dog and buried it," Craig said matter-of-factly. "Is it alright if I borrow your hose to rinse out my van?"

"I looked toward the street and saw a white van parked in front of the house. I told him it was alright and that the hose was curled up in the side yard near a faucet. I motioned in that direction and Craig stepped off the porch. Then I shut the door but within a few minutes, Craig was knocking again."

"Do you have some rags I can use?" he asked.

Frances remembered some old torn up towels and T-shirts

that her husband used to wash his own car. She got them from under the kitchen sink and gave them to Craig. She noticed that he had a piece of paper wrapped awkwardly around his hand. It looked. she thought, like he might have injured himself.

After that, she closed the door and returned to the family room.

Around thirty minutes later, she noticed she could still hear the water running. Wondering if Craig, perhaps, forgot to turn the faucet all the way off, she returned to the porch. Through the sliding doors of the van which were open, she was surprised to see Craig Anderson on his hands and knees. As she watched, he alternately squirted the hose on the floor and scrubbed using the rags. Frances was amazed by the diligence with which he carried out his task.

Frances said she then walked outside to the sidewalk and noticed that Craig had taken off his tennis shoes. They were sitting on the sidewalk alongside the van.

"Gee, Craig," she said her worried-mother-instincts breaking through, "You're going to catch cold."

Craig didn't respond. Instead, he stepped out of the van, walked to the driver's side and pulled the van forward. When he got out again, she asked him if he was moving since her son had a van and everytime someone moved, they asked him to help.

"No, I'm remodeling my bathroom and I needed to take the tub down to be refinished," he told her.

Sensing that Anderson didn't wish to talk, Frances went back in the house. But in a few minutes, Craig was at the door again, asking if he could wash himself.

"Yes, I guess you can," she said. She led him to the kitchen where he let the water run as he carefully rinsed his arms and hands over and over, "like a doctor scrubbing for surgery," she told the detectives. As she watched, he handed him paper towels. He used some of them to dab at his blue jeans.

Remembering the paper that had been wrapped around his hand when he first appeared at her door, Frances went to the medicine cabinet and returned with a bandage and gauze which she laid on the counter. However, he didn't use them.

"Okay, can I use your bathroom?" he asked her.

Frances, by then, was wishing that her husband would come home from work. "Oh, yes, of course," she muttered. When Craig emerged around five or ten minutes later, Frances was standing in the living room. She was shocked to see that he had taken off his blue T-shirt, which was balled up in his fist, and his hair was slicked down on his head. She thought he looked like he had doused his head under the sink.

"Do you have a shirt I can borrow?" he asked her.

By now, Frances wanted Anderson out of her house. She grabbed the first shirt she could find from a pile of laundry, one with gray and black stripes.

"Will this do?" she asked, handing it to him.

"Sure." Craig slipped the shirt over his head. "I'll wash those rags and send them back to you."

"That's okay, don't bother," Frances replied.

With a brisk, "Thanks," Craig walked toward the door.

"Oh, what time is it?" he turned and asked.

Frances looked at the clock in the living room. "It's 5:20."

"It's not as late as I thought," Craig declared.

After Craig left, she shut the door. Around ten minutes later, her husband came home.

"What's going on out there?" Walter Seedlock asked. He had seen the van and noticed as he pulled into the driveway that there was a man inside who appeared to be scrubbing the floor.

Frances summarized Craig's strange appearance and activities. Shortly after that, they looked outside again and Craig was gone.

When Kevin Seedlock came home a few hours later, she told her son about Craig's peculiar visit.

"Weird," Kevin murmured. Curious, he called Craig and asked him what he had been doing. Kevin had gone by the store that morning to purchase some caulking supplies and found a sign on the door that said something like "Closed on Veteran's Day."

Craig calmly explained he hit a dog and buried it somewhere in Los Altos. Kevin recalled that Craig said he had borrowed the van from a friend and told him he left a pair of tennis shoes and a shovel at Kevin's house. "Throw out the shoes," Craig told him.

Then Craig added, "By the way, don't talk to anyone about this. Especially don't talk to any detectives."

Kevin hung up still wondering what was going on. At the time he didn't connect it, though, to Denise Redlick's disappearance. Of course he had seen the posters about Denise and he was in the shop one day when a couple of police officers came in asking questions. But the Craig Anderson he knew was a real nice guy who had always been helpful and generous, extending credit to Kevin for painting supplies without charging him interest or asking him to fill out any tedious form. He never thought of Craig having harmed Denise or anyone else.

The next morning after the incident, Kevin was leaving for work when he spotted a pair of Nike Tennis Shoes, the ones Craig apparently left behind, on the sidewalk in front of the house. Kevin picked them up and walked over to the sideyard where he placed them by the garbage cans.

A few days later, Walter Seedlock was doing some yardwork when he noticed the tennis shoes at the side of the house. Walter picked up the shoes, which he knew weren't his, and wondered why Kevin had left them outside by the garbage. "They look good enough to use still," he said to himself, and took them back inside.

When the Seedlocks had finished telling Marriscolo and Collopy what they could recall, the detectives began collecting potential evidence. Collopy carefully removed a metal shovel, a pair of size eleven Nike Tennis shoes, a wooden pick handle that the officers thought had a speck on it that could be dried blood, and a white and yellow paper towel found in the juniper bushes at the front of the house. Mrs. Seedlock thought the towel might be one that Craig had used.

In the middle of the interview with Frances Seedlock, Marriscolo had called Chase and told him about the van. Back at the station, Van Etten had already called a half dozen car rental agencies in search of a van rented by Craig Anderson when Marriscolo called back with the additional tip provided by Walter Seedlock that the van had a Budget logo on its side.

Within a few minutes, Van Etten had found what he was seeking.

Like most young women on the Peninsula, Kathleen Wade had seen a few of the reports on television, read a few of the newspaper stories, and noticed the flyers in store windows over the past month about the mysterious disappearance of Denise Redlick. Being the same age as Denise, Kathleen felt extremely uneasy knowing that a woman could vanish in the middle of the day from a public parking lot in a quiet city like Burlingame.

On the evening of December 19th, she had started to watch the evening news when yet another story concerning the Redlick case came on. She was half listening as the reporter talked about a suspect being arrested in a related case.

Suddenly Kathleen felt a chill down the length of her spine as she sat mesmerized by the image on the screen.

"Oh my God! I know him!" she shouted to her husband who was in the next room. The mug shot of the blond suspect with the moustache and receding hairline looked instantly familiar and yet, Kathleen at the moment, couldn't precisely place the face. "I don't know exactly where or how, but I know him," she said again, rubbing her forehead. "It's got to be through work."

Kathleen went to bed that night pondering the image of the murder-for-hire suspect. By the time Holly Travers, assistant manager of the Budget Rent-A-Car Agency in San Carlos, called the next morning, Wade had made a decision.

"Kathy, the police are here and they want to . . ." Holly began to say.

But she hadn't even finished the sentence when Kathleen blurted out, "Tell them, yes! He's the one."

Van Etten had already confirmed with Holly over the phone that Anderson, displaying his own driver's license as identification, rented a Ford Econoline van at 3:05 p.m. on November 10th and returned it at 5:47 p.m. on November 11th after it had been driven ninety-five miles. While Holly was contacting Kathleen, Van Etten was driving to San Carlos to pick up copies of the rental agreement. By the time he got there, Holly had tracked down the van. It was being rented by the United States Postal Service at its San Mateo station for help in transporting the crush of Christmas mail. Over the phone, the detective told San Mateo postmaster

James J. Kehoe that one of the vehicles he was using might have been involved in a homicide. Kehoe immediately located the van which was at that very moment being used to deliver mail.

"By the way, the two employees who cleaned out the van around that time said they saw a stain on the floor that looked like blood," Holly excitedly told Van Etten before he left the agency to drive to San Mateo.

With a sudden sense of urgency, Van Etten drove more quickly than he should have and arrived at the post office at 1:40 p.m. where he took possession of the Ford Econoline. Resisting the temptation to glimpse into the rear of the vehicle until after county criminalists could examine it, Van Etten immediately headed the van toward Burlingame. As he rode, the metal walls and floor vibrated and rattled with every bump in the road. Not easily spooked, the detective couldn't help feeling uncomfortable. Like all the officers close to the case, Van Etten had come to feel he had known Denise. He couldn't help but wonder if the young woman who seemed so lovely and loving had met a violent and bloody death in the rear of the vehicle which he was now driving.

■ CHAPTER SIXTEEN ■

Sleuthing

At almost the same time that Van Etten reached the halfway mark of his drive back to Burlingame, Chase abruptly decided to make a trip to Redwood City to confront prisoner Anderson. He arrived at the jail at 1:00 p.m. where, from his side of the interview booth, he reiterated Craig's legal rights. Anderson again waived his right to have his attorney present.

"Look, Craig, I thought you should know what the publicity about your arrest has come up with," Chase grimly offered.

The commander proceeded to describe the interview with Frances Seedlock, the discovery of the tennis shoes that, upon a cursory examination, appeared to be bloodstained, and the locating of the van that Anderson had apparently rented around the time that Denise vanished. Chase talked slowly, allowing each point to sink in and to allow the suspect time to consider the implications.

"This doesn't look good for you," Chase warned. "Is there anything you wish to tell me now?"

Craig looked shocked. He stood stark still.

"At this point I'm going to have to invoke my rights," Craig finally said. "I better talk to my attorney before I say anything else."

Turning away, Chase quickly left without comment. Then the commander returned to the police station. On the way, he stopped at a liquor store to buy a bottle of champagne and plastic glasses. Making a rare exception to the department's "no booze" rule, he wanted the detectives to share in a toast to a job well done and to celebrate their sudden accumulation of evidence.

Back in his office, Chase popped the cork. Suddenly his phone rang. It was a deputy from the jail.

"I've just been passed a note from Anderson," the deputy said. "It says he wants to see you as soon as possible."

Chase brought Marriscolo up to date and took off. Within thirty minutes he was back in a jail interview room, face to face with Anderson once again.

"Have you got a tape recorder on you?" Anderson asked.

"No," Chase said, cursing his neglect to grab his pocket-size recorder as he dashed out of the office.

"Well, I want to tell you the whole thing, but I have to talk to my lawyer first," Anderson said.

Chase's face turned beet red but he said nothing. He couldn't believe that the suspect had lured him all the way down to Redwood City again for no apparent reason. He left without asking anything further.

By 4:30 p.m., criminalists Benny Del Re and Mario Soto from the San Mateo County Forensic Lab, were beginning their inspection of the suspect vehicle parked in the Burlingame Police Department garage.

Del Re, a young and ambitious worker who first came to San Mateo County as a criminalist intern in 1978, had plenty of experience in forensic serology, the examination of blood, saliva, semen and other body fluids collected as evidence in crimes. Benny figured that since his graduation from California State University at Sacramento in 1976, he had analyzed dried bloodstains more than five hundred times and had testified as an expert in the area of serology more than forty times.

Del Re listened as Marriscolo brought the criminalists up to speed on the potential significance of the van to the case, summarizing the interview with the Seedlocks, particularly Mrs. Seedlock's description of how she had watched as Craig scrubbed the cargo area floor. "What we're looking for," he told Del Re, "is blood."

"These people down at the Budget Agency said they thought they had seen a spot on the floor of the cargo area that looked like blood," Marriscolo said.

Benny unlocked the rear windowed doors of the vehicle. He stepped up into the cargo area carrying a large black case full of evidence testing and collection materials. Soto followed him.

By now it had turned dark outside and the police officers had set up floodlights in the basement garage to help illuminate the interior of the van. The first step of the inspection would be a careful, visual examination, looking for any suggestive reddish, possibly brownish, markings.

As the two criminalists ducked their heads, pushed their noses up against the metal walls, and quietly muttered their observations to one another, they shouted their findings back to the cluster of eager Burlingame detectives and sheriff's Lieutenant Mike Dow, the crime lab supervisor who had been intrigued by the unusual aspects of the case and decided out of curiosity to observe the inspection.

"Looks like there's something here," Del Re said after working his way from one side of the van's interior to the other.

"What have you got?" Marriscolo yelled back, barely able to contain his excitement.

"Well, we've got a lot of faint reddish-brown stains all over the place," Del Re hollered. "Can't tell you what they are yet, but they look a lot like they've been diluted with something."

Benny reached into this bag of supplies and took out a black marking pen. Working his way around the interior of the van beginning with the rear right door and ending with the rear left door, he labeled each panel with a number ending the sequence with nine. Then he returned to the beginning and circled individual and small groups of the faint stains, including two Soto found on the ceiling and one on the floor adjacent to the sliding doors on the right side of the vehicle. It took him twenty minutes to complete this initial, visual inspection. When he was done, he made a rough estimate of the number of spots. He guessed there were close to fifty.

The next step in the examination was a presumptive test for blood. While the two-step test doesn't differentiate between hu-

151

man and animal blood, it is a strong indicator that further inspection and testing is necessary.

Using cotton swabs, the two criminalists carefully dabbed ortho-tolidine, a chemical reagent, to each of the spots. If the spots changed color, Del Re knew they were most likely not blood. These spots, however, were remaining the same color. "Look at that!" he observed.

The most revealing part of the test occurs in the second step in which each of the spots is dabbed with a twenty percent solution of hydrogen peroxide, an oxidizing agent. If the spots turn any shade of blue, the substance has a very strong possibility of being blood.

Within seconds of coming into contact with the hydrogen peroxide, each of the spots began to turn a vivid blue.

Most of the stains, however, including the largest ones, were just too faint or diluted. But the two stains on the ceiling, and a third one that Benny located along the right side of the vinyl-covered passenger seat, were larger and more crust-like. After visually examining the surfaces to which the stains had adhered and deciding there were clean and free of contamination, Benny prepared to "collect" them to take them back to the laboratory for more precise tests that would take several days to complete.

He knew from experience that dried bloodstains on a nonabsorbent surface could be very brittle and easy to remove. Standing underneath one of the ceiling stains, Benny reached up with a small piece of clean, white glassine weighing paper in his hand and tapped the edge of the stain with forceps. The tiny crust of presumed blood flaked onto the paper. After folding the paper, gently sliding it into an evidence envelope and marking it, Benny repeated the procedure with the second ceiling stain and the stain on the passenger seat.

At 7:30 p.m., the two criminalists emerged from the van. Benny locked the rear doors and placed tape across the panels, indicating that the doors should not be opened again except for further evidence collection.

Although tests of dried bloodstains collected from the van wouldn't be completed for several days, Benny Del Re was able to tell Marriscolo the results of the test on the Nike tennis shoes the next morning.

"Looks like you scored," Del Re excitedly reported. Both shoes had smears—on the back of the right shoe and near the top eyelet, on both sides and in back of the left shoe—that reacted positively to the presumptive ortho-tolidine test. The investigators already knew, based on records from the Peninsula Memorial Blood Bank in Burlingame where Denise had been an occasional donor, that her blood type was A. Although there was not enough of the stain on the right shoe for further testing, he was able to subject the stain on the eyelet of the left shoe—by removing several tiny pieces of thread and attaching them to a thin piece of glass—to a species test and a multi-step test called absorption elution that identifies one of the four blood groups.

"It's human, Type A," Del Re informed the detective.

Marriscolo clenched his fists and looked away not wanting to betray the intense emotion he suddenly felt.

The criminalists returned to the police station first thing early Monday morning to conduct a search for fingerprints. Later, the crime lab's fingerprint evidence technician, Stanley Baker, used a fine, bristled fiberglass brush to lightly dust the interior surface with a black powder. The special powder clings to moist areas like those created by the touch of oily fingers and palms.

Baker, with more than twenty years of experience in fingerprint identification, was able to lift with special tape, seven prints —two of fingers and the remainder of palms—which he transferred to evidence cards.

Unfortunately, the only known inked print available to him for the presumed victim, Denise Redlick, was the right thumb print from her driver's license application, obtained from the state Department of Motor Vehicles. None of the prints lifted so far were from thumbs.

But Baker was able to identify the source of three latent lift cards.

Two of the palms belonged to Benny Del Re and one of the fingerprint cards was a perfect match for Lieutenant Mike Dow.

There was no further word from Craig Anderson. On Saturday, Chase returned to the jail to see him. Anderson came out but no longer appeared eager to talk.

"I spoke to my attorney," he said tonelessly. "He told me I shouldn't discuss anything with you at this time."

As Chase left, he had the feeling that he and Craig would never talk freely again. He was right. Shortly thereafter Craig's attorney called him and said his visits with Anderson had to stop.

Craig Anderson was one of two dozen shackled prisoners, all wearing orange coveralls, appearing before Municipal Court Judge Walter Harrington during an otherwise routine arraignment calendar on Monday morning. Not wanting to be inadvertently photographed, several of the prisoners turned their heads when they saw television and still cameras pointed at them from across the courtroom.

Craig momentarily made eye contact with his mother and father but, as if embarrassed, turned away. At no time did he acknowledge Joan and Harry Redlick and Joan's sister, Carolyn, who were conspicuously seated in the front row.

The Redlicks were quickly introduced to deputy district attorney Carl Holm whose judgment and optimism they would come to implicitly trust in the coming months. They couldn't have asked for a better advocate for their daughter in Holm, whose bushy, reddish-blonde moustache and beard and balding scalp gave him an appropriately scholarly appearance. A hard-nosed and extremely driven prosecutor, known for his dry humor and sometimes surly nature, Holm, who was of Swedish background, had once been a law professor at Southern Illinois University School of Law. But he had returned to California—where he grew up—because he missed the beaches and the sunshine.

Marriscolo, when he first contacted the district attorney's office to discuss the case, had said, "Give me the best." In Carl Holm, who had a deep compassion for victims—whether they were clean-cut college students or low life drug dealers—the detective got precisely what he requested.

Craig's parents had retained Dick Bennett, a well-known and

highly respected local criminal defense attorney, to represent their son who was being held on charges of soliciting murder of Michael Brunicon. Fearful for their son's safety in an overcrowded jail filled with drug dealers, armed robbers and assorted felons, they wanted Craig bailed immediately. But the bail set by the municipal court judge was impossible to meet.

Harrington read the charge and asked the defendant to enter a plea.

"Not guilty, your honor," Anderson answered in a barely audible voice. The judge then scheduled a preliminary hearing for January 5th and Bennett entered his motion asking that his client be released on his own recognizance.

"What we have here is a ruse by the Burlingame Police Department to keep my client in jail while they continue investigating the disappearance of Denise Redlick," Bennett said forcefully. He argued that the police had been conducting a fishing expedition, disrupting Anderson's personal life and business affairs, destroying his reputation with innuendoes for weeks.

"My client is really being held for a crime that no one is certain has even occurred, let alone whether Craig Anderson had anything to do with it," Bennett insisted.

The defense attorney went on to point out that Anderson had an absolutely clean criminal slate, that he was firmly attached to his family and business in San Mateo County where he had lived his entire life, and that he had no reason to flee if released.

But Holm, who attacked every case with a vengeance, insisted that investigators needed to keep Anderson behind bars. Search warrants issued last week, Holm said, resulted in "further evidence that the defendant was probably involved in the disappearance of Denise Redlick" although he did not elaborate in open court.

What Holm didn't say was that Craig, in his telephone conversation with Doug Rees the week before, had talked about taking a vacation sometime in January. Marriscolo and Holm feared that, as the investigation intensified, Anderson was plotting to perform a vanishing act of his own.

"While Mr. Anderson may have ties to this community, he

also has all the reason in the world to flee at this point," Holm declared.

Without hesitation, Harrington upheld the extraordinary $500,000 bail, guaranteeing investigators that Anderson would be wearing orange coveralls for an indefinite period of time.

In the courthouse hallway, Joan Redlick, her voice shaking with emotion, fielded questions from reporters. She fought back tears as she announced that she had made a personal appeal— "mother to mother"—to Shirley Anderson, asking for help in locating Denise's body. In response, the Redlicks were slapped with a restraining order prohibiting them from making any further direct contact with members of Craig's family.

"I imagine my daughter half-buried someplace," she said in a flat, exhausted tone. "We just want Denise back so we can bury her for Christmas."

Although Burlingame police hadn't given reporters leads on the stunningly swift developments in the Redlick case, reporters quickly discovered what was unfolding.

KGO-TV reporter, David Louie, who lived in the Burlingame area, had been driving by the police station on Friday night when he noticed the flood-lights trained on a vehicle in the screened basement garage, partially visible from busy California Drive. With a reporter's curiosity, Louie called Chase and wound up with an "exclusive"—the first report concerning the van rented by Craig Anderson and the detection of possible bloodstains in the cargo area.

Following up on Louie's story, San Mateo Times reporter Janet Parker Beck, who had once been Denise's teacher, asked Chase if the bloodstains in the van had been further identified. Chase revealed that the specks of blood had been determined by the Crime Lab to be type A, as confirmed by records from the Peninsula Memorial Blood Bank where Denise had been an infrequent donor.

Beck's story was headlined, "Blood In The Van Same Type As Redlick's." But Chase told the reporter that the newly acquired evidence was far from enough to justify murder charges and the investigation was far from over.

"It will just be added to everything else we have," the commander said of the red-brown stains in the rented van that was locked and parked in the police department's secure basement. "We have to first prove that Denise Redlick is dead."

PART THREE

The Trials

■ CHAPTER SEVENTEEN ■

Solicitation of Murder

For the first time since their daughter was born, Joan and Harry Redlick were forced to endure Christmas, Denise's favorite holiday, without her.

And Craig Anderson, a man for whom, as one of his former girlfriends put it, "image was everything," spent a lonely Christmas in jail, his bail too high to be met.

San Mateo County Jail was a long way from the comfortable house in which Craig had lived.

In a bleak and dreary maze of narrow hallways on the fourth floor of the Hall of Justice, Craig Anderson's quarters were in cell C4, a "tank" in the rear of the jail, an especially gloomy section completely void of windows and sunlight. Craig and eleven other men charged with serious felonies ranging from armed robbery to murder shared the unit, roughly the size of a two-car tandem-style garage. Each man was issued a four-inch thick, plastic wrapped mattress and assigned a berth on a steel-frame bunk bed. On weekends, when jail overcrowding became a particular problem, deputies tossed another mattress or two on the floor. Each tank contained a single toilet, sink and shower, and a metal picnic-style table with four stools bolted to the cold metal floor. The cracked stucco walls, painted a pale yellow-beige euphemistically known as "mushroom," amplified the deafening blare of televisions suspended from the ceiling, one to each tank. Shoved under the bunks, spilling out into the meager walking space, were cardboard boxes containing each prisoner's personal possessions including legal documents, books, letters and toiletries. The most exercise Craig could hope for was a weekly basketball game— with each prisoner grabbing a pair of well-worn high top tennies that might, if he's lucky, be in his size—on an outdoor court with a view of the municipal court dome across the street. But most prisoners chose to stay indoors, either because returning to their dingy cells after an hour in the fresh air might be unbearably depressing, or because they feared that the few valuable possessions they left behind in their cells would be stolen by the time they returned.

One luxury, however, in C4 was a pay phone, allowing inmates to make an unlimited number of telephone calls (providing the recipients would be willing to accept the "collect" charges) throughout the day. Craig called a number of his old friends from Mills High School and from his summers at Svedahl during his jail stay, complaining that the Burlingame Police Department "has it in for me." For the most part, however, he acted, as one long-time friend said, as if nothing out of the ordinary had recently happened in his life. When asked pointed questions about his case, he would abruptly cut off discussion "on the advice of my attorney."

Although the van and the tennis shoes had proved to render valuable evidence in the Redlick case, none of the remaining items seized through the search warrants had been useful. Eager to more directly connect Craig with Denise's disappearance, Marriscolo obtained another search warrant, based on eyewitness information provided by Mrs. Seedlock, for the San Carlos house, this time specifically seeking "a pair of blue jeans with spots, a blue T-shirt with a possible spot on it, any and all rags and towels terrycloth type to be examined for the presence of blood."

In the presence of Dick Bennett and one of Craig's brothers on December 27th, Marriscolo and Van Etten again picked through Craig's personal property for an hour, seizing several towels and shirts from cabinets and closets. Marriscolo used a gauze pad to lift a suspicious red crusty substance from a ridge beneath the lid of the washing machine in the kitchen.

But the crime lab examined all the items over the next few days and was unable to detect any additional evidence of blood.

Time eked by. The flurry of phone calls to the Burlingame Police Department concerning the whereabouts of Denise Redlick had subsided. But public interest in her plight had not.

Finally, January 15th, the day of Craig Anderson's preliminary hearing on solicitation of murder charges came. It was four days before Craig's thirtieth birthday.

Every one of the one hundred seats was filled, and milling spectators stood in the hallway when the defendant, shackled at the wrists and ankles, was escorted by two armed sheriff's deputies into the brightly lit northern district municipal courtroom in South San Francisco. He exhibited no outward signs of anxiety, discomfort or embarassment. In fact, some observers believed he seemed rather cocky and self-assured.

However, as the prisoner quickly scanned the many rows occupied by Denise Redlick's relatives and friends, he could not have overlooked the myriad of white carnations pinned to jackets, coats and sweaters. Later Harry told a reporter that the flowers were a symbol of that concern for Denise and of support for the belief that Anderson held the key to her whereabouts. "We're sharing our concern and showing that we're interested in following this all the way through," Harry patiently told another reporter as he waited for the hearing to begin.

Anderson's contingent of supporters was much smaller. His parents, his two brothers and sister, and several other relatives and family friends sat in a cluster on one side of the courtroom in San Mateo. They complained throughout Craig's court appearances that they, with the help of their attorneys, had to fight for the few seats that they needed. In an irate letter to the district attorney's office, one of Craig's cousins later recalled the humiliation of having a woman with a broad smile on her face approach her in the hallway and, not knowing she was related to the defendant, inquire, "Can you point out Denise's parents?"

"Who are all these people and did they come on a chartered bus?" Craig's incredulous cousin asked.

Before the hearing began at 11:30 a.m. Judge Margaret

Kemp, a former deputy district attorney who abandoned her private practice as a defense attorney to become the county's first female judge, listened to defense attorney Dick Bennett argue his motion to have the public, including the press, excluded from the hearing under Section 868 of the state Penal Code to "protect the defendant's right to a fair and impartial trial."

"I am informed, and believe, that two nights ago, channel 7 broadcast my client's photograph at least five times in the approximate five-minute period of time and a reward for Denise Redlick's person was increase from $10,000 to $15,000," Bennett told the judge.

"The point, very simply, that I am making, your Honor, is, number one, my client is charged with solicitation for purposes of murder, that being the homicide of a Michael Brunicon, not Denise Redlick, having no relation to Denise Redlick. Secondly, my client in the articles has been characterized by the Burlingame Police Department as a prime suspect in the disappearance of Denise Redlick. Most importantly, no charges have been filed."

Bennett felt that non-lawyers might not be aware that a preliminary hearing is not a trial and may ascribe to it a level of legitimacy and credibility that it does not merit.

"That is not the atmosphere, coupled with the press being present, for Mr. Anderson to feel that he is having a fair hearing; to feel there isn't somehow some large group of people who have presumed his innocence. All we have to do, judge, is to project that on out and the people who project it are the press, naturally."

"The press picks up," Bennett went on, "who are here, the press picks up what is said, and it will be too late in my judgment unless the court closes this preliminary hearing for Mr. Anderson, on either matter, to get a fair trial in approximately two or three months."

However, Holm, knowing from informal discussion with Bennett that he was to make this motion, had analyzed things a different way. The way he saw it, keeping the hearing open to the public wouldn't hurt the defendant's constitutional rights one bit.

"The irony is the more publicity, the less likely any instance of any publicity is going to cause a substantial prejudice to the defendant's rights to a fair trial," Holm asserted.

Kemp, whose big eyes and smooth voice contrast with her tough demeanor on the bench, looked thoughtful.

"All right. The court has considered Mr. Bennett's motion and is going to deny the motion under 868. The court cannot find that by having this hearing open that there will be substantial prejudice to the defendant's right to a fair trial. The motion is denied."

And, with that, the prosecution's first witness, Michael Brunicon, approached the bench.

Brunicon wore faded denim jeans, a plaid flannel shirt, a hooded grey sweatshirt and his long hair was loosely tied back in a ponytail. As he slid into the witness' box and glanced at the sea of unfamiliar faces before him, he looked stiff and uncomfortable.

Holm led the witness through a series of questions about his marriage, separation and divorce from Lucy Larson. He described his appearance back in 1984—during the period in which Craig allegedly solicited his murder—and recalled Lucy having a number of pictures of him in her possession; photos that Craig might have seen. He remembered only one occasion when he encountered Craig, face-to-face: when Craig and Lucy came to Brunicon's storage locker to take away a waterbed. He had also talked to Craig briefly on the phone several times when he was making arrangements to pick up his daughter.

Cross-examined by Bennett, Michael said that Craig "was very rude on the phone."

"Did he ever threaten you on the phone?"

"No."

"Did he ever say, 'I'm going to kill you?' "

"No."

"I am going to hurt you?"

"No."

"I am going to get you?"

"No."

"Sort of funny, isn't it?"

"No, it's not funny," said Brunicon frowning, obviously not the least bit amused.

Following Brunicon to the stand was Emad Musa, the San Francisco liquor store owner who was the subject of one of the charges filed against Craig.

"At some point in 1984, approximately the middle of the year, did you receive a phone call from someone purporting to be Craig Anderson?" Holm inquired.

"Yes, I did."

"And, could you tell us what the defendant told you or asked of you in that conversation?"

"Well, basically, he just, he said he had a problem and that he would like it taken care of."

"All right. Now, did he say what the problem was?"

"I thought I knew what he was implying but I didn't want to push it."

Bennett was listening carefully.

"I move to strike as speculative on behalf of this witness," the defense attorney interjected.

"I think, excuse me," Holm said and abruptly stopped.

"The objection is overruled," Kemp said.

Holm pressed further, realizing that his witness needed to be more specific. Finally, after several more of Bennett's objections to speculation, Musa testified that Craig "said he didn't want to see this person anymore."

"Mr. Musa," Bennett approached the witness on cross, "did Mr. Anderson ever tell you he wanted you to kill somebody?" The witness squinted his eyes thoughtfully, "He never said 'kill,' to my best recollection."

"Did he ever identify this person as male or female, this person who was harassing him?"

"Not to the best of my recollection," Musa shrugged.

"Did he ever tell you he would give you money, ever talk about any money?"

"No, he didn't."

Bennett smiled. "Did he ever tell you whether or not he wanted this person injured or harmed in anyway? Did he ever say, 'I want this person harmed,' 'I want this person injured,' words to that effect?"

"Not to those words, no."

"Did he ever describe height, weight, age, how it would happen, where it would happen or anything of that sort?"

"No, he did not."

"No names were ever mentioned?"

"No, he did not."

The preliminary hearing broke for lunch and resumed at 2:35 p.m. Statuesque brunette, Lucy Larson, took the stand. After taking the oath and settling in the witness' chair, Lucy stared for a moment at Craig. He quickly looked away.

Holm led her through a description of her stormy relationship with Craig, the argument in Hawaii over her having worked as a cocktail waitress, and the incident back home when he allegedly struck her in anger when she was attempting to leave his home.

The prosecutor asked her what Craig thought of her former husband.

"He expressed that anyone that rode that type of motorcycle and hung out in bars, and that, were a low-life," she said.

Lucy also said Craig was "insanely jealous of me having any type of contact with a male, and even in a working atmosphere, he would never want me to even have male friends, per se."

The next witness was Doug Rees, who was in the uncomfortable position of testifying against his former business partner and ex-fiance's brother. He recalled hearing Craig, in the warehouse one day in June 1984, around a week to ten days after Lucy came into the paint shop with bruises and injuries that she said were inflicted by Craig, asking Richard Weeks, "if he would do away with Lucy's ex-husband." The two men talked for about twenty minutes, in all, but Rees said he heard only that part of the conversation.

"Did the defendant ever express to you his feelings toward Lucy's husband?" Holm asked.

"Well, he didn't like him personally," Doug said. "He didn't like what he stood for." Craig thought Michael "was scum."

Bennett pulled out a copy of Rees' statement to the police.

"Do you remember telling Inspector Marriscolo that you thought he was joking at the time?" Bennett asked.

"That's my feeling personally. It wasn't said in a joking manner though. He wasn't laughing when he said it. Craig sometimes said angry things about people, things like, 'I'm going to get that bastard,' and would then cool off." Under persistent questioning by Bennett, Rees said that would happen perhaps twice a month, which Bennett calculated to be twenty four times a year, minimizing the significance of his alleged exchange with Weeks.

Finally, the prosecution's key witness, Richard Weeks, took the stand.

He recalled Craig Anderson asking him, possibly around the beginning of June 1984, for help.

"He said that he wanted a person killed," Weeks testified. "He didn't give me a purpose. He just said that he wanted him out of the way and he said he was willing to pay for it." Craig gave him a piece of paper on which he had scribbled the intended victim's description and schedule, indicating that he got off work at 5:00 p.m. and that he would be home around 5:20 p.m. Craig, Weeks testified, also said that "he didn't care if the daughter got taken too, but he didn't want anything to happen to Mrs. Brunicon," meaning Lucy.

As Weeks described Craig taking him to the apartment building in Mountain View where he believed Brunicon lived, Judge Kemp suddenly called the two attorneys to the bench. She was concerned that the witness might be incriminating himself in conspiracy to commit murder and thought he should consult with an attorney.

After a five-minute recess, Weeks returned to the bench. With Kemp advising him that he had the right to consult with an attorney, Weeks decided he would, instead, forge ahead with his testimony.

That evening, he conveyed that he went to Craig's house where Craig gave him $1000 in cash.

Bennett, in a rapid-fire manner of questioning, zeroed in on the conversation, secretly tape-recorded by the police, in which Anderson ultimately gave Weeks $300. He forced him to admit that he told at least fifteen lies during that conversation. Among the lies were that the police were after him with an arrest warrant and that the police had obtained the scrap of paper on which Anderson had written the descriptive information about Brunicon.

"Now Mr. Weeks, when you walked into Craig Anderson's home, were you aware that there was reward money with reference to the disappearance of Denise Redlick?" Bennett asked.

"I was aware of reward money," Weeks said. "I state for the record and whoever else wants to know, I am not concerned with any reward money. I don't care about it. I don't want it."

In a further attempt to destroy Weeks' credibility, Bennett grilled him on his narcotics use. Weeks admitted to using cocaine, amphetamines and marijuana in June 1984 when the solicitation allegedly occurred. Bennett tried to pinpoint him as to how frequently that use occurred (although Holm successfully objected to the questioning) until Weeks finally lost his cool with the retort, "Can you tell me how many times you went to the bathroom last . . . ?"

Bennett angrily interrupted as the courtroom erupted in laughter, forcing Judge Kemp to call for order. "I am asking you, sir, whether or not you were on drugs in June of 1984?" Bennett demanded.

"I cannot give you a direct answer exactly how many times. I am terribly sorry, I didn't keep a record," the witness responded with mock haughtiness.

Bennett then grilled Weeks about why he found it necessary to lie to Anderson on December 11th.

"Because I thought it would help bring out the facts," Weeks said.

"By lying? By telling Mr. Anderson a whole spat of lies about the police?" Breaking in, Holm objected to the "argumentative" nature of the question and was sustained. Bennett asked it again.

"Because I felt compelled to do my civic duty," Weeks contended.

With the prosecution's evidence concluded, Bennett asked that, at the very least, the solicitation count related to Musa be dismissed. But Kemp asked Anderson to rise and ordered him to stand trial on two counts of solicitation of murder, setting a January 30th arraignment date in superior court.

Then, Bennett requested that Anderson's "incredulous" $500,000 bail be lowered.

"When bail was set, we were informed that the reason that bail was going to be set was that, immediately thereafter, the office of the district attorney would bring some other and more serious charges against Mr. Anderson," Bennett directed to the judge.

"We are still waiting," the defense attorney boomed, stressing the word "still." "Mr. Anderson has been in custody for 28 days at $500,000 bail on an eighteen-month-old solicitation charge. That is not, judge, pursuant to any reasonable schedule."

Bennett suggested that the judge set stringent conditions, like pulling Anderson's passport and requiring him to contact a probation officer every third day, in setting a reasonable bail or even releasing him on his own recognizance.

"This man is extraordinarily cooperative as are all the members of his family," Bennett said.

Holm quickly protested. "Every witness that has come to me and discussed this case regarding the solicitation of murder, for obvious reasons, has expressed fear of the defendant now they have become aware of the solicitation and are concerned that the defendant not be released from jail."

Bennett, however, found it incredible that witnesses could be "scared like heck of him now, but weren't scared for eighteen months when this thing happened. That's not right, judge."

But Kemp was not swayed by Bennett's arguments.

"With regard to the bail, the court feels that there is substantial likelihood that the defendant could, in fact, flee given not only the seriousness of this charge but the potential charges against him," she firmly announced. "The court is further concerned by the clear and present danger which I think exists to the witnesses in this matter and is going to leave the bail set at $500,000."

With that, in unison, the roomful of Denise Redlick's supporters stood and applauded the judge's decision. Afterward, outside the courtroom, Harry and Joan Redlick appeared visibly pleased that Anderson would remain in jail. They told reporters that as long as he was in custody, the chances of finding their daughter were improved.

"Of course, anyone capable of soliciting for murder is capable of murder," Harry dispiritedly said.

■ CHAPTER EIGHTEEN ■

Beyond a Reasonable Doubt

With Anderson firmly in jail, the prosecutors pressed on hoping to add to what little tangible evidence they already had collected to back up their contention that Denise Redlick had been murdered. Marriscolo had been talking with criminalist Benny Del Re about the possibility of taking the blood stain analysis one step further than identifying the crusts from the van and the blood on the tennis shoe as Type A. That, the investigators realized, might not provide the jury with an indisputable reference point for determining that Denise Redlick had been slain in the van. Since the entire population of the world can be divided into just four inherited genetic blood marker types—A, B, O, and AB, the detectives wondered if, in fact, they could use a technique known as electrophoresis to more specifically link Denise Redlick with the rented vehicle by comparing the dried blood crusts with samples of Denise's parents' fresh blood.

Electrophoresis uses electric current to separate enzymes and other inherited proteins in a blood sample. Then, specific chemicals are applied to "stain" the proteins and make them more visible. Each enzyme type—indicated by the presence of different proteins—produces a distinctive, easily recognizable pattern of bands which can be identified to determine the genetic type of blood sample. As with the more broad ABO typing system, enzyme and protein marker systems can be used to divide the population into groups and, in forensics, more specifically include or exclude a victim or a suspect from the realm of criminal possibility. For example, the combination of Type O blood, found in fifty percent of the population, and the enzyme phosphoglucomutase (PGM for short) Type I, which occurs in sixty percent of the population is found in thirty percent of all people. As Del Re explained it to Marriscolo, the more genetic marker systems that can be typed, the smaller the population group possessing the characteristic will be.

At that time, crime labs were using around a dozen enzyme and protein marker systems as genetic markers for dried blood stains. Del Re knew that through electrophoretic testing of Denise's parents' blood, he could create a genetic profile of what Denise's own blood protein and enzyme profile would be.

On January 22nd, Inspector Marriscolo accompanied Joan and Harry Redlick to Peninsula Hospital just a few blocks from the Burlingame police station, where a registered nurse drew two vials of blood from each of Denise's parents. He delivered the vials to Del Re who identified Harry's blood as Type A and Joan's blood as Type O, a genetically logical combination for producing a Type A daughter. Then, Benny conducted several electrophoretic tests of the parents' blood sample, identifying them with several specific genetic marker groups.

But the criminalist became concerned that the size of the three bloodcrust samples from the van, considering how much had been already used up for the earlier species and ABO typing tests, would make it difficult to conduct further enzyme testing. In his judgement, electrophoretic enzyme tests of the dried bloodstains would use up most or even all of the samples that were left, precluding his lab or any expert ultimately hired by the defense from conducting the species and ABO tests over again, if necessary, as a double check.

After discussing the situation with the District Attorney's Office, the prosecution decided that the enzyme tests of the dried blood would not be performed, afterall, leaving the Type A match between Denise's blood and the blood in the van as the most specific comparison available.

But Carl Holm still wasn't satisfied that everything possible had been done to uncover evidence that Denise Redlick had been inside the van.

On Thursday afternoon, January 23rd, at Holm's request, Marriscolo drove the van across the San Mateo-Hayward Bridge to Cooper Lasersonics Incorporated, the world's largest manufacturer of medical lasers, in Pleasanton. Doctor Edward German, a forensic scientist with Cooper's Plasma Kinetics Group, had agreed to conduct a laser-enhanced fingerprint examination of the van. Benny Del Re and Carol Holm met Marriscolo at the lab.

As German himself explained in one scientific paper, "The laser is not a miracle machine." By far, he said, the three best latent print detection techniques available in 1986 were cyanoacrylate (the Super Glue ingredient) fuming, dusting with powders, and ninhydrin, all of which had already been used, to some extent, in examining the Redlick case evidence. According to German, lasers weren't of much value in detecting latent prints until the early 1980's when forensic researchers discovered the value of combing laser light with chemical techniques. When the item of evidence has already been examined by conventional cyanoacrylate or ninhydrin methods, the supplemental laser-chemical analysis merely changes the color of the previously developed ridge detail so that it can be more brightly illuminated, German explained.

Combined with the supplemental chemicals, laser examination in 1986 could be expected to recover additional identifiable latent prints in about fifty percent of carefully selected cases. When used more broadly in examining all types of evidence in all types of cases, the success rate would drop to about thirty percent.

German donned special goggles as he passed the copper vapor laser, which emits a greenish-orange light, over the interior of the Ford van. The scientist thought he saw several areas in which fingerprints might be lifted.

Then, the interior was retreated with cyanoacrolyte followed by an application of a biological dye, Rhodamine 6G, giving the metal panels and floor a pinkish tint. Finally, the laser was again passed over the panels so that photographs could be taken of eight newly enhanced prints, three of fingers and five of palms.

Marriscolo, Holm and Del Re spent more than eight hours at Cooper Lasersonics, observing and assisting in German's test. Then Marriscolo drove the van back to Burlingame and parked it in the police station garage.

The ball was back in the county crime lab's court to make sense of the new prints. As Holm had suggested, criminalist Stanley Baker, the fingerprint identification expert, began his detailed comparison of the laser-enhanced prints with the thumbprint from Denise's driver's license, her only known positive print, and with latent prints removed from dozens of Denise's personal possessions removed by Marriscolo from her bedroom or bathroom including her sunglasses, photo albums, a ceramic vase, a diary, several perfume bottle, a toothpaste tube, curling iron and a black leather purse. Each comparison turned up negative.

As a last resort, Marriscolo contacted the Bank of America and asked for documents that Denise might have come in contact with in the course of her work. Bank officials gave the Burlingame police a file of papers, including overdrafts and job performance evaluations, that would have been touched by Denise when she signed each of them. Marriscolo processed each of them with ninhydrin, producing numerous latent prints which he turned over to the crime lab. Again, Baker compared them with the driver's license thumbprint and the lifts from the van without success.

Marriscolo was disappointed but not defeated. "Maybe the district attorney can't use the fingerprints to prove that Denise Redlick had been in that van," he said to Holm later that day. "But Craig Anderson's attorneys can't use them to convince a jury that she hadn't been there, either."

Still despite all of their convictions that Craig Anderson had killed Denise, the task of proving it continued to be onerous and Holm knew that if the more serious charge of the murder of Denise Redlick wasn't filed against Craig soon, a judge would be obligated to lower his bail. Over the next three weeks, Holm, Assistant District Attorney Steve Wagstaffe, Fox and Marriscolo sat down to discuss that dilemma many times.

Weighing heavily on their minds was the knowledge that if Anderson was tried and acquitted and Denise's body, possibly along with additional incriminating evidence such as a weapon, were found after the trial, the one-time defendant could not be forced to stand trial on the same charges again.

"He could stand up and say 'I did it,' and there's nothing we could do," Wagstaffe observed. His constitutional rights would have protected him.

The prosecutors could recall only one previous case in San Mateo County in which a murder charge had, in fact, been filed before a body had been found. In that 1977 case, witnesses claimed that the defendant had given an acquaintance a fatal karate-kick to the head, disposing of the body in a dumpster that was eventually hauled off to one of the county's huge landfill sites. The district attorney's staff debated the possibility of digging up the body, but learned after contacting landfill officials that excavating the dumpsite would cost more than $150,000. In fact, they weren't certain that they could identify the right dump or even the right location in the dump. However, when the defendant decided to plead guilty to a lesser charge of manslaughter, the problem of not having a body was resolved.

In the other cases which had happened elsewhere and appeared somewhat similar, the murderer had always admitted he was aware the person was dead, placing the blame on someone else, or confessed to the crime, or there were eyewitnesses or hard evidence. But one case had some common elements as trying Craig Anderson for the murder of Denise. It was the dramatic conviction of L. Ewing Scott in 1957.

Wealthy Pasadena socialite Evelyn Throsby Scott, twice divorced and twice widowed, met and married L. Ewing Scott, her fifth husband in 1949 after a whirlwind courtship. Her new spouse, a handsome and charming but dismally unsuccessful businessman, promptly took charge of Evelyn's considerable financial affairs. Her fortune was estimated to be worth nearly $1 million. But one day in May 1955, Mrs. Scott vanished. When concerned friends, who considered Scott a fortune hunter, began inquiring about her whereabouts, Scott said she had suffered a mental breakdown and had gone away for treatment in the East.

Later, when investigators began asking tough questions, he claimed that she had sent him out for a can of tooth powder and, when he returned, she was gone.

However, the presumption of death was established when police officers probed the backyard of the couple's Bel Air home and found Mrs. Scott's dentures and eyeglasses buried. Like Denise Redlick, the victim was regarded as a woman with consistent and responsible habits who would hardly have gone away without these two intimate possessions.

Scott was arrested in April 1957 while he was a fugitive trying to enter Canada in a new car purchased with his missing wife's money. Found guilty and sentenced to life in prison, Scott still denied that he killed his wife. However, later, when he was paroled, he described the slaying to the author of a book about the case.

Though Scott ultimately admitted the slaying, the bottom line in People vs. Scott was a District Court of Appeal ruling in 1959 that death can be proven by purely circumstantial evidence. "The undisputed facts point unerringly to a single conclusion. The evidence of appellant's guilt was convincing. The judgement is affirmed." The United States Supreme Court refused to review the conviction.

As Holm carefully examined People vs. Scott, he realized that L. Ewing Scott's behavior prior to his arrest was far more self-incriminating than that of Craig Anderson and that there had been much more evidence of death. Scott had also been charged with forgery and grand theft in connection with his dead wife's estate and had fled the country as investigators began to pin down the murder charges.

"We don't have that kind of thing with Craig Anderson," Holm said in one of his many staff meetings on the Redlick case. "We haven't got the same weight of evidence of guilt to show the jury that the prosecution had in the Scott case."

Moreover, to Marriscolo's dismay, the testimony he had painstakingly gathered about Craig's former girlfriends, with allegations that he had been abusive or violent toward them, would not be admissible even though that information had been disseminated in search warrant affidavits that had been summarized by the press.

Holm said that the experiences of the other girlfriends weren't "sufficiently similar", the standard required by law, to the case of Denise Redlick for a judge to allow them to be discussed. Even Lucy Larson who had, in the murder solicitation case, testified that Craig allegedly assaulted her, would not be permitted to make those statements if Craig was indicted for the murder of Denise Redlick.

"What did he have to do, murder them all to make them relevant to this case?" Marriscolo asked in frustration.

"What would be needed," Wagstaffe patiently explained, "would be an example of Anderson forcing one of his girlfriends in a vehicle against her will. The premise could then be that if it had happened to another woman, it could certainly have happened to Denise Redlick as well. An example of where he hit a woman would not be sufficient," the assistant district attorney said.

Though Holm, like Wagstaffe, played devil's advocate as he and the police continued to gather evidence, he also was convinced that all the remaining pieces of the puzzle added up to form only one logical picture: that Craig Anderson had killed the missing girl. Marriscolo, who felt that everything possible had been done to eliminate anyone else as a suspect, was growing more and more exasperated with the delay in filing murder charges. The detective, who had also spent many hours reading up on every case which even seemed remotely similar, had come away wondering if they were ever going to be able to prove Craig's guilt beyond a shadow of a doubt despite their convictions.

"It's really a simple story," the detective told Fox one particularly long day. "When you tell it to a jury, they've got to see it," he said emotionally.

Though the detectives investigated every lead looking for new evidence, with Anderson in jail nearly two months, it was becoming very clear that short of finding a body, the investigators had gathered all the proof against Craig that they were ever going to get. Waiting any longer, Holm and Wagstaffe agreed, would mean that memories, like those of Mr. and Mrs. Seedlock, would dim and that was worrisome in a circumstantial case.

But what really triggered the District Attorney's office next move was a superior court judge's warning on February 19th that if the more serious charges weren't filed soon, he would be obligated to reduce bail in the solicitation case.

"There's no advantage in waiting any longer," Holm said at a staff meeting on the case that day. Fox and Wagstaffe concurred.

Late that afternoon, Marriscolo's phone rang. It was Carl Holm.

"We're ready," Holm told the inspector. "Go for it."

The detective knew, immediately, what the prosecutor meant. It was finally time to book Craig Anderson on murder and kidnapping charges.

"And we're going for the special circumstance," Holm added. That meant that Anderson would face the additional charge that he had murdered Denise Redlick while committing a kidnapping. Under California Penal Code section 190.2, the punishment for a murder when the attached special circumstance is determined by the jury, is a choice between life in prison without the possibility of parole, a so-called LWOP—or the death penalty. The district attorney's office would determine closer to the trial date, if he would seek death in the case of Craig Alan Anderson.

On Thursday morning, Marriscolo's adrenaline was pumping as he drove to the courthouse in Redwood City, met with Holm to obtain the typed arrest warrant, and drove back to the central county courthouse in San Mateo. Municipal Court Judge Phrasel Shelton quickly signed the one-page document inserting, for the minimum amount of bail, the words "no bail," and a search warrant authorizing the Burlingame Police Department to draw a blood sample from the prisoner in anticipation of the defendant claiming that the blood inside the Ford Econoline and on his tennis shoes had been caused by a self-inflicted accidental wound.

At 2:00 p.m., Marriscolo drove to the Hall of Justice in Redwood City and took the elevator to the fourth floor. In his hand he clutched the paper which was the climax of so many weeks of long hours and dedicated detective work.

"I've got a warrant here and I want to serve it in person," Marriscolo told the deputy in charge of the jail. Normally a warrant could be delivered to a prisoner through the jailers, but the Burlingame detective had waited too long for this one not to savor the moment.

Craig was brought to one of the booths used by attorneys to visit clients in custody. If the prisoner was surprised to see Marriscolo, who had kept his distance in the past, he didn't show it. Craig kept his eyes straight ahead, his face expressionless.

"I've got a warrant for your arrest," Marriscolo quickly announced, trying to keep his jubilant feelings from showing. "You're being charged with the murder and kidnapping of Denise Redlick."

The detective thought he saw Craig tremble, but he couldn't be sure.

"I don't want to talk to this guy," the prisoner said.

"There's more," the detective said. "I've also got a search warrant. Judge Shelton says you've got to let me have the jail nurse draw a blood sample."

"Forget it," Anderson snapped, looking agitated and angry. "You're not getting my blood," he scowled as he turned his back and asked a deputy to take him back to his cell.

"We'll see about that," Marriscolo called over his shoulder.

Marriscolo told the lieutenant in charge of the jail at the front office what had happened. "Let's hold him down and take it anyway," the deputy suggested. "You've got the order."

The idea of forcing Anderson to give a blood sample was tempting. But the detective also thought it might cause problems this case didn't need.

He shook his head. "No, I'll get in touch with his attorney," Marriscolo replied. "We'll get him to cooperate."

The next morning, District Attorney Fox called a press conference. A half dozen reporters regularly assigned to the courthouse and a couple of television camera crews gathered in the DA's conference room, one floor below the jail. Fox, usually known for his quick laugh and cheerful nature, began with an appropriately grim tone.

"The two and one-half month investigation of Denise Redlick's disappearance has led the district attorney's office to conclude that Craig Anderson kidnapped and killed his ex-fiance," the grey-haired elected official reported. "We believe that the circumstances of the case are such that it does justify the filing of charges. Miss Redlick's whole life pattern would not lead a reasonable person to conclude that she had simply skipped out."

When Craig appeared in municipal court later that morning for arraignment on murder and kidnapping charges, he had at his side a new attorney replacing Dick Bennett. The substitution came as a surprise to courthouse insiders who knew Bennett, a local, as a trusted and familiar face who had worked opposite all of the experienced deputy district attorneys in San Mateo County. His successor, Nathan Cohn, was a well-known, high profile San Francisco trial lawyer whose reputation as a criminal attorney was acclaimed but as far as the San Mateo County District Attorney's Office was concerned, he was an outsider.

Nathan Cohn, sixty-seven, had begun practicing law in San Francisco before many of the attorneys he was squaring off against in the courtroom by the 1980s had even been born. A trim, six-foot-one and bald, Cohn was a well-established, well-paid veteran of both civil and criminal law who kept company with some of the most famous attorneys in San Francisco, people like Melvin Belli and Charles Garry. His Criminal Law Seminars in the 1960's resulted in the publication of three books bearing his name and his stature among his legal peers led to his being elected the first president of the American Board of Criminal Lawyers in 1976.

Cohn had read about the Redlick case but hadn't paid much attention to it when he received a call from Craig Anderson's father. Cohn was the author of a column, "Thinking Out Loud," in a local weekly newspaper whose publisher was a client of Cohn's and a friend of Ron Anderson's. Craig's father was looking for the best legal advice money could buy and, with the publisher's recommendation, called Cohn who agreed to accept the challenging case.

For Nate, the Anderson case had a special appeal. In the 1950s, Cohn was a young defense attorney with an impressive trail record. "I was knocking them out up here," he later said. "I didn't know what it was that I was doing right. All I knew was that everytime I went into court, the jury would say 'Not Guilty!' or I'd at least get a hung jury. For some reason, I was lucky."

During that period, he attracted the attention of an attorney advising one L. Ewing Scott who had wanted him to fly to Los Angeles immediately to consider representing Ewing, recently returned from Canada to stand trial on charges of murdering his missing wife.

"I've got something to do tonight," Cohn told the lawyer, "But I can get down there on Monday morning." The two attorneys made arrangements to meet at the courthouse.

But, over the weekend, Scott settled on another attorney and, by Monday morning, the trip to Los Angeles was no longer necessary.

When Craig's parents called Cohn about representing their son, Cohn's keen mind immediately flashed back to the Scott case. From what he could see, the authorities had a great deal more evidence against L. Ewing Scott than they had against Craig Anderson.

Cohn decided that his newly-acquired client was getting a bum deal. The defense attorney believed that the Burlingame police had led the news media down a calculated path and that reporters had blindly followed. He regarded Marriscolo's search warrant affidavit as an intentionally inflammatory gimmick to suggest that Craig "is a wild man beating up women" and that Denise's parents' public pleas for the return of their daughter's body to give her a Christian burial added unjustifiable credibility to the illusion of a crime.

That morning, Cohn had gotten Superior Court Judge Thomas Jenkins to lower his client's bail in the solicitation case to $50,000, but it was a strictly academic issue since the no-bail murder warrant for Craig in the Redlick matter had already been served.

When Cohn met Craig's family outside the arraignment courtroom at 11:00 a.m., the hallway was packed with what Cohn began calling "the white carnation group" , an assembly that "looked more to me like a lynch mob than a bunch of sympathetic people. Everybody was antagonistic to the Andersons."

The arraignment was brief. Craig entered "not guilty" pleas and Cohn's first motion, a request for a gag order, was denied. "By this time, getting a gag order would be like trying to close a hole in the ship when it's three-quarters full of water," Cohn later admitted.

A few minutes after the arraignment, Marriscolo met with Cohn and Craig Anderson's private family physician at the county jail. This time, the prisoner was cooperative although still obviously annoyed. As a county jail nurse observed, the physician withdrew enough of Craig's blood from his left arm to give Marriscolo the two vials the county Forensic Lab needed to be tested and typed.

Marriscolo waited impatiently. The days of testing seemed to take forever. Benny Del Re finally called. Craig Anderson's blood Type was O.

According to the criminalist, there was no way the blood splattered in the van could have come from the murder suspect.

Searching for a presumed murder victim on the San Francisco Peninsula is a lot like searching for a needle in a haystack. Over the years, many murder victims have been dumped within the forest of the mountainridge that separates the densely populated bayside from the sparely populated oceanside, and throughout any of the many county and regional parks. Usually, remains are found by hikers who wander away from well-worn trails or by truck drivers who park their rigs and step off the edge of the road to stretch their legs. In fact, in December just a few days before Craig was arrested, a serviceman traveling through the area who stopped to relieve himself at an Interstate 280 offramp stumbled upon the body of a woman twenty feet down a steep embankment who had been dead for a day or less. Initially there was some suspicion that the victim was Denise Redlick. But dental records later identified the victim, shot once in the head, as a

San Francisco State University student. It was one of several false alarms that would occur in the search for Denise.

Marriscolo was absolutely convinced that she was dead and anticipated that Denise Redlick's remains would probably be found in a similar chance way. But with the trial of her alleged killer approaching, the inspector decided that concerted, deliberate efforts to find her body should not be abandoned.

Working within the framework of the rental van's mileage, proximity to the Seedlock's Palo Alto household and tips provided by people who knew Craig Anderson who said he like to drive along Interstate 280 and sometimes went jogging at a community college track in Cupertino, the detective began to focus on an area of Santa Clara County. In a preliminary step toward identifying the parameters, Marriscolo spent one morning in the area with a California Highway Patrol helicopter crew taking aerial photographs. A productive search of the expansive area, he realized, would require the help of numerous agencies.

Two days before the search, Marriscolo and Sergeant Tim McHenry and Detective Dave Hayes, the San Mateo County Sheriff's Office search and rescue experts, met at a restaurant with Lieutenant Keenan Kirby from the Santa Clara County Sheriff's Office and Rangers Raleigh Young and Dave Camp, to plan their search strategy.

The Santa Clara County authorities said that the areas they had in mind were already popular for illegal dumping and that previous searches in other investigations had turned up useful evidence including several bodies.

With their direction, five specific roadways were selected for the search—Montebello, Mt. Eden, Stevens Canyon, Moody and Page Mill—with a command center in the middle of Stevens Creek County Park. The seven hundred seventy-seven-acre park, accessible from several directions, is bisected by Stevens Creek Reservoir.

At 9:00 a.m., on Saturday March 22nd, under sunny skies, more than fifty volunteers and several dozen observers including Carolyn and John Kristovich, Denise's aunt and uncle, and Nick and Ann Circosta, Denise's godparents, gathered at the command post where they spent the day sipping mugs of coffee. Ten agen-

Denise with her family (left to right: Joan, Mike and Harry Redlick) at high school graduation.

Denise Redlick and Craig Anderson.

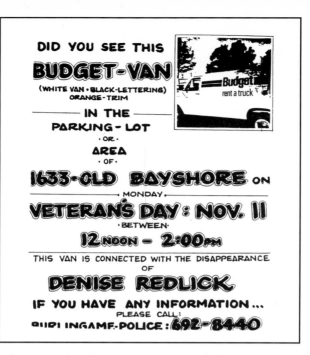

DID YOU SEE THIS

BUDGET-VAN

(WHITE VAN • BLACK-LETTERING)
ORANGE-TRIM

—— IN THE ——
PARKING - LOT
· OR ·
AREA
· OF ·

1633·OLD BAYSHORE ON
· MONDAY ·
VETERAN'S DAY : NOV. 11
· BETWEEN ·
12 NOON – 2:00 PM

THIS VAN IS CONNECTED WITH THE DISAPPEARANCE
OF

DENISE REDLICK

IF YOU HAVE ANY INFORMATION ...
PLEASE CALL:
BURLINGAME·POLICE : **692-8440**

Flyer circulated concerning Denise's disappearance.

Harry Redlick meeting with volunteers in front of the building where his daughter was last seen.   *Courtesy of The San Mateo Times*

Tom Marriscolo
Photo by Mike Russell

Judge Carl Holm
Photo by Mike Russell

The van in which bloodstains were found.
Photo by Mike Russell

The site where Denise's body was found.
Photo by Mike Russell

cies from the two neighboring counties were represented. During the day, members of the Bay Area Mountain Rescue, rappelling off cliffs some fifty to one hundred feet into a ravine, found seven abandoned autos, all of which were searched, to no avail.

A ripple of nervous excitement spread through the group anxiously waiting at the command post when it was learned, through radio communications, that climbers had come across a pair of woman's boots. No one had forgotten that Denise, when last seen, was wearing a pair of grey and black leather boots. The boots were relayed from the site where they were uncovered to Carolyn Kristovich who gave them a hasty examination.

"These aren't my niece's boots," she announced with a mixture of sadness and relief.

Throughout the day, searchers in various locations, connected by radio, found several purses, bits of clothing and the apparent evidence of a robbery—a safe with a hole sawed out of one side.

The two CRDA dogs recruited for the search sniffed here and there, but showed little interest in most of the terrain, suggesting that there was probably nothing of significance to be found.

"Unfortunately recent rains may have washed away evidence," Detective Hayes, who was assigned to public relations, told reporters. At the end of the day, Marriscolo explained that the area, about sixteen miles from where Craig washed out the van, had seemed like an ideal place to stash a body.

"But we deal with logic," he said wearily, "Who can really know how someone, who is committing a murder, thinks?"

■ CHAPTER NINETEEN ■

Bad Blood

A standing-room-only crowd of spectators, sporting white carnations on their lapels, packed the gallery. During the two-day hearing before Municipal Court Judge Richard Gravelle, they would hear more than twenty prosecution witnesses.

That Joan Redlick was the star witness, there was little doubt.

On March 7th at Craig's preliminary hearing on charges of murdering and kidnapping Denise Redlick, Joan Redlick answered a question posed by Assistant District Attorney Steve Wagstaffe with a chilling display of bitterness.

Wagstaffe was trying to set the stage for his direct examination of Denise's mother.

"Mrs. Redlick, do you have any children?" the prosecutor innocently asked.

"I have a son and I HAD a daughter," the witness, with no hesitation shot back staring heartbrokenly into Craig Anderson's eyes.

It was the first time that Joan had made eye contact with Craig since his arrest in December. But the contact was momentary. In an apparent nervous quirk that would continue through the remainder of his days in San Mateo courts, Anderson blinked incessantly. Unlike the hearing in January when the defendant had seemed cocky and self-assured, he now seemed passive and compliant.

Wagstaffe firmly but gently led her through a series of questions concerning the morning that Joan last saw Denise and the evening in which she failed to return home as expected.

"By eleven o'clock that evening, I knew something had happened to her," she said. "By one o'clock in the morning, I knew she was dead."

Without a body, eyewitness or murder weapon, Wagstaffe spent much of the hearing trying to establish that Miss Redlick was a happy, stable woman who, despite the emotional trauma of her broken engagement, was eager to get on with her life. There was simply no reason for her to suddenly disappear.

When defense attorney Nate Cohn objected to Wagstaffe's line of questioning, the assistant district attorney convinced the judge that Miss Redlick's "state of mind" is among the most important evidence in the case and that it was "certainly out of her character" to disappear.

Joan testified that, in fact, all of her daughter's personal possessions—her make-up, her spare glasses, all of her clothes, and her cherished family photos—remained at home. And that when she left home that morning, she appeared "very happy."

Harry Redlick, for the first time, publicly described the wounds that he had seen on Craig's body when he came to the Redlick's house, at their request, on November 14th.

"I noticed when he came in. It wasn't that cold a day and he had on this sort of ski sweater that came up around the neck and came away done here at the arms," Harry said, gesturing as he spoke. "At first I didn't think anything about it and we went upstairs." While sitting there, he said, he detected the scratch that ran up the back of Craig's hand and along his neck.

"Those scratches, were they going in every which way direction?" Wagstaffe asked.

"No. They were made just nice and straight," Harry recalled.

Cohn, in his cross-examination, tried to make the point that Craig willingly came to the Redlick house that night, implying that he had nothing to hide. It was the first of many occasions that would turn into a battle of semantics between the defense attorney and the prosecution's witness.

"He came to visit your house?" Cohn asked.

"Right. Well, at my wife's request," Harry said.

"At you wife's request?" Cohn asked again.

"Not voluntarily."

"Well, did she use a gun on him?" Cohn sharply challenged the witness.

Harry was perturbed. "He never offered to come over, to help in any way. She said, 'Would you please come over, Craig?' I listened to the conversation," Harry explained.

"Fine. So he came over after you invited him or asked him over?"

"Requested that he come," Harry insisted. "Not invited."

"Oh, you requested," said Cohn. Turning to face the witness he asked, "He doesn't work for you, does he, sir?"

"Oh, no," Harry answered with amazing patience.

"So, if he didn't want to, he wouldn't have had to come over, would he?" Cohn hammered away.

"No," Harry had to agree.

Then Cohn focused on Craig's mannerisms as they sat in the family room. Harry had to concede that Craig did nothing to hide or disguise the scratches.

"He couldn't hardly do anything," Harry said. "They were so obvious."

"He didn't wear gloves?"

Harry was incredulous. "No. Would you come to somebody's house and wear gloves and keep them on?"

"So he didn't wear gloves?" Cohn said.

"No."

"Didn't have his hands bandaged?"

"No, he did not."

The exchange became even testier when Cohn asked about the Saturday when Craig had found Denise at the beauty salon and they had spent the afternoon up the hill near Interstate 280 talking about their relationship. Harry insisted that they drove separate cars because "she was afraid of Craig" and that they sat in Denise's car when they got there. "She would not go there in his car," Harry said.

"You sure?" Cohn said.

"I'm sure."

"Didn't she tell you that they met at the beauty parlor and went up in one car and sat there for five hours talking?"

"They did . . . if you want to be semantically correct, they did not meet. He went into the beauty shop. She had no intention of seeing Craig. She had no intention of talking to Craig," Harry declared.

"Mr. Redlick . . ." Cohn began.

"Craig sought her out. You're misleading me," Harry angrily responded.

Judge Gravelle, sensing the growing tension, told the witness to, "Calm down. Just listen carefully to the question and just answer the question he's asking."

"I'm not trying to do anything wrong," Cohn apologized. "I'm just trying to ask you some questions. I have a job to do and I'm doing it."

The most significant testimony during the preliminary hearing was provided by Frances Seedlock, who described Craig washing out his van and then washing himself, "like a doctor washes and scrubs before an operation," a description that would linger in the minds of courtroom observers for a long, long time.

Benny Del Re, the San Mateo County criminalist, described how he analyzed the most tangible evidence in the case—the dried bloodstains in the rented van. He testified that samples collected from three areas were Type A—the same as Miss Redlick—while Anderson's own blood was Type O. However, under cross-examination that represented only the tip of the iceberg in what was to come later from the defense concerning the disputed bloodstains, Cohn asked if Type O blood can appear to be Type A if exposed to the elements for a period of time. Del Re admitted that it could.

"But safeguards are taken to make sure that doesn't happen when you take the sample," the criminalist explained.

Wagstaffe ended his presentation of the evidence by calling one surprise witness, something that a prosecutor can more easily do in a preliminary hearing than in a trial. Wagstaffe summoned Ron Anderson, Craig's father, to the stand. Cohn objected but, after a recess, the judge allowed the questioning to proceed.

Wagstaffe questioned Ron Anderson about the business

records for the San Carlos store which, since Craig's arrest, had been shut down. The prosecutor wanted to see those records to determine if there were any evidence that Craig had opened the shop on November 11th.

"Where are those records today, sir?" Wagstaffe asked.

"Most of them are in my possession," Anderson said, explaining that they were with him at that very moment.

Wagstaffe asked the judge's permission to examine those records. "They're potential evidence."

Cohn objected on the grounds that the records should have been subpoenaed. But Wagstaffe told the judge that Ron Anderson had refused to talk to the district attorney's office and that the prosecution couldn't subpoena the records unless it was known where they were being kept.

Gravelle denied Wagstaffe's request.

"I think it's purely speculative as to whether any record the witness might have would reflect whether or not the defendant was present," the judge said. But he added, "The testimony that the court has before it, seems to clearly indicate that the defendant was not present at his business on November 11, 1985 at any time during the day."

Wagstaffe, however, proceeded to ask Ron Anderson about any contact he might have had with his son on Veteran's Day. Anderson couldn't recall if he had talked to Craig on the phone that day, either at work or at home.

"Do you recall, as you sit there and testify today, sir, Craig telling you at some time that he was indeed working on that day?"

"I can't answer that yes or no," Ron Anderson said.

"In other words, you don't have a memory of that?"

"No," the witness responded.

After the prosecution had presented its case, Cohn came forward to argue fervently and vehemently for dismissal of the charges.

"This is probably the flimsiest charge of murder I've ever heard of," Cohn said. "There is no proof of the death. There is no proof of the body. There is no proof of the weapon. There's a proof of a disappearance of a girl and that's it.

"There's absolutely no jurisdiction for this court to hear this case and make a holding in this county because you've got absolutely no evidence that a crime was committed," Cohn continued. "This girl could have gotten into a car with another person and driven to San Jose or she could be in Los Angeles."

Stepping slowly to the front of the courtroom, Wagstaffe made a wide sweeping gesture with his hands. He felt that if the defense attorney were correct, then "all somebody has to do is completely dispose of the body and that's it. Unless the body is found, there cannot be a prosecution for murder. The Scott case stands for the proposition it does not take that."

Wagstaffe explained that if a kidnapping starts in one county and ends when the victim is murdered in another county, the jurisdiction is in both counties. "And there's strong, certainly a strong suspicion here that you can conclude that Denise Redlick was kidnapped against her will by leaving her car doors open," he said.

Judge Gravelle agreed that there was, in fact, sufficient evidence to hold Craig Anderson on both charges, murder and kidnapping. Furthermore, he retained the defendant's no-bail status.

And, as Judge Gravelle walked down the steps to return to his chambers, the spectators, most of them again wearing white carnations, stood and applauded his decision.

■ CHAPTER TWENTY ■

For the Defense

Nate Cohn had made a tactical decision, a good one the prosecution acknowledged, to postpone Craig's solicitation of murder trial and to proceed to trial as quickly as possible in the Redlick case, refusing to "waive time." In any criminal case, the defendant has the right to ask the court to disregard the legal requirements for a speedy trial. But from the day Marriscolo issued Craig's arrest warrant on Denise's murder, Cohn insisted that the arraignment, hearing and trial should proceed like clockwork. It made sense for the defense to press for the more serious case to be heard first and it was also true that the faster the so-called evidence was heard by a jury, the less time there would be to perhaps find a body or any more compelling evidence.

But Cohn was angry. Everywhere he turned he was running into obstacles. His client, a seemingly decent and reputable businessman who had never before been in trouble with the law, was being treated like the lowliest of criminals. In a document filed with Superior Court on March 24th, Cohn ticked off examples of how Craig Anderson was being singled out by the authorities for treatment that violated his constitutional rights.

Cohn made several vehement claims including:

*When Craig was brought into court for his first preliminary hearing, he was bound by leg shackles. "This was done before he was officially charged with any violent crime," Cohn said.

*When Cohn arrived at the jail on March 1st for a scheduled appointment with Craig, he was forced to wait twenty-five minutes to see his client. Then, instead of being brought to the cubicle he had requested, which he understood to be soundproofed, he was led to another cubicle. He and his client, he said, could hear deputies talking outside and, presumably, their own conversation could be heard by the deputies. As a result, they were unable to have a confidential talk about the case.

*An order depriving the defendant of visitors had been made by jail authorities on February 24th because Craig had "failed to obey an order of the medical department." Cohn was baffled by the allegation since Craig had no reason, at that time, to see a doctor or a nurse. When Craig's parents arrived that evening to see their son, they were turned away without explanation.

*At Craig's arraignment on murder charges in Redwood City, a deputy standing outside the courtroom refused to let in Craig's mother, father, brothers and other relatives and friends. The deputy told Cohn that there were no seats, but when Cohn went inside, he found seven or eight vacant seats near the front of the courtroom. When the judge entered, Cohn brought the problem to his attention and the judge subsequently ordered the bailiffs to escort the Anderson contingent, steaming outside, to the vacant seats. But according to Cohn, only Mr. and Mrs. Anderson were ushered in, leaving the rest of Craig's family to sit outside.

Each time Cohn entered the courtroom on behalf of Craig, it furthered his belief that his client's ability to obtain a fair trial had been seriously eroded.

"I would look in the hallway and see a sea of white carnations," he said. "They had already convicted him."

Cohn was standing outside the courtroom one day with Shirley and Ron Anderson when a stranger approached him.

"Mr. Cohn, I always thought you were a nice person," the man, apparently there for the Anderson case, said.

"Well, I'm glad you felt that way but I hope you haven't changed your mind," Cohn declared.

"But you're defending this guy!" said the stranger. "How can you do such a thing?"

Cohn couldn't believe it.

"Somebody has to defend him. It's his right. He is presumed not guilty until he's proven guilty," Cohn said. "If you catch me putting on phony evidence or lying or doing something unethical in the courtroom, then maybe you SHOULD feel differently about me. But all I'm trying to do is present a straightforward case." He shook his head disgustedly. "Even my wife has been attacked."

Carolyn Cohn had gone to a fashion show at a church in Burlingame, ironically, the same church where Craig and Denise would have been married, just after the preliminary hearing on the murder charge when she was approached by several people who had strong opinions about the case.

"What's your husband representing that guy for?" one asked.

"That guy is as guilty as sin," said another.

Craig's parents had also experienced the community's hostility. In a declaration filed in Superior Court, Shirley Anderson listed numerous complaints about how her son and her family had been treated.

On the day that Craig was arrested, Shirley and her daughter attempted to have a lunch brought in to their son while he was being temporarily held at the Burlingame station. "We spent the entire afternoon trying to get Commander Chase to meet with us or at least grant permission for Craig to be fed," Shirley wrote. "We were unsuccessful on both counts."

The Burlingame police, she said, proceeded to announce Craig's arrest at a press conference, even though Craig hadn't yet been able to meet with his attorney who was tied up in court. And, only after a bailbondsman arrived at the station late in the afternoon did Chase emerge to announce to the Anderson contingent that the bail was, in fact, an astronomical $500,000—not $50,000 as they had originally been led to believe—on a "bogus solicitation of murder charge."

Craig's mother and father felt that in court, the Redlick's supporters turned into a "vigilante group" who attempted and "almost succeeded" in preventing her from even using the restroom by blocking her way.

Later, at the county jail, she was denied visitation rights on two occasions because her son had merely declined breakfast and was, therefore, listed as suicidal, she said. At one point, he was even placed in solitary confinement.

According to Shirley Anderson's declaration, family members had received so many annoying phone calls that they had been forced to change their phone numbers. Craig's elderly grandparents had also been the target of harassment, she further stated.

"Even with all the intimidation and harassment, it has not caused me to lose my concern or my love for the missing woman, Denise Redlick," Shirley Anderson wrote. "We are a Christian family full of love and compassion and will always remain that way."

Meanwhile, San Mateo County District Attorney Jim Fox received several letters complaining of Craig's mistreatment.

Said one author, "Your subordinates, with the help of Burlingame Police, have taken a case of a missing person and changed it into 'Murder She Wrote.' With the flimsiest circumstantial evidence I have ever seen or heard about, your office has taken away a man's freedom, his business, his reputation and his future. Worst of all, you have tormented his family."

A cousin of Craig's who had attended the hearing accused court officials of favoritism.

"I feel sorry for the Redlicks and their loss, but all this wasted time and public money being spent on their antics instead of looking for their daughter, Denise, is very saddening" she wrote. "What a terrible price my cousin, Craig, has to pay because of a broken engagement."

Fox, however, quickly responded to the criticisms.

"Our office does not have any desire to 'railroad an innocent man,'" he said, "However, based upon the evidence available, we do not wish to see an individual escape prosecution and punishment for a crime which he has committed."

There was, however, one development favorable to Craig in mid-April. Fox, on April 12th, told reporters that he and his staff had decided not to seek the death penalty.

"Based on our evaluation—the facts of the case and the background of the defendant—we have concluded that this is not an appropriate case for the death penalty," Fox said. The decision was based on Anderson's lack of criminal history and the prosecution's belief that the defendant "was probably emotionally disturbed because of rejection by the victim."

But because of the alleged special circumstance of kidnapping, Anderson was still facing the chilling prospect of spending the rest of his life in prison.

For the prosecution, the defense strategy of not waiving time meant they had to move quickly to tie up the loose ends of their case. Since Holm and Wagstaffe had anticipated that Craig would force the case to court as soon as possible, they had made certain that they had enough evidence to try the case from the day they filed charges. "We resisted pressure to file it quicker because we wanted everything ready to go," Holm said. In fact, since January, only one new witness—a relatively insignificant one—had surfaced. It was the father of one of Craig's three original alibi witnesses who corroborated his son's revised version of what happened on November 11th.

But, in any criminal case, many hours are spent on details that may play only a small—but potentially very important—role in the trial testimony. For example, Sergeant Jack Van Etten had spent a tedious four days calling every car and truck leasing agency, more than one hundred ten businesses, in the San Mateo County Pacific Bell phone directory to find out if a Craig Alan Anderson or Anderson Paint Company had rented a vehicle on November 9th, 1985.

The police had learned that when Denise arrived at a friend's birthday party that evening, she was visibly shaken, having felt that a van had been following her as she walked in the dark from her car to the apartment complex recreation room where the party had been held. Since this was just a few hours after Denise's marathon meeting with Craig, when she told him their relationship was absolutely finished, the investigators wondered if he perhaps had an earlier, aborted plan to kidnap her. But Van Etten's exhaustive phone calls turned up nothing.

In a further effort to bolster the contention that the van was rented to kidnap and murder Denise, Commander Chase, in his own car, traced over the route that he presumed Anderson would have covered on November 11th. Then Chase drove from the Budget agency in San Carlos to Anderson's home (.7 miles), to the Redlick home in San Bruno (twenty miles), to 1633 Old Bayshore

(6.6 miles), to the Seedlock home in Palo Alto (twenty-two miles) and back to the Budget agency in San Carlos (11.6 miles). The total mileage—60.0 miles—was well within the ninety-five miles logged on the van's odometer by the time Anderson returned it.

All of the witnesses were interviewed again by Holm, Marriscolo and Wagstaffe and a few of them provided additional information. Chris Morganti told the prosecutors that she had taken notes, which she saved, of her conversation on November 14th with Craig. She turned over the notes, jotted on a small note pad, to Marriscolo who placed them in the evidence locker. In the course of conducting second and third interviews with potential witnesses, Marriscolo found several more people who remembered seeing suspicious scratches on Craig's body around the middle of November.

Just a few days before the trial was to begin, Holm and Marriscolo went to Joan and Harry's house to persuade the victim's parents to turn tape recordings of conversations with Craig over to the prosecution. Because the tapes were not made in any official capacity, they were legally the Redlicks' property. Joan, in fact, was reluctant. She feared that anyone reading raw transcripts of the tape might find them complimentary toward Craig and that she might, in her surreptitious attempt to have Craig reveal something about Denise, appear to trust him. Ultimately the tapes were turned over to the police and copies were made for Nate Cohn.

It was a decision that Joan would later regret.

With the trial date rapidly approaching, Cohn began delving into his best line of defense, to challenge the validity of the crime lab's work on the dried bloodstains in the van and on the tennis shoes.

The way the press described it, Cohn thought with indignation, it was as if the interior of the van was covered with blood. As he looked at the San Mateo County Forensic Lab's reports concerning the forensic blood tests, he deduced that only three small crusts of blood were removed. Yet, he knew that even a tiny amount of a victim's blood is enough to convict a murder defendant given the right—or wrong, depending upon whose side you are on—set of circumstances.

Luckily Nate had heard about a scientist-turned-courtroom consultant who might be able to help him get the bloodstains thrown out of court.

Benjamin W. Grunbaum, a grey-haired and bespectacled native of Poland, came to this country in 1946, to study at the University of California at Berkeley. While working on a doctorate in analytical biochemistry, he became interested in research, by a noted biochemist at UCB, into the identification and individualization of body fluids. In 1963, Grunbaum accepted a position in the anatomy-physiology department as an associate research biochemist working on a study, funded by the National Aeronautics and Space Administration, into the effects of weightlessness on the metabolism or primates, work that earned him several awards from NASA. In addition, he wrote a dissertation on differentiating body fluids among schizophrenics, the mentally ill, alcoholics and normal people that earned him his masters degree in criminalistics in 1964.

Along the way, the biochemist developed an instrument called the Sartophor, to assist in the microanalysis of blood, both in crime labs and clinical labs. The system originally was licensed by Beckman Instruments and marketed under a different name, but a German Company, Sartorias, later purchased the license and gave the device a new name. Grunbaum receives royalties from the worldwide sales of the equipment.

In the mid 1970s, Grunbaum was asked to direct a five-year study for the California Office of Criminal Justice and Planning, using electrophoresis to analyze blood samples from twenty-two thousand Californians, representing various ethnic groups, compiling information about the frequency of various proteins and enzymes which serve as genetic markers. Grunbaum's final report, "Distribution of Gene Frequencies and Discrimination Probabilities for Twenty-Two Human Blood Genetic Systems in Four Racial Groups," was published in the Journal of Forensic Sciences in 1980.

According to Grunbaum, the system that he outlined was

used by laboratories in several European countries although it was adopted by a few crime labs in this country.

Meanwhile, his publications began attracting the attention of criminal defense attorneys who sought him out for help in interpreting the results of crime lab evidence.

"The first thing I would do," Grunbaum said, "is ask to see the laboratory data." He looked for how the criminalist derived his results. "The notes were the most shocking thing I had ever seen in my life. They had nothing to do with science." The biochemist formed the opinion that crime laboratories operate in a virtual vacuum in the United States, with no licensing of technicians or standardization of their techniques.

"Every one of them thinks he is the reincarnation of Sherlock Holmes," Grunbaum argued. "Thousands of them in this country think they can do whatever they want since there is absolutely no supervision." Criminalistics, he claimed, is the only science in which one can routinely find examples of "methodology drift," taking an established or published laboratory method and employing variations of those techniques from one lab to the next, without any verification that the altered methods actually work.

In an article published in The California Defender, the journal of the California Public Defenders Association, in 1985, Grunbaum wrote that both prosecutors and defenders would benefit if crime labs were subjected to quality assurance programs. He proceeded to outline his proposal for such a program, including mandatory licensing and proficiency testing of crime laboratory technicians. Without such standards, the "quality of physiological stain analysis in United States crime laboratories may range from excellent to very poor."

"The (crime lab) analyst is also subject to a certain bias, because he is intimately acquainted with the details of the crime under investigation and may have formed opinions regarding the guilt of a suspect," Grunbaum wrote. "To be completely objective, he would have to be unaware of the facts of a case before he did any analysis."

In his campaign for crime laboratory reforms, Grunbaum began collecting data from proficiency tests, administered by the

Collaborative Testing Service Incorporated, for crime labs across the country that opt to subscribe to the program. In his lectures, published papers and courtroom testimony, he liked to emphasize the proof that crime labs do make errors. For example, in a 1985 test requiring technicians to identify the ABO type of two fresh blood specimens on clean cotton cloth, two of the sixty-two labs returning their results made errors. Both misread the Type O stains as Type A. Those two errors, he contended, could represent two defendants who are unjustly convicted of a crime.

Although Grunbaum had been described, by some, as an opportunist carrying out a personal vendetta because the scientific community has not chosen to accept his way of doing things, the biochemist felt that he was on a lonely crusade only because no other knowledgeable, working scientist had bothered to become as familiar with forensic laboratory practices as he.

"The totality of the scientific community would challenge this work if they knew about it," he contended.

Three weeks before the trial date, Grunbaum, a charming and congenial man who still speaks with the trace of a Polish accent, sat in Cohn's San Francisco office examining the San Mateo County Forensic Lab's "bench notes" from its testing of the dried bloodstains in the van and on the tennis shoes. The name of the criminalist who had performed the tests stuck out like a sore thumb. Benny Del Re had worked as a research associate for Grunbaum during the OCJP grant study at University of California at Berkeley from 1976 to 1978 after his graduation from California State University at Sacramento. Del Re, in fact, had come to disavow Grunbaum's study of a new electrophoresis system and claimed that he once declined to have his name included on one of Grunbaum's scientific publications about the research because he didn't think Grunbaum's proposed methods—acceptable in a clinical laboratory where fresh blood samples are being analyzed—worked in forensics.

"The bottom line is that there's a lot of sour grapes on Grunbaum's part," Del Re said. Ben Grunbaum, he said, could have turned the work around into something useful for the forensic community and taken credit for it. "Instead, he chose to fight everyone and go off on a crusade," Del Re claimed.

Grunbaum remembered Del Re as a "very, very good technician" in the Berkeley lab. But Benny, he said, "was under the
misapprehension that he was there to do research. He was strictly
a technician."

Grunbaum silently scanned the documents that Cohn had
obtained through routine discovery. With a critical eye, he traced
the complex procedures that were used to determine that the
bloodstains in the van were Type A. It took the biochemist only a
few minutes to reach his conclusion.

"Mr. Cohn, I believe that you should challenge these test results," Grunbaum declared. "In my opinion, they are scientifically
unacceptable and inadequate to support a conviction."

It was just what Cohn was hoping to hear. The professor, in
his distinctive English, went on to explain that the defense should
make a motion to exclude the prosecution's evidence that the
bloodstains were of the same blood group as Denise Redlick. He
felt the basic problem was that the techniques that Benny Del Re
had used to reach his conclusions concerning blood typing, varied from published, standardized methods.

Cohn was eager to hear more and to begin preparing for this
strategy. But as the defense attorney asked a few more questions
about bloodstain evidence and the complicated science surrounding the forensic tests, Grunbaum became uneasy. Successfully
challenging the evidence, he believed, depended heavily on inten-
sive, well-thought out scientifically ground cross-examination. He
felt that it was too late in the game for Cohn, despite his experience and reputation as one of the city's leading criminal defense
attorneys, to become adequately versed on the subject. Delicately,
he broached that potential problem.

"Mr. Cohn, you're a wonderful lawyer, one of the best in San
Francisco," Grunbaum said, stroking the attorney's ego. "But in
order for us to work together and for you to understand this issue, it would take an enormous amount of time. I think it would
be extremely prohibitive." To Grunbaum's relief, Cohn sat down
and listened without seeming offended.

"But I know someone who could be a tremendous asset to
you, who might be able to come in just for this phase of the case,"
the biochemist went on. "Would you consider it?"

Cohn knew it was more than a request. It was clear to Cohn that Grunbaum would be unwilling to work on the case without this other attorney's help. Although he had never before, in forty years of practicing law, asked another attorney to step in to handle a portion of his case, he relented.

"His name is Robert Brower," Grunbaum went on. "And I am very impressed by his work."

In 1983, Brower had been working as an insurance defense attorney, paid by insurance companies to represent policy holders who had been sued for liability, when his law firm partners assigned him to represent Grunbaum, then a University of California employee, in a defamation suit. The suit had been filed by the owner of a private laboratory who had been hired by San Mateo County to analyze evidence in a 1980 trial that ended in the conviction of David Roundtree, a co-defendant in the slaying of a Burlingame man and the rape of the man's wife, on first-degree murder, rape, robbery and burglary charges. Grunbaum, testifying for the defense, claimed that all of the prosecution's blood, saliva and semen test results were invalid. Roundtree's court-appointed defense attorney, in his motion for a new trial, filed a report by Grunbaum who severely criticized the work of the private laboratory criminalist hired by San Mateo County. The criminalist, in turn, filed a defamation suit against Grunbaum.

"That was the first time in my life that I had anything to do with bloodstains," said Brower. He spent six months studying the complexities of blood evidence although the plaintiff eventually dropped the litigation.

But Brower had come to "realize what Grunbaum's all about."

"He was simply trying to promote the idea that criminalists do not have licenses and are not controlled by any government agency. The quality of their work can vary from very good to very bad," said Brower. In 1984, Brower was the author of an amicus curiae, or "friend of the court" brief, filed in Grunbaum's behalf with the California Supreme Court in People vs. Brown, a murder case out of Riverside County that addressed that very issue.

In their brief, Brower and Grunbaum pointed to the results

of voluntary forensic laboratory proficiency tests as proof that dangerous errors do occur in physiological fluid analysis."

The bottom line of their controversial paper was that "until criteria for reliability are developed, accepted and observed, the forensic analysis of dried blood and body fluids must be considered unreliable."

The rebuttal brief filed by the Riverside County District Attorney's Office contended that Grunbaum misrepresented the error rate in proficiency tests and mistated that the methods used by forensic laboratories for analysis of physiological stain evidence "have been impartially and objectively evaluated."

The Brown Amicus Curiae briefs were circulated among criminalists throughout the world. Although they would not be the deciding factor in the Brown case (which was ultimately appealed to the United States Supreme Court on other issues and upheld), they would put into print arguments that would continue for years to come.

When Grunbaum contacted Brower asking if he could meet to discuss a pending San Mateo County murder case, the attorney agreed as a favor to a friend.

Grunbaum arranged to have Brower and Cohn meet at Grunbaum's home in the quiet valley town of Moraga, just east of Oakland, on the Saturday before the trial was to begin. Cohn arrived in his vintage Rolls Royce, parking it next to the corral, which was "most impressive to the horses," Grunbaum jested.

For several hours, the three men sat in Grunbaum's sunny living room and discussed the bloodstain evidence. Like Grunbaum, Brower saw numerous points on which to seriously challenge the San Mateo County Forensic Laboratory's findings.

"The bloodstain evidence is worthless," Brower told Cohn. Besides the fact that the van had been used by many people after Craig Anderson and that forty percent of the population has the same blood type as Denise Redlick, Brower felt that the lab had taken certain liberties in processing the blood crusts—which if adequately demonstrated to the court—could throw a very dark shadow over the findings.

"But," said Brower shaking his head thoughtfully, "the real

key to discrediting the crime lab's work will lie in a very through cross-examination of Benny Del Re."

While the defense team heavily weighed the best strategy for counteracting the prosecution's most significant evidence, Holm and Wagstaffe had already taken steps to make sure they would enter the bloodstain hearing with both guns drawn.

CHAPTER TWENTY-ONE

Peremptory Challenge

Nate Cohn still wanted a change of venue. As the trial date grew closer, he continued to collect newspaper articles and to take note of television coverage of the case.

On Monday, May 5th, Cohn made one last-ditch effort to have Craig Anderson's trial moved to another county. At 1:30 p.m., Cohn and Holm stood before Judge Walter Capaccioli, who had been assigned to the trial that morning by the presiding criminal judge, to argue the issue. The defendant, making his first courtroom appearance in several weeks, looked pale and ill at ease as the final preparations for his murder trial began.

Capaccioli, a thin and dark-haired man known for blending a firm judicial style with tongue-in-cheek humor, discussed reading the motion for the change of venue along with the supporting documents and recent newspaper articles that Cohn had submitted just that morning.

"Your honor, since meeting with you at lunchtime, I found two more newspaper articles," Cohn said. He handed the clerk photocopies of articles dated May 3 from The San Mateo Times and the Peninsula Times Tribune, both describing the Burlingame Police Department's version of events leading up to the trial.

The defense attorney, standing at the table next to Craig, said he had also subpoenaed tapes from several television stations but the stations had not responded. In addition, Cohn reported that he heard one of the stations on Sunday night had televised an interview with Holm saying he had "very substantial evidence" to convict Anderson while another station, "And I didn't see it myself, your Honor," had shown footage of officers conducting a weekend search in the Mountain View area for Denise's body, even though there is no evidence that there is a body to find, he insisted.

Cohn scornfully suggested that the police department contacted reporters and invited them to photograph the search.

"I think the police department is deliberately setting these things up so that they would get the county in the state of mind that my client cannot get a fair trial, your Honor."

Furthermore, Cohn told the judge that "the mother of the girl" was interviewed, saying that she only wanted to find her daughter's body so she could give it a decent Christian burial.

"All through this entire program, there would seem to be no doubt being expressed by anyone that there was a dead body somewhere and that my client committed a murder. Yet," Cohn said exasperatedly, "There is no evidence of a murder at this stage."

Cohn went on to cite a relevant Supreme Court ruling that a change of venue must be granted when the defendant shows there is a "reasonable likelihood" that, without a change, a fair trial cannot be obtained. And, in Cohn's opinion, reasonable likelihood does not mean that prejudice must be more probable than not.

The defendant, Cohn argued, is entitled to a trial in another county "not only when the preponderance of circumstances calls for such results but also whenever a defendant has shown even a reasonable likelihood that he will not receive a fair trial."

Cohn had submitted numerous sworn statements, provided primarily by friends and relatives of his client, to support the change of venue motion. In a four-page report, Shirley Anderson said that the news media had, since her son's arrest, been presenting a one-sided picture of the case, slanted from the Redlick family's point of view. The mother of the accused killer vented her frustration and disappointment with a legal system that, in her opinion, was failing to protect her falsely accused son, and a community that had already labeled him a murderer.

"I have watched the Redlick family produce and direct the news coverage, especially Channel Seven, to focus their camera on my family and me in an attempt to cause us to lose our dignity and self-respect," Mrs. Anderson declared. "My children have watched their brother be considered guilty until proven innocent and have wondered where the judicial system exists that they studied in the Burlingame School District. The people in the city and county I once loved have turned their heads away from us at markets, stores and restaurants in the area.

"Because of the publicity generated by the Burlingame Police Department and the San Mateo County District Attorney's office and most especially the white carnation group of Joan and Harry Redlick," Craig's mother continued, "it is not possible for my son to receive a fair and impartial trial in San Mateo County and quite possibly anywhere in the entire Bay Area. All my family and I have asked for is fairness."

Also submitted in support of the venue change were letters from several San Mateo County residents who, by their own admission, were friends or relatives of Craig Anderson. The common thread was one of indignation over the biased nature of news coverage and the manner in which the Redlick contingent had taken over the courtroom at each hearing, sometimes leaving the Andersons with nowhere to even sit.

Some letter writers objected to the public displays of affection between the Redlicks and the prosecutors. One example cited occurred at the preliminary hearing in March where a woman wearing a white carnation approached Marriscolo at the prosecutor's table, leaned down and kissed him on the cheek.

"The prosecuting attorney and his associates seem not only on very friendly terms with the Redlick family, but have acted in an unprofessional manner and seem very biased in this case," wrote one observer.

A declaration had also been filed by Nate's own wife, Carolyn, who said she had talked to a number of people in the area who were familiar with the case and all had made up their minds —from what they had read in the newspapers—that her husband's client was guilty. Mrs. Cohn said she and her husband had Easter dinner in South San Francisco on March 30th with ten other people. At least seven of them were certain of Anderson's guilt.

"It was also expressed that Anderson's only chance would be if he selected a jury in Australia or Chile," Carolyn Cohn said.

Holm, however, looked relaxed and confident as he listened to Cohn's renewed attempt to move the trial elsewhere. He had no doubt, based on the information submitted by Cohn so far, that the trial would be held in San Mateo County. Rarely were trials moved to different jurisdictions since the cost and inconvenience is enormous. In recent years, only one San Mateo County murder trial, the retrial after a hung jury of a young man accused of killing his affluent parents to reap the benefits of the estate, had been moved to another county due to the effects of pre-trial publicity. While the disappearance of Denise Redlick and the arrest of Craig Anderson had been heavily covered by the media, many other cases had remained in the county with just as much, or even greater, pre-trial publicity.

Calling the defense attorney's supporting documents "woefully inadequate," the prosecutor said it would be foolish for the police department and district attorney's office to intentionally enflame San Mateo County residents, as suggested by Cohn, in a way that would justify a change of venue. In fact, Marriscolo had taken great pains to make sure that the press was unaware of the weekend search but reporters who tune their radios into police frequencies, easily find these things out.

In addition, most, "if not all" of the affidavits in favor of a change of venue were supplied by friends or relatives of the defendant, people with a natural bias, he pointed out.

Jury *voir dire*, can weed out potential jurors who walk into court with a bias, Holm believed. "The test is whether a juror, notwithstanding some knowledge of the case, would be able to put it aside and render a fair and impartial judgement." Holm said. "And, from experience in cases more publicized than this, that can be done."

"Submitted?" Capaccioli asked the attorneys, who nodded that they were indeed finished arguing the issue.

"As I read the law, the court has to consider the nature of the charge and the frequency and timing of the publicity, the evidence, if any, of continued community interest and the size of the community as well as the standing of the victim and the accused in the community," the judge explained.

According to the judge, extensive publicity alone would not justify a change of venue. Furthermore, he felt that a thorough *voir dire*—questioning of the potential jurors—would eliminate any possible pre-trial publicity problems.

"Therefore, under the totality of circumstances, I can't say that there has been a showing that there is a reasonable likelihood the defendant will not receive a fair trial. Therefore, the motion for change of venue is denied."

A visibly disappointed Cohn then raised the possibility of individual, *in camera*—in chambers—questioning of each of the prospective jurors so that one person's answers to questions about prejudice due to pre-trial publicity doesn't affect anyone else's.

Holm objected to such a measure because it would take weeks. Again Capaccioli ruled against the defense.

Still undecided, however, however, was the prosecution's most critical evidence, the submission of the results of examining of dried blood samples, the issue raised by Cohn. Holm and Cohn agreed to delay a hearing on this matter until after the jury had been impaneled.

Ninety San Mateo County residents who were on the prospective jurors roster lifted their right hands and took an oath to tell the truth in ceremonial courtroom 2M.

The room, often used for more festive events, including swearing in of new judges, is not designed for the benefit of spectators. Because of poor acoustics, only those who sit in the first few of some fifteen rows can hear the dialogue.

Seated in the front row, on opposite sides of the courtroom, were the defendant's parents and the victim's parents. Despite Joan Redlick's impassioned letter to Craig's mother on her daughter's behalf, they had not spoken a single word to one another since Craig's arrest six months earlier. The friendship and love

209

that had grown out of the engagement party in February 1984 were gone forever.

"Good morning ladies and gentlemen," Capaccioli began. "I am addressing myself to the people who have been summoned here as prospective jurors with respect to the trial that's pending before this court."

The noise in the courtroom subsided as the judge went on to explain what would occur over the next few days.

"The process of jury selection is called Voir Dire," he said, providing the proper pronunciation. "That's a French phrase which very loosely means 'to speak the truth.'

"Now, sometimes the questions that are asked by the court or by the attorneys may appear to you to be tedious and some-what personal but, I assure you, it is not an attempt to unnecessarily invade your privacy. What it is, is a legitimate desire on the part of the court to select a fair and unbiased jury. So please don't feel embarrassed by the questions or that your ability or integrity are in any way being challenged. I assure you they are not."

Unlike any other time during the trial proceedings, the attorneys, during jury selection, have a chance to exchange words with the people who will ultimately judge the merits of their case. But it's also a chance for the attorneys, if they choose their jurors carefully, to tip the scale of justice in their own favors.

The clerk drew from a revolving wooden container the names of twelve prospective jurors to sit in the jury box below a bank of windows that allow the street noise, and occasionally, the pounding of basketballs on the floor of the jail exercise yard two stories above, to filter in.

"Now, I'm going to introduce to you Mr. Craig Anderson," the judge said. "Mr. Anderson, would you please rise and face the jury?" Awkwardly, the defendant, wearing the same blue-grey suit and dark blue tie that he had worn on the night he met Joan and Harry Redlick, stood and faced the judge.

"Thank you, sir," said Capaccioli, waving at Anderson to be seated. "Do any of you know Mr. Anderson or are in any way acquainted with Mr. Anderson?" None in this initial group did. Then the judge read a summary of the charges—first-degree murder with a special allegation of kidnapping and a second count of kidnapping—and clarified that the district attorney would not be seeking the death penalty. That would come as a relief to those prospective jurors who hadn't even known they had walked into a murder case.

The message, however, was clear. This was a serious matter.

Capaccioli, explaining that the trial might last up to three weeks, excused several people who might suffer an "undue hardship." The judge said he expected the case to be over with before early June.

Then, it was time for the attorneys, with Cohn getting the first crack, to question the panelists.

For the defense attorney, *voir dire* would be the only chance to weed out jurors who might have already formed an opinion concerning his client. He repeatedly asked panelists if they had read or seen anything about the case, including the many posters circulating around the county.

Cohn, who had objected to Holm's earlier portrayal of Denise as "the victim," asked each prospective juror if they understood there is no evidence before them, yet, that anybody is a victim and that the district attorney "has to prove all the material allegations of his charge before he can do anything other than bring a verdict of not guilty."

One of Cohn's courtroom quirks, frequently apologizing for misunderstanding answers to questions, surfaced early. "I'm getting deaf," he said on one such occasion. When the judge asked one prospective juror to repeat his answer because he, too, hadn't heard, Cohn interjected with a smile, "Usually I'm the one who doesn't hear. I'm the one who's getting old."

Judge Capaccioli countered, with a sigh, "We're both getting old, Mr. Cohn."

Some who watched the trial would describe Cohn as a bumbler. Over and over he would say to prospective jurors and witnesses, who appeared baffled by questions that made misstatements of the evidence, "I'm not trying to confuse you," or "I'm not playing games with you." Critics would feel that it was Cohn who was confused, not the witness, while many others knowing or having heard of Cohn would feel that his reputation of having a bewildered facade was all part of his own game, that he was still sharp as a tack.

Holm's questions focused on acceptance of the concept of circumstantial evidence which would be the foundation for his case. In a variety of ways, he asked if each person could find the defendant guilty of murder without establishing the existence of a body.

Holm offered this example: Suppose you assume that it snowed during the night? Then suppose you see tracks in the snow leading to the house. Can you assume that someone came home after the snow had fallen?

Cohn, however, turned the examples around, asking one juror if he could also see that, perhaps, someone had walked away from the house backwards.

"So, all circumstantial evidence isn't conclusive, do you understand that?" he said to the panelist who answered that she did.

There were times, even as early as jury selection, when Holm's wry sense of humor would get under Cohn's staid skin. After Cohn's twist on the snow scenario, it was Holm's turn to question the same individual. He rose from his chair and took a dozen steps backwards to turn and face the jury.

Capaccioli was not amused.

"Mr. Holm, that's unnecessary."

Cohn immediately stepped in. "Your Honor, this might be funny to Mr. Holm, but this is not funny to my client or to his parents or the parents of the girl. I don't think this is funny at all."

The prosecutor, looking just a little sheepish, offered, "I'm sorry." Then under his breath, but loud enough for the court reporter to write it in his transcript, "I was trying, just trying to see if I could do it."

Concerning the lack of a body, Holm asked several jurors if they had any doubts that Jimmy Hoffa, the former Teamster's Union president who vanished on July 30, 1975, is, in fact, dead. Cohn objected to the Hoffa analogy.

"It's an unfair question. There is no way they could possibly know if Jimmy Hoffa is dead," Cohn declared. Holm was simply implying, he claimed, that one can determine from reading that newspapers that something is a fact. Capaccioli, however, allowed the question as a means of identifying a prospective juror's beliefs.

The voir dire, at times, demonstrated Cohn's keen sensitivity to prejudicial language. Besides objecting to Denise's portrayal as a "victim," he also protested when Holm referred to finding the defendant guilty "beyond a reasonable doubt." Cohn insisted, several times, that the terminology should be "beyond all reasonable doubt." When he interrupted Holm for a third time to make that point, the judge, his patience wearing thin, chided both attorneys and told them to stop arguing.

"Let's get on with this," the judge said. "It's frustrating enough."

Holm had also decided well in advance to ask the panelists questions about their relationships with their children, so that he could identify those jurors who might see how Denise Redlick, at twenty-three, could still be close enough to her parents to keep them posted of her whereabouts everyday.

It was no coincidence that, of the five men and seven women finally impaneled, seven were parents of adult-aged children.

Throughout the entire three days of jury selection, Craig Anderson, serious-faced, conferred quietly with Cohn, seldom glancing at the people who would decide if he was a murderer. But midway through *voir dire* on Thursday, Anderson finally had a reason to smile.

That happened when Peter M. Fena was called to step into the jury box. Fena, who had known Craig since they were both in their late teens, had known that Anderson's trial was occurring sometime in May. When he received a notice to appear for jury duty in the mail, however, it never occurred to him that he would be called to sit in judgment of Craig. He walked into the courtroom, saw Anderson in his business-like suit and tie, and murmured half to himself, "Oh no, I don't believe it."

But he also figured that he would be dismissed without hesitation.

Fena immediately volunteered to the judge that he was a friend of the defendant, that they had been playing football every Thanksgiving for the past eleven years.

Capaccioli looked curious.

"What kind of game is that?"

"Well, you've heard of the Rose Bowl and the Orange Bowl?" Fena said.

"Yeah, I have," Capaccioli responded, as if to say, "Who hasn't?"

"Okay. We play in a game called the Toilet Bowl." The courtroom erupted with laughter. "And we've done that since we graduated from high school." But Fena also pointed out that he also knew two of the people on Holm's potential witness list including Denise's cousin, Lori Voreyer who had been a close friend of his wife's since high school.

Under the strange circumstances, Fena was not eager to serve. "No matter what happens, someone's going to end up hating me," Fena said, realizing he was caught in the middle.

However, Fena felt he had to answer with an honest, "Yes," when asked if he could be "fair and impartial" if selected for the jury. Three hours later, after a lunch break, Cohn used one of his peremptory challenges to dismiss Fena.

In fact, Cohn's use of peremptories, with all twenty-six exhausted when the prosecutor still had five remaining, backed him into an awkward corner just after the afternoon break on Thursday.

Cohn had used his last challenge to excuse one of the prospective jurors when William E. Larson was called to fill position number eleven.

Larson quickly informed the court that he was familiar with the case. A high school teacher for ten years until his retirement, Larson was concerned about criminal trial appeals that cause verdicts to be overturned for seemingly superficial reasons. He did not wish to be one of those reasons.

Larson said he knew Joan Redlick as a "very valued secretary" at his high school. He also had "a little insight as to her problem" through mutual colleagues, people who talk to her everyday, at school.

"Would the fact that you know people that know her in any way influence your decision?" Judge Capaccioli asked.

"Conceivably," Larson responded.

"How?"

"Well, I think I have more information, heresay, than most people would."

"It's not wrong to have an opinion," the judge declared. "It's not wrong to have this information." The judge wondered if Larson could put the information aside and decide the case on the basis of evidence presented in court.

"Yes," was Larson's adamant reply.

Cohn was alarmed. He began firing questions at juror number eleven, zeroing in on the possibility of pre-trial prejudice.

"I would like to say that I am not biased," Larson told the defense attorney.

"You would like to say? Would you say it?" Cohn demanded, with an air of suspicion.

"I will say it. Yes, yes, yes!"

Cohn continued to grill Larson, asking him if he were aware that a group of people wearing white carnations had shown up to support the Redlicks at previous hearings. Holm objected to the irrelevance of the question and Capaccioli sustained the objection. Cohn, angry now, asked to approach the bench. After the attorneys returned from their brief conference with the judge, Capaccioli ordered Cohn to ask a different question.

"Is there anything at all that you have heard that would incline you in any way to believe that a crime has been committed in this case?" Cohn asked, trying a new approach.

Larson's answer was not one that the defense attorney, whose case was largely based on the possibility that Denise Redlick had simply run away somewhere to be alone, wanted to hear.

"It seems to me that we are in court for a reason and there must have been a crime committed somewhere or we wouldn't be sitting here. I'm not saying who did it, but a crime has been committed. There is a young lady missing and it's my impression that she has not gone off on her own recognizance."

"I see. You have that impression?"

"Yes, yes."

"You have an impression that a crime has been committed and that Mr. Anderson . . ."

"He has nothing to do with it," Larson stopped the question

short. "A young lady is missing and that is a devastating thing for everyone."

"That I don't argue with," Cohn, now on the defensive, answered.

After several more questions, Cohn looked at the defendant and asked whether Anderson had ever been in one of Larson's summer school classes. Anderson, looking up finally, said Larson was "vaguely" familiar.

When Cohn had finished, he asked for a hearing, outside the presence of the prospective jurors, to indicate why Larson should be disqualified by the judge. Capaccioli, however, said none of Larson's answers would exclude him from serving as a juror and told Cohn he would have to state a specific grounds for disqualifying Larson. Disgusted, Cohn said he would drop the matter for the time being.

By the end of the afternoon, the jury, with Larson holding seat number eleven, had been impaneled. Among its members were an office manager for an airline catering company, a United States Postal Service clerk, a manager of marketing, planning and international sales for a major corporation, a retired telephone company executive, a media supervisor for an advertising agency, an airline cargo agent and a liquor store manager. The youngest member, a loan service clerk for a savings and loan company was also the daughter of a San Mateo County Sheriff's Department detective.

Eight of them had some exposure to the case, mostly having seen posters of Denise or a television report on the search for her presumed body.

Holm and Wagstaffe had wanted a jury of well-educated, intelligent individuals who could make logical deductions without having to be presented material in black and white. Yet, they didn't want people with scientific or similar backgrounds, people who would need to have all the evidence fit neat little formulas. This would have to be a jury that could rely on common sense, Wagstaffe said.

The prosecutors were relatively happy with what they got.

Cohn was livid.

After the jurors had been sworn in and admonished not to

read anything about the trial, watch any television programs about the trial, or discuss the trial with anyone, they were told when to return and then dismissed.

When all of the jurors had filed out of court and the bailiff closed the doors behind them, Cohn again asked for a change of venue. "The voir dire," he argued, "has shown my client can't receive a fair trial. To make matters worse, the assistant district attorney has unfairly used his challenges primarily to dismiss those people who had not heard about the case," he complained. "And, then there was Mr. Larson.

"There is no way in the world that man should have been allowed to sit on this jury. If he had told the truth . . ."

"I think he DID tell the truth," the judge interjected.

"Well, I don't believe it. I don't believe it at all. I don't believe the attitude of that man in the jury box, his look, that smart-aleck"

Again, the judge cut him off. Capaccioli accused Cohn of arguing with Larson, asking him the same question over and over, impugning the man's integrity.

Capaccioli said that, in fact, he had been impressed by how little the jurors seemed to know about the case. Saying that "there is still no evidence that Anderson can't receive a fair trial in San Mateo County," the judge once again denied the change of venue.

With no body, no murder weapon, no eye witnesses, and a defendant who insisted he was innocent, the trial was finally ready to begin.

■ CHAPTER TWENTY-TWO ■

Opening Statements

On the kind of warm, sunny May day Denise would have loved, Joan and Harry Redlick, accompanied by their son, Mike, and their daughter-in-law, Lynn, who was five months pregnant, made their way to the eighth floor of the Hall of Justice in San Mateo County to attend the first day of Craig Anderson's trial for the murder and kidnapping of their daughter.

By the time Bailiff Peter Kutch unlocked the double mahogony doors to courtroom 8D at 9:25 a.m. on Tuesday, May 13th, the hallway was filled with reporters and spectators waiting to secure premium seats for the opening statements in People vs. Anderson. After more than six months of speculation in the media over what had happened to Denise Redlick, there was a feeling in the air that, finally, the truth might be forthcoming.

Joan, in a dark printed dress that emphasized how thin and pallid she had become, and Harry took up places that first morning on a slick, oak bench just outside the courtroom, waiting to be called as witnesses.

"I just wish this were over with," Joan whispered to Harry as he protectively draped his arm around her shoulders while watching their friends and relatives file through the doors. Mike and Lynn secured seats in the front row of the gallery, behind the prosecutor's table, and looked down the row to the left to find that Shirley and Ron Anderson had claimed seats at the opposite end. Cohn, who had felt badly that his client's family had grown to feel as if they had been ostracized from the community over their oldest son's arrest, stood nearby, chatting with Mr. and Mrs. Anderson and trying to ease the obvious tension.

"Relax," he whispered. "Everything will be fine."

At precisely 9:30 a.m., the court became still as two deputy sheriffs escorted prisoner Anderson, who was waiting in a holding cell in a hallway behind the courtroom, to his seat to the left of Nathan Cohn. Before he sat down, one deputy unlocked and removed the chain shackling the defendant's hands to his waist so that he would be free to jot notes on the yellow legal pad placed in front of him. In his stylish blue-grey suit, he looked as he did the night of his first blind date with Denise. Only his pale complexion was a reminder that he no longer had the freedom to jog along the streets of San Carlos as he once had.

Kutch stepped into the hallway to summon the jurors and ask them to take their seats. Finally, Judge Capaccioli appeared in the doorway behind his platform and stepped up to his black leather chair.

"All rise, court is now in session," Kutch bellowed as he noticed that some spectators were still scrambling for seats.

Judge Capaccioli announced, "I'm going to now instruct the clerk to read the information."

The clerk began, "In the Superior Court of the State of California in and for the County of San Mateo. People of the State of California, Plaintiff, versus Craig Alan Anderson, Defendant, C-15906. Information.

"The District Attorney of the County of San Mateo hereby accuses Craig Alan Anderson of the crime of felony, to wit:

"Count one, violation of section 187, Penal Code, California, that the said Defendant on or about November 11, 1985, at and in the County of San Mateo, State of California, did willfully, unlawfully, and feloniously, and with malice aforethought, murder Denise Redlick, a human being.

"Special allegation, Penal Code Section 190.2 (a) (17).

"It is further alleged that the murder of Denise Redlick was committed by the Defendant Craig Alan Anderson, while the Defendant was engaged in the commission of and attempted commission of an immediate flight after having committed and attempted to commit the crime of kidnapping, in violation of Penal Code Section 207 within the meaning of the Penal Code Section 190.2 (a) (17).

"Count two, violation of section 207, Penal Code, California, that the said Defendant on or about November 11, 1985, at and in the County of San Mateo, State of California, did willfully, unlawfully, and feloniously, forcibly steal, take and arrest Denise Redlick in the County of San Mateo, State of California, and did take the said Denise Redlick into another county and another part of the said San Mateo County.

"Dated March 17, 1986.

"James P. Fox, District Attorney, by Steven M. Wagstaffe for Carol W. Holm, Deputy."

While he read the charges, Craig Anderson kept his eyes fixed on the floor and did not look up.

"The Defendant has entered a plea of not guilty to the charges and entered a denial to the special allegation."

The first matter before the jury was Capaccioli's reading of preliminary instructions of law to give the jurors a foundation for examining the evidence that would be presented to them over the next three weeks. Many of the instructions dealt with the behavior of the jurors, themselves. For example, one instruction routinely given to jurors in felony criminal cases is an order that they not make an independent investigation of the facts of the case or the laws surrounding them. "This means, for example, that you must not, on your own, visit the scene, conduct experiments or consult reference works or persons for additional information," the judge said.

While the vision of a juror sneaking out to the scene of the crime in the dead of the night, notebook and camera in hand, might made dramatic fodder for a made-for-television movie, it is against the law. And the instruction, when given in San Mateo County, had a special significance. Just five years before Anderson's trial, a juror in a high-profile capital murder case, transferred to San Mateo County from Sacramento on a change of venue, in which the defendant was charged with the execution-style slaying of two California Highway Patrol officers, traveled to the scene of the slaying and reported back to his fellow jurors

220

during a week of difficult and apparently deadlocked deliberations. The jury's verdict, which resulted in the judge's pronouncement of the death sentence, was eventually overturned by the
state Supreme Court because of the juror's misguided sleuthing.

Of particular importance in Anderson's case were instructions concerning circumstantial and direct evidence. Capaccioli
explained, as jurors already began taking diligent notes on little
pads that were given to them by the bailiff, that both types of
evidence are acceptable in proving or disproving the charges.
"Neither is entitled to any greater weight than the other." In addition, he told the jury "that if circumstantial evidence has two reasonable interpretations, it is the jury's duty to adopt the interpretation which points to the defendant's innocence and reject that
which points to his guilt."

After thirty minutes of instruction the jury was finally ready
to hear the opening statements.

Although jurors are instructed that nothing the attorneys say
can be considered evidence, Carl Holm knew that the opening
statement would lay a critical foundation for his circumstantial
case. The jury, both he and Wagstaffe felt, must learn enough
about Denise Redlick to care about her and understand how it
could not be believed that she would simply disappear, unless she
were a victim of foul play.

Holm walked to the podium, faced the jury and solemnly
began outlining his case against defendant Craig Anderson.

"In this trial, you are going to come to meet and get to know,
but never see, a wonderful young woman by the name of Denise
Redlick," Holm softly began, his voice slowly building to a cre-
scendo. "You're going to learn a great deal about Denise from her
friends, from her acquaintances, from her family. You are going
to learn about her habits. You are going to learn about her
desires, her dreams. You're going to learn about her activities during the last year. You're going to learn about certain things that
are going to surprise you and shock you."

"She will be described by all her friends, her relatives, everyone who came in contact with her as a wonderful human being, a
loving, dependable, sincere, unique person," Holm declared. "She
was interested in the welfare of other people. She was a happy

221

person, looking forward to her life. She had various events planned in her life that she was going to participate in which she never got the chance to do.

"The evidence will show," the prosecutor went on, "that Denise did not just get up and vanish into thin air. She had plans the day she disappeared. She had plans for trips. Those plans were interrupted and eliminated and canceled by that man right there, the defendant who sits before you in judgment in this case."

As Holm abruptly turned to his right and thrust his index finger toward Craig, the defendant continued to stare straight ahead. There was no reaction to Holm's accusation.

Holm described Denise and Craig's whirlwind courtship and engagement, the break-up that occurred after he struck her, how upset she had been by his attempts to reconcile, and how, on November 9th, exactly one week before the date of the cancelled wedding, Denise ended her relationship with the defendant, once and for all. He described Craig's sudden appearance at the hair salon and how, after talking for four hours, Denise reportedly told him, "I don't love you anymore."

"She was upset about the contact by the defendant that day but she was happy and excited that she thought she had put this relationship behind her," Holm told the jurors, enraptured by the story they were hearing.

"Denise thought that she had put behind her what was causing her the mental stress. But she was mistaken, gravely mistaken. For on November 11th, Veteran's Day, Monday, a holiday, the defendant kidnapped her, the evidence will show, and murdered her," Holm said, pausing to let his accusation linger. "For, if he couldn't have her, no one else could either."

The deputy district attorney went on to outline key points of evidence that Denise had not just run away—that she left behind all her personal possessions and that she never again used her credit cards and bank accounts. Stepping toward the front of the courtroom, Holm used a pointer to show the jury, on a black and white aerial photograph of the Peninsula, the many areas that had been searched for evidence of Denise without finding any trace of her.

The prosecutor described Craig's statement that he had

worked on Veteran's Day and how witnesses would testify that the paint shop was actually closed. He told the jury how several witnesses would describe scratches they had seen on Craig's neck and hands. Then, Holm showed the jury a color photograph of the van that was rented by the defendant and noted that the rental company employees observed a stain on the floor that they believed to be blood.

"That van was eventually processed by laboratory personnel, scientists from the crime lab," Holm said, glossing over an area of evidence for which the admissibility had not yet been determined. "You'll hear more about that later."

Holm went on to describe how a witness, Frances Seedlock, would testify that Anderson had washed the van at her house on the late afternoon of November 11th after telling her he had run over a dog, killed it and buried it.

"Some of the witnesses' testimony, you may not understand how it fits into the picture until the conclusion of the case and when the arguments are made," Holm said. "So when a witness comes in and testifies just for a few minutes, listen carefully, because what they say may be extremely important in this case."

Holm concluded by promising the jury that the prosecution would prove beyond a reasonable doubt "and to a moral certainty that the defendant is guilty of murder of that wonderful human being, Denise Redlick, and that he is guilty of kidnapping, also."

During a fifteen-minute recess, Cohn and Holm conferred with the judge and agreed that although all other potential witnesses would be excluded, the parents of the presumed victim would be permitted to observe the trial. Joan and Harry now joined Michael and Lynn in the front row as Cohn stepped forward.

Nate Cohn, tall and imposing, spoke in a quiet, firm voice. "There is clearly no evidence that Denise Redlick is dead. We don't know where she is.

"He was in love with her," Cohn said of Craig. "And he is still in love with her."

Cohn's approach was to try to sow several seeds of doubt in the jurors' minds. He suggested that a "suspicious-looking man," a man who looked nothing like Anderson, was seen cruising through the lot on the Monday in question. Furthermore, absolutely no one saw the white Budget van, with the conspicuous rental agency logo on the side, in that same lot that afternoon.

The defense attorney described the argument that led to Denise and Craig's broken engagement. According to Cohn, both Denise and Craig had a lot to drink at the wedding and he became angry with her because she had danced with another man before dancing with Craig.

"She started hitting him on the arm and, finally, he was driving the car and he slapped her," Cohn declared.

"Craig was very much in love with her, or is very much in love with her, and proceeded to do everything he could to make it up to her," Cohn said. On Saturday, Nov. 9, Craig and Denise agreed to get together the following week and Denise promised Craig she would call him.

Cohn advised the jury that the evidence would show that Craig rented the van to remove debris resulting from remodeling the bathroom in his house and that, at the rental agency, he had requested a pickup truck but none were available so, at the suggestion of the rental agent, he registered for the van.

The next day was Veteran's Day. "The evidence will show that when the police department searched the shop, they found the receipts for the three sales on that date," Cohn said.

Cohn said that Craig went to the Seedlocks' house that afternoon to talk to Kevin Seedlock about a painting job. When Kevin wasn't there, Craig decided to wait for him. Then, being "a meticulous person," he decided to wash out the van before returning it. Craig told Mrs. Seedlock, according to Cohn, that a "neighborhood dog had done his business on his lawn."

After learning of Denise's disappearance, Craig went to the Redlick house one night where Denise's parents discussed what he had done to cause the breakup between him and Denise, Cohn stated. "They kept after him for about two hours and he just couldn't take it. He was worried about Denise. He didn't like all this guilt being thrown at him as to why they broke up and he left."

Cohn spent several minutes explaining to the jury how Kevin Seedlock originally told police that Craig had said he left a shovel at the house and how the police had actually confiscated a shovel as evidence. "Later on it was proven, the police found that shovel belonged to the Seedlocks," Cohn said. "So there's no way in the world, the evidence will show, that Craig would have ever said get rid of the shovel."

Cohn also discussed the circumstances of Denise's disappearance, pointing out that the office building is in a busy location and that no one saw the white Budget van in the vicinity at that time. "The evidence will show that there's no way that Craig knew she was going to her cousin's or was sticking around there for an hour and a half waiting for her, no way.

"Now, the evidence will show that Craig did not see her that day. And, the evidence will show that he didn't kill her, couldn't kill her. There's no evidence that she's dead.

"And, with that in mind, I'll leave it to you. And, thank you very much."

CHAPTER TWENTY-THREE

The Prosecution's Case Begins

The opening statements had taken nearly two hours. After a short recess, prosecutor Holm had the clerk mark the photograph of Denise Redlick—the same one printed on thousands of posters which had been circulated throughout California towns—as exhibit No. 1. Then he called his first witness, Charles Nan, to the stand.

The dark-haired Nan, visibly upset, quietly rose as the clerk addressed him, "State your name, please?"

"Charles Gerard Nan," he supplied.

The clerk continued, "Spell your middle and last name, please."

Nan spelled his name slowly and deliberately.

"Thank you. Would you be seated in the witness stand?" the clerk replied.

Nan took a seat.

Judge Capaccioli motioned to the witness, "Mr. Nan, would you move that microphone close to you and the chair as close to the mike as you can?"

Nan pulled the microphone closer to him and nudged his chair closer.

"Fine, it should pick up your voice. Go on."

Carl Holm adjusted his wire-rimmed glasses and began. "Good morning, Mr. Nan."

"Good morning, sir," Nan replied.

"Where do you work?"

"I'm employed at the Bank of America."

"How long have you worked for the Bank of America?"

Nan looked away as if thinking, "Since October, 1983."

"And, at some point in 1985, did you work at the San Francisco Bank of America?" Holm asked.

Quietly, Nan replied, "Yes, sir, I did."

In a few questions, Holm elicited the personal information he needed for the record and then proceeded with Nan's relationship with Denise Redlick.

"And can you tell us when you first met Denise Redlick?"

"I met Ms. Redlick in January." Nan paused, then realized that the answer was not what the prosecutor had asked. "Pardon me, in 1984." Nan, unhesitating, went on to describe Denise as Holm asked, "Could you characterize for us what type of person Denise Redlick was?"

"She was a vivacious, fun-loving type girl who was very high on life, very close to her family, who really cared about people, and she just really enjoyed life and enjoyed what she was doing."

"Was she personable to the customers that came to engage in transactions at the Bank of America?" Holm asked.

"Yes, sir. Very much, sir."

Holm began building a picture of Denise's character.

"Was she dependable?"

"Yes," Nan shook his head.

"Was she prompt in her times when she would come to work and engage in the various requirements she had at the Bank of America?"

"Yes."

"Did you learn—at some point during 1985—that she had plans to marry?"

"Yes, sir."

"Do you recall when that was?"

Nan's brow wrinkled, "Approximately late January, early February, 1985. I don't recall the exact date."

"And did you learn to whom she was going to marry?"

"Yes, sir."

"Who was that?"

"Mr. Craig Anderson."

Holm continued calmly questioning his witness, almost as if they were talking quietly over a cup of coffee.

"And what was her demeanor then when you learned that she was going to marry?"

Nan brightened. "Very joyous, very excited, bubbling."

Then Holm's voice hardened.

"Did you notice if her demeanor changed in relationship to this engagement with Craig Anderson during the year of 1985?"

Nan's smile faded.

"Yes, sir."

"Could you describe how it changed?"

Nan leaned forward, obviously confused. "Are you speaking of after the engagement was called off?" he asked.

"Let me rephrase the question," Holm said slowly. He thought a moment and continued, "At some point, did you learn anything about the engagement being called off?"

"Yes, sir."

"Would you tell us when that was?"

"September 30th, 1985."

"Did she speak to you about it?"

Nan seemed perplexed, but Holm pressed on, "Did you learn through her?"

"She came into work one morning, and she had announced it to the few of us who had already arrived, and then I spoke to her about it a few days later."

Holm took a deep breath, "Okay, what was her demeanor at that point when she announced the ending of the engagement?"

Nan responded quickly, "She was very relieved that it . . ."

Quickly, Cohn stepped in, "Objection, your Honor. That calls for an opinion and conclusion. He has no qualifications to say that she was relieved."

Capaccioli nodded, "Sustain the objection in the form it was stated . . . asked."

Holm shook his head. "Beg your pardon?"

Slowly, the judge repeated, "I'm going to sustain the objection in the form it was asked."

Holm stroked his beard for a moment and then proceeded.

"Did Denise express her attitude toward breaking up this engagement?"

"You mean directly to me?" Nan questioned.

"Yes," Holm replied firmly.

"No, I can't say that she actually directly said, but it was very visible that she was relieved."

Holm turned to a different subject.

"Between the end of September, 1985, and November—middle of November—did you from time to time receive phone calls from a person identifying themselves as Craig Anderson?"

"Yes, sir," Nan replied and could not help himself scowling.

"And for whom were those phone calls?" Holm asked quickly.

"Miss Redlick."

"And did you tell Denise Redlick that the calls were for her?" Holm looked toward the jury.

"Yes, sir," Nan replied.

"Did you tell her who was calling her?"

"I don't exactly recall, sir."

"Did you notice how she reacted to those calls in October of 1985—the ones that you answered from Craig Anderson?"

"Yes, sir," Nan said responsively.

"Could you describe that for us?"

Nan sighed, and then relied, "She was visibly shaken by these telephone calls, extremely upset, unable to go on with her normal duties and her job performance, very adversely affected."

When Holm continued and asked Nan about plans he and Denise had made for the evening of Monday, November 11th, Nan described how Denise had never returned his calls to decide on their meeting place, even though, previously, she had always been dependable when it came to such matters.

Then it was the defense's turn.

In cross-examination, Cohn made two points: Denise had been seeing a psychologist just before her disappearance, and Nan had told Marriscolo early in the investigation that Denise

229

was being harassed by another girl, who was an ex-girlfriend of Craig. Both points were efforts to show that Denise's life was in turmoil, and that, perhaps, she had a reason to quietly slip away.

Nan, however, corrected his statement, saying that he understood that the mystery woman was harassing Craig, not Denise.

After recessing for lunch, the next witness to be called was Lori Voreyer—the last person to see Denise before she vanished.

Lori, for six months, had been carrying a special burden on her shoulders. She had encouraged Denise to do what she herself would have done if she were in her cousin's shoes—tell Craig, once and for all, that their romantic relationship was finished. Lori also felt guilty for having had her back turned when Denise walked out of the travel agency and toward the parking lot on November 11th. Her testimony would force her to relive those painful memories.

"Good afternoon, Miss Voreyer," Holm said gently, "Would you tell us where you live?"

"I live in San Bruno," Lori replied in a soft, tense voice.

"And are you married?" Holm asked.

"Yes," she murmured.

"And are you related to Denise Redlick?"

"Yes."

"Could you tell us what your relationship is?"

"She was my cousin."

Holm picked Denise's photograph from the table. "And I'd like to show you People's Exhibit #1. Who is that?"

"Denise Redlick."

"How long have you known Denise?"

Her voice quivered. "All of her life."

After a few routine questions, Holm looked searchingly at Lori.

"Could you describe for us what kind of personality she had?"

"She was . . ." Lori cleared her throat, trying to control of her emotions, "It's kind of hard. She was a very loving and giving person, the kind of person that everybody likes. She always felt sorry for the underdog. Very happy-go-lucky. Just the type—like I say—the type of person that you would—anybody would—try to befriend, very pleasant."

"All right. Was she a dependable person?"

"Oh, yes," she said, brushing away a tear.

Lori Voreyer, as had Charles Nan, reinforced the verbal portrait being carefully drawn by Holm of Denise—a warm, loving, dependable young woman. "She was a person who was very high on life," Lori stressed, "very close to her family, who really cared about people. She just really enjoyed life and enjoyed what she was doing."

When Holm asked about Denise's demeanor on becoming engaged, Lori replied, "Well, I'd say, at first, she was very excited and seemed to be very happy, and, later on, she was getting to be very withdrawn and somewhat into a shell—almost like not herself—like as though someone was trying to put their influences on her as to what to wear, how to look, and to—kind of—be in the background."

"Was this like Denise—to be that way, in the background?" Holm asked.

"No, not at all," Lori said.

After the break-up, Denise slowly started becoming herself again, "building up more confidence about herself, going to exercise class, getting her hair done, getting her nails done, taking care of herself more," Lori claimed.

Holm asked how Denise seemed to feel about her relationship with Craig at that point.

"She felt almost like a sense of duty to take the phone calls from Craig, to listen to him. She didn't know how to make it final."

Cohn was on his feet, objecting to the witness' attempts to "read somebody else's mind." Capaccioli sustained the objection, although Lori had subtly made the point that Denise was finding it difficult to make a final break with Craig.

Lori was asked to testify about Denise's travel plans for November, recalling her conversation with Denise on Monday morning and her subsequent arrival at the travel agency at 12:40 p.m. Lori testified that she booked several hotels for Denise and Chris to stay in during their upcoming trip to New York and that

Denise was looking forward to the trip. She continued that Denise left the agency around 1:40 p.m., after saying she planned to stop at Mervyns department store to buy a few items of clothing for the trip.

Denise's airline tickets, she added, were never used, eliminating any question about whether she might have gone to New York by herself. Harry Redlick had returned the tickets to Lori and credit was issued sometime around the Christmas holiday.

Denise, Lori said, never called that evening, as promised, to obtain Lori's brother-in-law's phone number in New York.

"Since that date, have you ever seen Denise?" Holm asked.

"No."

"Have you ever had any telephone conversation with Denise since that date?"

"No."

"Have you ever had any other communication or contact with Denise from that date?"

One more time, Lori would answer Holm's question with a sharp, decisive, "No."

During Cohn's cross-examination, Lori showed—on a diagram of her office building and the surrounding area posted at the front of the courtroom—that Denise left the travel agency in broad daylight, when the weather was clear, in an area with plenty of business traffic.

Cohn also brought up the meeting that Craig and Denise had on Saturday, November 9th, pointing out that the couple had gone to a "secluded area" near Camp Sawyer Road to talk, indicating that Denise trusted him and had no reason to fear him.

In his redirect examination, Holm—seizing upon the opportunity opened by Cohn's questions—asked Lori what Denise said she and Craig talked about on November 9th.

"Mr. Cohn asked you about a conversation you had with Denise on the 11th, where you spoke about her seeing the Defendant for a few hours on Saturday the 9th?"

"Yes," Lori said, sighing heavily.

"Did you . . . did she . . . Denise, tell you what she talked about in terms of that conversation on the 9th with the Defendant?"

"She briefly told me what was said."

"What did she tell you?"

Cohn raised his hand. "Excuse me, I'm going to have to object to that as hearsay."

Holm quickly interjected, "I'm entitled to get before the jury the entire contents of the conversation that the Defendant's attorney asked about on the 11th."

Judge Capaccioli announced, "There's no objection by you if it's hearsay. What is it being offered to prove?"

Holm argued, "Her state of mind regarding her relationship with the Defendant, but also to explain and not to leave a false impression about the portion that Mr. Cohn asked this witness about. It's akin to if a portion of a writing were introduced, the whole writing may be introduced to give context."

Cohn objected, "I didn't ask what the conversation between my client and Miss Redlick was. I asked if there was a conversation. Now he wants to go have this lady tell the jury what someone else told her they conversed about with someone else."

Holm waved a hand, "No. He asked her about the fact that she met and spoke for five hours, and how they went there, and where they went, and things like that."

Judge Capaccioli again questioned, "What's it being offered to prove?"

Holm said, "Her state of mind."

Capaccioli questioned, "How is that relevant?"

"In terms of her relationship with the Defendant bearing on the charges, the 207 charge, lack of consent," Holm shook his head decisively.

"All right. It's overruled," Capaccioli firmly said.

Holm looked back at Lori, "You may describe for us the . . . what Ms. Redlick told you happened or how she described a conversation between herself and the Defendant.

"How she described it?" Lori questioned.

"Well, what she said, let's put it that way."

"She said that basically that he wanted—he expressed that he wanted—to give the relationship another try, and that it was very difficult for her, but she finally told him that it was all over, and she did not feel the same way about him."

"Okay, Did she say anything else about what went on?"

"Yes, she also said that he told her that if he ever found out that she got back with Mark, that she'd be sorry. She was very scared about that."

Cohn jumped up, "Objection, your honor. That's way out of line."

Holm countered, "It goes to her state of mind, as I mentioned before."

Capaccioli shook his head negatively, "I'm going to sustain the objection and admonish the jury to treat it as though they never heard it."

But they had. Holm had gotten across his first inference that Craig Anderson was a man who couldn't take no for an answer.

Holm tried a different tact, "What was her demeanor at that point when she was speaking to you?"

Lori moaned, "She had a very scary look on her face that scared me."

Two more witnesses testified that day how the police, on the morning of November 12th, became involved in the search for Denise—San Bruno Police Sergeant Robert Metcalfe, who found the Triumph while investigating the missing person report, and Burlingame Officer James Potter, who took charge of the Triumph as it was towed from the parking lot at 1633 Old Bayshore.

The jurors, although they wouldn't yet know the significance, learned from the testimony of both officers that the driver's door of the sports car—parked in approximately the fourth or fifth space at the east entrance to the office building—was unlocked. Later, as Denise's friends and family testified, they found out about Denise's seemingly obsessive habit of locking car doors.

Cohn, in cross examination of Officer Potter, began his attempt to show that investigators had failed to adequately consider suspects other than Craig. But Cohn, unable to find an acceptable way to ask Potter about such reports, was frustrated in that effort.

"Did anyone tell you about any suspicious people being in the area?" Cohn asked Officer Potter.

Before the officer could answer, Holm objected on the grounds that it was hearsay. Capaccioli overruled his objection. He then objected that it was ambiguous.

"What's meant by a suspicious person?" Holm asked.

Capaccioli agreed and sustained the objection, telling Cohn to be more specific.

But, throughout cross-examination of Potter, Cohn kept trying to introduce the information that Potter had—on November 14th—talked to a delivery man who had recalled seeing a "suspicious man" in a black van at the Old Bayshore building around 1:15 p.m. on November 11th, the same time that Denise was leaving the building.

Over the next three days, Holm also called a variety of witnesses to testify about the relationship between Denise and Craig. Rossana Hanak, who worked with Denise at the Bank of America on El Camino, was one. She had known Denise as a fellow employee, helpful, considerate and caring. Rossana, like many others whose acquaintance with the young woman was peripheral, had been caught up in the futile hope Denise would be found, and, since she handled Denise's account at the bank, she had carefully watched it for any signs of activity—some indication that Denise was still alive. Holm queried this knowledge during his examination.

"I'd like to show you People's Exhibit 4 and ask you if you take a look at what's inside there, see if you recognize those documents?"

"They're the statements of Denise's accounts," Rossana said slowly.

Holm asked several questions concerning the accounts and then focused in, "Have you investigated the account to determine if any withdrawals had been made from that account?"

"Yes, I have," Rossana sighed.

"Have there been any withdrawals from that account since November 11th of 1985?"

"No."

For Denise's family, gathered in the courtroom, the simple facts in these and the next few witnesses' testimonies were final punctuation marks separating Denise from the life she had once led.

Although Rossana was an acquaintance and coworker who, like other near strangers, felt touched by Denise's mysterious disappearance, Chris Morganti, with whom Denise was to travel to New York, was a very good friend who had shared many close times with the missing girl. Unable to contain her emotions, her husky voice broke as she testified that Denise appeared happier after breaking up with Craig.

"She wasn't sad. She felt good that she had made that decision."

Holm watched the words' impression on the jury.

"Did you see her from time-to-time after October 1st of 1985?"

"Yes."

"How was her demeanor or outlook on life during October?"

Chris was steadfast, "that she wanted to get on with her life and go back to normal, seeing her friends more, going out and doing things with her girlfriends."

"All right, and that included you, I assume?"

"Yes."

"Did you make plans with Denise for taking a trip?"

"Yes, I did."

"Do you recall about when it was that you made those plans with Denise?"

"Around the middle of October."

"And where were you planning to go to?"

"Back east to New York."

"And how were the two of you going to get there?"

"We were going to fly."

"And did you obtain tickets for that purpose?"

"Yes."

"Do you recall about when it was?"

"That we got the tickets? The end of October."

"And I assume you had a ticket and Denise had a ticket; is that correct?"

"Yes."

"When was this trip suppose to begin?"

"November 14th."

"And when would you return from New York? Do you recall?"

"I'm not sure; it was like ten days later."

"Were you going to someplace besides New York?"

"We were going to fly into New York, stay a few days, and then travel down toward Washington, D.C."

"Would you describe for us Denise's feelings toward this . trip?"

"She was excited. She had everything planned. She was looking forward to it."

"Do you know if she had purchased any new clothing for that purpose?"

"Yes, she had purchased a few new things, and she had everything ready that she was going to take."

"Did you ever make that trip on November 14th?"

"No."

"Did you eventually get the money back for the tickets?"

"Yes, we did."

"Would you tell us why you didn't take that trip to New York?"

For a moment, Chris's voice broke, "Because Denise was missing since the 11th."

"Did you speak with Denise sometime the week of October . . . excuse me . . . November 9th, the week before the trip—on the phone or in person?"

"Yes."

"Did you make plans to get together at sometime on the weekend of Veteran's Day weekend?"

"Yes."

"What day were you going to get together"

"I talked to her on Saturday, and we were going to get together Sunday night, the 10th."

"What time—do you recall—did you speak with Denise on Saturday?"

"About 7:00 p.m."

"What was her demeanor or attitude then?"

"She was rushed—on her way out going to a party—so she was basically just rushed, and she said she'd talk to me on Sunday night."

"Okay. Did you see her Sunday night?"

"Yes, I did."

"Where?"

"At my apartment."

"This is in Millbrae?"

"Yes."

"And what was her demeanor then?"

"She was very excited."

"About what?"

"She was excited about the trip. She was excited. She had just gone to dinner with her family. She was just real up."

"Did she describe anything that happened to her regarding the Defendant, Craig Anderson?"

Chris paused and bit her lip, "Yes, she did."

"Did she describe to you her intentions regarding her relationship with the Defendant?"

"Yes."

"Could you tell us what it was?"

"She said that they were not going to stay in contact. They were going to stay apart from each other, and she felt good about it that she had cut it off, and that's how it was going to stay."

"Did you make plans then on Sunday night for purposes of contacting each other later that week before the trip on the 14th?"

"Yes."

"What did you decide?"

"She was going to call me or try and get in touch with me Monday afternoon. If not, she said she'd talk to me Monday night when she got home."

"Did she describe to you her plans on Monday, what she was going to do on Monday?"

"Yes."

"What did she say on Sunday she was going to do on Monday?"

"She told me she was going to meet Lori, and I was going to

meet her also, but she didn't know for sure what time she was going to go. If she didn't call me in the morning, she was just going to go. She had an errand to run, pick some things up at Mervyns, and watch a football game that evening. So if she didn't talk to me that afternoon, she'd talk to me that evening."

"Did she describe where she was going to go to watch that football game on Monday?"

"No, she said she was going with some friends."

"Did you ever speak with her on Monday, the 11th of November?"

"No."

"Did that surprise you?"

Cohn raised his hand, "Objection, your Honor, whether it surprised her is not relevant."

The judge looked up, "Sustained."

Holm stroked his beard a moment and went on, "Let me ask you this, was Denise reliable about her statements of intention to contact you?"

"Yes."

"After that Sunday, November 10th, did you ever see Denise Redlick again?"

"No."

"Have you ever seen her since then?"

"No."

"Have you ever spoken with her since then?"

"No."

"Have you ever had any type of communication either written or oral from her?"

"No."

"Do you have any idea where she is?"

"No."

On further redirect, Holm asked Chris, "Did you ever drive with Denise either in her car or her parents' car and she was the driver?"

"Yes."

"And did she have any particular habit or custom about the manner in which she locked the car door?"

Cohn stood up, "Objection, no foundation."

Judge Capaccioli agreed, "Sustained. You have to lay a foundation."

Holm took a deep breath, "How often would you say you've gone with her in a car?"

"How often?" Chris looked perplexed.

"Uh huh."

She shrugged, "Maybe once a week."

"And would she be driving these times?"

She nodded, "Most of the time."

Holm moved in, "Would this be through the five years that you've known her?"

"Uh huh, yes."

"And would there be times when the two of you would get out of the car and go someplace after you got out of the car?"

"Yes."

"And could you describe for us her habit in terms of whether she locked the door when she left the car or not?"

"She always locked the door."

Cohn shook his head, "Objection, your honor. Ask it be stricken. She can't testify she always locked the door. She was with her once a week."

Capaccioli said, "It was overbroad. Sustained. You can rephrase it."

Holm flushed, "What was her habit and custom on those times you were with her for five years once a week in terms of whether she locked the door or not?"

"When I was with her, we were in the car, getting out of the car to go," Chris's voice broke for a moment, "She always locked the door."

"Was there any particular time you commented about that to her?"

"Yes, there was."

Again Cohn interrupted, "Objection, Your Honor, calling for hearsay."

The judge disagreed, "She's testifying to what she said."

Cohn was staunch, "So, what's the difference. It's still hearsay if it's offered to . . ."

Holm said impatiently, "It's not intended to prove anything other than what she said." Capaccioli asked, "How is it relevant?"

Holm frowned, "It's relevant as to a comment on Denise Redlick's actions in locking or unlocking the door. It was something that . . . a unique situation."

Capaccioli questioned, "You mean this is for the purpose of only determining, describing the utterance, and then measuring the response of Denise to that utterance?"

Holm shook his head, "Yes."

Capaccioli nodded, "I'll allow it and strike it if I'm not satisfied that that's what it is for."

Holm asked, "Was there an occasion when you commented to Denise about her locking the door?"

"Yes," Chris answered quickly.

"Where was that?"

"In the driveway of my parents' home."

"And what city was that in?"

"Pacifica."

"And what . . . could you describe what happened?"

"We were in my car, and I was driving, and we went there to drop something off, and I pulled into the driveway, and we both got out, and she locked the door, and I teased her that we were running in for just a second to drop something off."

Cohn interrupted, "I would object to what this lady said, Your Honor."

The judge's voice was impatient, "Grounds?"

"On hearsay. Self-serving."

Capaccioli announced, "Overruled."

Holm could not suppress a smile, "Thank you." Turning to Christine, he continued, "Go ahead."

Capaccioli looked toward Cohn, "And the fact that it is self-serving is not an objection. You know it and I know it."

Cohn nodded, "I understand."

Holm turned again to Chris, "You can continue."

"So we got out of the car in the driveway of my parents' home, and she locked the door, and I teased her, and she just laughed and laughed, and still locked the door, something that she always does."

Cohn again intervened, "Objection, ask that that be stricken."

Capaccioli said, "Grounds?"

Cohn answered, "Hearsay."

Capaccioli glanced at Holm, "Do you want to respond?" Then he went on to answer his own question, "If it's not hearsay, what is it relevant to prove, state of mind or habit?"

Holm nodded, "Correct."

"Overruled."

Holm continued, "So you said that she what—after you teased her?"

"After I teased her, she laughed and still locked the door, and we went into my parents' house. When we came out, I had to unlock the door for her to get in."

On cross-examination, Cohn attacked Christine's testimony about the lock. Figuring that Denise drove her car about half of the times that the two women went out together means they really only were in the car, with Denise at the wheel, about twenty-five times a year, Cohn assumed.

"You don't know—you don't have any personal knowledge of what she did when you weren't in the car with her, do you?"

"No," Chris conceded.

During the testimony of Michele McKindley, many of Denise's friends and relatives in the audience, including Joan Redlick and Carolyn Kristovich, burst into tears.

"Everyone needs a best friend like Denise," said Michele, who spoke clearly and calmly, despite the obvious pain of losing her closest friend, "She loved life, loved to laugh and smile, and thought of everyone else first and herself second."

"Was she dependable?" Holm asked.

"Oh, yes, you could trust her with everything." With Denise, she remarked, she shared her innermost secrets. But Denise's "true best friend," Michele said slowly, was her mother. She looked at Joan, who was sobbing openly. "They had a relationship that every mother and daughter dream of. There was honesty and trust, without question or doubt."

With her dad, Michele recalled, Denise was also unusually close. She traveled with him and even took wind-surfing lessons with him. Michele twisted a strand of her dark hair and looked away for a moment. Later, after she pointed her finger at Craig to identify the defendant—who continued looking down at an invisible spot on the floor—she spoke about two phone conversations that she had with Craig after the couple had broken up.

Holm adjusted his glasses and asked in a firm tone, "Did you ever receive a phone call from the Defendant regarding that class reunion?"

Michele shook her head knowingly, "Yes, I did on that Monday, the next Monday, the 28th."

Holm moved in even more forcefully, "And what did the Defendant ask you, if anything?"

"Michele paused and then went on, "Craig wanted to know if Denise had a good time, and if she had danced with any boys at the dance, and made comments about their relationship, and what was going on, and what was happening, and wanted to explain things to me. And, at that point, Craig told me that he thought Denise was a selfish, spoiled little bitch—is what he said —and that things were not working out the way he wanted them to."

After finishing his questions on that subject, Holm turned to a second telephone conversation.

"Did you have a phone conversation with the Defendant where he asked you about other male friends of Denise Redlick?"

"He called me the Thursday after Denise was missing, after he had left the Redlick house."

During that conversation, Craig—who had just watched the KTVU News update on the search for Denise—wanted to know "who the two guys passing out fliers were on television." One was Mark Gooch and the other was a friend of Mark's, she stated.

Michele also noted that Mark Gooch, Art Thomas and Barry Rush—all of whom had dated Denise in the years before Craig came into the picture—helped distribute flyers to spread the word about Denise's disappearance.

"To your knowledge," Holm said, facing the jurors to make sure they paid close attention, "did the Defendant ever try to find, or participate in trying to find, Denise?"

"Absolutely not," Michele firmly replied.

Did Craig ever express any concern about Denise's whereabouts? Not a word, Michele declared. Did he appear to be upset about her disappearance? No, she insisted.

"Okay. When was the last time you had any contact with Denise?"

"November 7th."

"And that was by telephone?"

"Uh huh."

"Have you heard from Denise Redlick ever since that date?"

"No," she sighed heavily, "I haven't."

"Have you ever seen her since that date?" Holm asked.

"No, I haven't."

"Have you received any communications from Denise anywhere that might give you some clue as to where she is?"

"No. No, I haven't."

Cohn had apparently heard a different version of the first conversation between Craig and Michele.

"Did you tell Craig at that time that Denise had a good time, but she would have had a better time if she and Craig had been there together?"

"No. I told Craig she had a better time without him being there."

"Didn't you tell him she would have had a better time if she hadn't broken the engagement?"

"No," she said vehemently, steadfast in her remembrance of the Denise she had known.

■ CHAPTER TWENTY-FOUR ■

The Prosecution's Case Intensifies

The prosecution's most compelling evidence was the Budget Rent-A-Car van and what the San Mateo County criminologists had uncovered inside the vehicle. Although Holm and Wagstaffe didn't know yet if they would be permitted to tell the jury about the blood type and that the crime lab found that it matched that of Denise Redlick, they began bombarding the jury with testimony that would, at the very least, give the impression that something clandestine had occurred in a van rented by Craig Alan Anderson on the day that Denise Redlick vanished.

Charles Cantrell, the Budget agency employee, testified that he and another Budget worker, José Rodriguez, cleaned out the van rented by Craig Anderson. Cantrell was able to name the specific van—although there are about fifty in the Bay Area Budget agency fleet—because it had an unusual characteristic.

"Is there anything unique about that particular van that makes it stand out from all the other vans in that area?"

"The steering wheel."

"What about the steering wheel?"

"The steering wheel emblem—or inside the steering wheel—is, I guess, you could say deformed. It's totally opposite from the steering column itself."

"And do you know which particular van that picture represents?"

"Well, like I said, I was familiar with the van because of the steering wheel. That's how I knew that van, because when you got into it, you could just . . . the feel of it, you knew which one it was."

"Now, the portion in the middle of the round steering wheel, the portion that goes kind of up from the left, up to the left parallel to the floor, and up to the right, is that different than any of the other vans in our location?"

"Yes, it is."

"And in what way is it different?"

"Well, in some vans, you know, even in cars, okay, you'll have steering wheels that will be a little cocked, you know, but this one looked like it was made that way, you know, that's how easy it is to describe. It felt like it was made this way."

"Okay, so that particular steering wheel is different from all the other steering wheels from all the vans in your location?"

"Right," Cantrell nodded.

"Do you know what particular van number that particular van with that different steering wheel belongs to?"

Cantrell looked perplexed, "Excuse me?"

"Let me rephrase it," Holm began again, "That van in People's Exhibit, I think 16, with the—let's term it—funny steering wheel. Do you know which numbered vehicle it belongs to?"

"9110."

"Okay, and is that represented by People's Exhibit 9, that other photograph?"

"Right. Right," Cantrell firmly insisted.

"Okay. Now, I'd like to direct your attention to Tuesday, November 12th, 1985 in the morning. Did you have occasion to go inside 23-9110, the van shown by those photographs and examine the interior?"

"Yes, I did."

"And did you notice anything unusual about the floor in the back of the interior of that van?"

"The stain in the back of the van," Cantrell said excitedly.

"What was unusual about the stain in the back?"

"The color, just—you know—it just dawned on me as a different kind of stain."

"What did it look like to you?"

"Blood," he announced.

"All right, and did you do anything with that stain?"

"Tried to clean it."

"And were you successful in cleaning it at that point?"

"No."

"Would you describe for us approximately how big that stain was when you saw it?"

"In diameter, like this," he gestured, "like a puddle, a good size puddle."

Holm pounced, "Indicating about eighteen inches in circumference?"

"Right, eighteen-twenty inches, yeah."

"And do you recall about what time it was that you noticed that particular stain in the bottom of the back of that van?"

"About around 9:30 in the morning."

"And did you . . . in what way did you try to clean that particular stain?"

"With a strong degreaser, ammonia type thing that will take any marks up—you know."

"Prior to that, before that date, were there other occasions that you would have examined that particular van's interior and noticed something like that before?"

"All I can say is . . . as far as that is—you know—any time we do get a van in, and something needs to be cleaned or done to it, it's done—you know."

"Okay. Had you driven, or been in that van, before November 12th, 1985?"

"Yes."

"Prior to November 12th, 1985, had you ever seen that stain in the back of that van before?"

"No, I haven't."

Holm looked at the jury, "Thank you, I have no other questions."

Capaccioli looked at Cohn, "You may cross."

Cohn drew out that no one bothered to even note the stain in the vehicle inspection report. However, Cantrell said that inspection reports of vans are less stringent than in cars, since more wear and tear is expected. Whereas a floor stain in a car might be written up, a van's might not be.

Following Cantrell, the next witness, quiet, forceful Kathleen Wade, firmly connected Craig Anderson to the white van with the upside-down logo and an interior speckled by curious red-brown stains.

"I'd like to direct your attention to November 10th, 1985. Did you have occasion to rent a van to a person you learned to be Craig Anderson?"

"Yes," Kathleen Wade answered, looking Holm straight in the eyes.

"Do you see that individual in the courtroom today?"

Her eyes swept the courtroom and fastened on Craig, "Yes, I do."

"Would you describe where he's seated or standing, and what he's wearing today?"

"He's seated at the table to my right, in a blue suit and tie."

Holm raised his hand, "May the record reflect identification?"

Judge Capaccioli murmured, "Yes, it may so reflect."

Holm went on, "Do you recall—let me ask you this—are certain documents prepared in order to reflect a rental transaction?"

"Yes," Kathleen nodded.

"I show you Exhibit 13, if I may." Holm placed the document in front of Wade. "Your Honor, People's Exhibit 13 is a rental agreement which appears to be in the name of Craig Anderson, rental agreement number 011885." He addressed Wade, "Would you take a look at that copy? Do you recognize it?"

Wade's voice gathered momentum, "Yes, I do. It's my writing."

"Would you tell us what happens when someone comes in to rent a particular vehicle from your store?"

"We ask for identification, driver's license, and some type of security on the vehicle."

"When you say security on the vehicle, what are you referring to?"

"We obtain a credit card or some type of deposit from the individual."

"And when you ask for a driver's license, what do you do with the driver's license?"

"We record all the information off the driver's license—name, date of birth, driver's license number, physical description—onto our rental agreement."

"Do you compare the photograph on the driver's license to the person before you?"

"Yes."

Holm addressed the bench, "Mr. Cohn has seen and I have asked to be marked a certified copy of a Department of Motor Vehicle driver's license as Exhibit 14 in the name Craig Alan Anderson."

Turning his attention again to Wade, "Ms. Wade, I'm going to show you People's 14, this copy of a driver's license. Does it show a photograph of a person on it?"

"Yes, it does," she nodded.

"Does that copy of a driver's license look familiar to you?"

"Yes."

"Is that a photograph of the Defendant?"

"I would say so, yes."

As Wade continued her testimony, Holm made sure to again tie the Ford van #23-9110 to Craig Anderson.

"Now, I'd like you to take a look at People's Exhibit 9. Do you recognize a photograph of that particular van?"

"Yes."

"Is that the van you just mentioned, 23-9110?"

"Yes."

"What other kind of information would you want from the customer on November 10th besides the data that you already mentioned?"

"The period of time they intended to keep the vehicle, or if they intended for any other individual to be driving the vehicle and whether or not they wish to have any collision coverage, medical coverage, cargo coverage, the name of the employer, business phone number."

"Did the defendant indicate how long he wanted the truck for . . . or van, rather?"

"The latest "Expected To Return Time" would have been November 12th."

"By the way, November 11th, what time did you close? That would have been Monday."

"6:00 p.m."

"You mentioned as for any employer and telephone number, what was the purpose of that?"

"Just to have the means of contacting the customer."

"Would you ask the customer—here Mr. Anderson—whether it was to be used for personal business or work business?"

"Yes."

"And what was his answer?"

"Personal business."

Wade also brought to court contracts from November 3rd to December 6th for the rentals of the same van that had been rented by the defendant. No records could be found, she said, for rental of the van after December 6th, when the United States Postal Service leased the vehicle.

On cross-examination, Cohn tried to get Wade to concede that when Craig dropped in the office on Sunday, she told him no pick-up trucks were available. She said that was not true.

"Do you remember him saying that he was fixing his bathroom, and he had debris and garbage from his backyard he wanted to take to the dump?"

"No. I don't," Wade replied.

"You have an absolute conviction he didn't tell you that?"

"That's correct."

Holm, in redirect, hammered away at the point that a pick-up truck—which would have been the logical choice for hauling yard debris to the dumps—was available on November 10th and was not being reserved by another customer, either that day or the next, but the defendant did not choose to rent it.

"You don't recall him asking you for the pick-up and you

telling him he couldn't have that?" Cohn tried again in his recross examination.

"I don't recall that, no." Wade again insisted.

While continually adding details to its picture of Denise's wholesome character throughout the first and second weeks of the trial, the prosecution also brought before the jury twenty-eight witnesses who had a single purpose—to testify that they had rented Budget Rent-A-Car van No. 23-9110. They singularly agreed that they had rented the van at sometime during the month or so after Denise's disappearance, and that neither they nor any of their passengers had bled in the rental vehicle. Those called included a caterer, delivery workers for an automobile sales magazine, a painter, a real estate appraiser, a woman who hauled her furniture when she moved, along with three friends who helped her, and eleven United States Postal Service employees who, during December, had been inside the van during the time it was rented to help with the delivery of Christmas mail. The Postal Service's own fleet records—since the Budget Agency had been unable to find any records for that period—were used to identify each of their drivers.

All testified that they had not cut themselves, nor bled while in the vehicle.

In his obsessive thoroughness, Holm would include, among all the witnesses connected with the van, Julius Fukatsch, who confirmed that his brother-in-law used his name to drive the van and deliver the automobile magazines, and, through a Chinese interpreter, Chun Ye, who would say that he did not enter the van while working for a painter who had testified he had rented the van.

Cohn did succeed in getting one Postal Service employee to say that she might have had a "minor paper cut" while on the job, but "nothing really to cause any blood."

With other witnesses, such as the caterer, Cohn would attempt to show that materials carried in the cargo area might have spilled, suggesting that they might have caused a stain. That, however, would be meaningful to the jury only if Cohn could convince the jury that the stains could have been caused by anything other than blood.

The long litany of rental van customers seemed to some unnecessary and tedious. But, for Holm, the precariousness of proving his case with neither body nor witness made thoroughness imperative.

With their evidence on the van in place, Holm and Marriscolo knew that the next crucial point depended heavily upon the testimony of Frances Kramer Seedlock.

It was Thursday when they called her to the stand.

Frances Seedlock sat ramrod straight and stared directly ahead—avoiding eye contact with the defendant—as she settled into the witness' chair.

Mrs. Seedlock had shown at the preliminary hearing in March that she was unshakable. She would demonstrate her strength—despite her frail appearance—again.

After setting the scene—the Seedlock Palo Alto home—for the jurors, Holm led the key witness through a long series of questions concerning Craig Anderson's surprising arrival on her doorstep at 4:05 p.m. ("I looked at the clock automatically.") on Monday, November 11th. He had parked his white rental van outside on the street, in front of the house.

Craig, she recalled, asked if her son, Kevin, was home. Mrs. Seedlock told him Kevin, a painter who worked for Craig, wouldn't be home until 5:30 or 6 p.m.

"What did he say then?"

"He said that he'd killed a dog and that he had buried it and could he borrow the hose to rinse his van down." She had pointed to the hose in the yard. Craig also asked for some rags. She gave him four or five torn up old towels and then she left him outside as she went back into the house.

Around twenty-five to thirty minutes later, she testified, she went back outside.

"I saw the Defendant in his bare feet, and his tennis shoes were on the sidewalk, and he was washing the van out," Mrs. Seedlock declared.

"In what way was he washing the van out?" the prosecutor probed further.

"He was hosing it, then he got down and he was scrubbing it." The sliding doors on the sidewalk side of the vehicle were open and Craig was inside, facing toward the rear doors. He was crouched down, on all fours, scrubbing the floor "very vigorously" with rags.

"Did you comment or say anything to him at that point?" Holm asked.

"I only said—when I went out and saw him in his bare feet—I said it was cold, and, I said—you know—I was surprised to see his tennis shoes off. They were sitting there and I said, 'Gee, Craig, it's cold out. You're going to catch cold.' "

"Did he respond to your statement?"

"No," Mrs. Seedlock declared.

"Was he very communicative that day?"

Again, she answered, "No." She asked him if he was moving, since that seemed a logical reason to rent a van. But, instead, he said he was remodeling his bathroom, had removed the tub, and taken it to be refinished.

Mrs. Seedlock then went into the house and, shortly after that, Craig came to the door and asked if he could wash up. When she said he could, he proceeded to wash himself in the kitchen sink with "very hot water" as she handed him paper towels. The witness pantomimed Craig's actions, lifting her hands and forearms with clenched fists pointed towards her face and then rubbing his hands together. When he was finished, he asked to use the bathroom. He came out with his shirt off, his hair close to his scalp, as if it had been washed. Craig asked to borrow a shirt and Mrs. Seedlock gave him one and he put it on. He had his own blue t-shirt rolled up in a ball in his fist.

Craig said he would wash the rags and send them back to her, but she told him not to bother. As he left, he asked what time it was and she told him it was 5:20 p.m.

"He said it wasn't as late as he thought it was," she recalled.

With that, Holm was through with direct examination. Cohn was visibly eager to begin his cross, since he saw numerous areas where he could rip the woman's testimony apart. He had grown tired of people telling him, "Why don't you just get Craig to go dig up the dog?" In fact, Cohn had told them, there was no dog to dig up; Mrs. Seedlock had her story all wrong.

Mrs. Seedlock, however, stuck to her guns.

"Now, you had some conversation with him (Craig) regarding why he wanted to wash up the van, is that what you are telling us?" Cohn inquired.

"I had no conversation," she insisted.

"You said he told you that he killed a dog and had to bury it?"

"Right."

"Now, do you recall him telling you that he just cleaned out his yard and he had been fixing his bathroom and had taken things to the garbage and wanted to clean out the van, because . . ."

The witness looked him straight in the eyes, "No, sir."

"Did he mention that a neighborhood dog had droppings on his property . . ."

"No, sir."

". . . and it was in the van?"

This time, the judge advised Mrs. Seedlock to wait until the defense attorney finished his question to respond. But again, she firmly replied, "No, sir," to the completed question.

"Did you notice a cut on his hand?" Cohn asked.

The witness said that, yes, Craig was holding a piece of paper on his hand when he came to the door and that she had, in fact, given him a bandage and gauze while he was washing. Later, Holm would clarify, in further direct examination, that Craig told her he had cut his finger, but she never saw any blood.

Then, Cohn moved on to Mrs. Seedlock's interviews with Marriscolo. Mrs. Seedlock had been advised not to mention the defendant's first arrest for solicitation of murder. To have brought that before the jury could have resulted in a mistrial. The witness gingerly worked around it as Cohn, who may have been hoping that she would slip, skirted dangerously close to the issue.

The witness said her husband called the police.

Cohn hoped that the jury might feel that the Seedlocks had an ulterior motive.

"The reason he put the phone call through to the police was

because you had seen these reward posters offering a $10,000 re-
ward (for information in finding Denise), isn't that correct?"

"No, sir," she politely responded.

"Did you remember the reward posters?"

"No, sir."

"Did you know anything about Denise Redlick having been
missing before that date?"

"No, sir."

"How did you find out that she was missing?"

"I read it in the *Chronicle* the next morning, on the 20th." It
was the day after Craig's arrest for murder solicitation.

Cohn asked her if she had told Marriscolo that Craig left
tennis shoes and a shovel at her house. She said she had. The
police inspector took the two items away as evidence, but, the
witness said that she later found out the shovel belonged to her
husband and hadn't been left there by Craig.

Kevin Seedlock's direct testimony was even stronger than his
mother's. The young witness had, in fact, a dual purpose on the
stand. Holm has zeroed in on the first point immediately.

"On November 11th, 1985, did you have occasion to go to a
job site, a place you were working in San Carlos?"

"Yes, sir," Kevin answered politely.

"Did you go with Jeff Hale?"

"Yes, sir."

"And what time did you get here? Do you recall, approximately?"

"Nine-thirty."

"And what were you planning on doing at that job site that
day?"

"Putting in a few hours of work."

"What was the weather like that day?" Holm queried as if
passing the time of day.

"It was not very good. It was raining."

"And the few hours of work that you were going to put in,
what kind of work were you going to do on that job site?"

"We arrived at the site, we figured it was only good condition
to do so much with, so we planned to caulk cracks and stuff."

Holm smiled, "Could you explain to us what caulking cracks means?"

"Just sealing an open crack."

"Cracks at a home or a business?"

"Yes, a home."

"Is that preparatory to painting the home?"

"Yes, sir."

"Did you need additional equipment that day in order to do the work you had planned?"

"Yes, sir."

"What additional equipment did you need?"

"We needed more caulking."

"Did you start your caulking . . . back up . . . did you go someplace that morning for the purpose of getting some caulking?"

"Yes, we looked over our supplies and we figured we needed more."

"Okay. Did you start caulking before you left to get some more?"

"No, sir."

"Do I understand that you wanted to have enough to finish the caulking job?"

"Well, to keep us busy."

"Did you go someplace together with Mr. Hale in order to get more caulking?" Again, Holm repeated the innocent question he asked a few minutes prior.

"Yes, sir," Kevin answered.

"Where did you go?" Holm pressed on.

"To Roy Anderson Paints."

"And is that the one that you mentioned on Brittan in San Carlos?"

"Yes."

"How close is it to El Camino Real, would you estimate?"

"I'd say half a block."

"Half a block?"

"Yes."

"Did you arrive at the San Carlos Roy Anderson Paint Store in the morning?"

"Yes, sir."

"About what time did you get there, do you have any idea?"

"Quarter to ten."

"Was Jeff with you then?"

"Yes, sir."

"And when you . . . I assume you got out of whatever vehicle you went in and went to the store?"

"Yes."

"What did you notice about the store, was it open?"

"No, sir."

Then Holm prepared his bombshell.

"And did there appear to be any people inside the store?"

"No, sir."

"Did you see any sign on the store doors of any sort indicating whether the store was open or closed?"

"There was a sign on the door."

"What did the sign say?" Holm looked piercingly.

"The sign said 'CLOSED. VETERAN'S DAY'," Kevin answered firmly.

"And was it Veteran's Day that day that you went there?"

"Yes, sir."

"After you noticed the sign, did you try the door or see if anybody . . . if the door was open in any event?"

"No, sir."

"Did you leave?"

"Yes, sir, we left."

"Pardon me," Holm said, wanting to reinforce the impression he'd left.

"We left."

Later Holm went after his second point, asking Kevin, "After you had lunch at the Belmont Brewery, was this with Jeff?"

"Yes, sir."

"You went to Jeff's house?"

"Yes."

"What happened then?"

"We watched the football game on TV."

"Which football game was that?"

"Monday Night Football, the 49er's."

"Do you know who they were playing?"

"Denver."

"Do you remember anything unusual about that game?"

"It was snowing. I guess there was an incident where somebody threw a snowball on the field."

"After you watched the game, was this at Jeff's place?"

"Yes, sir."

"Did you return home?"

"Yes, sir."

"And when you returned home, did you learn anything . . .
did you learn the Defendant had been over to your home earlier
that day?"

"Yes, sir."

"Did you call the Defendant?"

"Yes, sir."

"What did you tell the Defendant when you spoke with him
on the telephone?"

"I asked him what he was doing at my house that day."

"And did he answer your question?"

"He told me that he had hit a dog, and that he had needed to
clean out his van."

"Did he say where he had got this van?"

"No, sir."

"Pardon me?"

Kevin reconsidered, "He borrowed a van from a friend."

Holm smiled, "Did he say anything more about how it was
he hit this dog? Where it was?"

"He mentioned that he had hit the dog in Los Altos."

"Did he say anything about burying it; do you recall?"

"Yes."

"Did he say where he had buried the dog?"

"Los Altos."

"Any particular place? Did he say anything in particular
about where in Los Altos?"

"No, sir."

"Did you react or respond . . . excuse me, withdraw that,"
Holm thought for a minute, "Did you say anything to him after he
told you that he hit this dog and buried it?"

"I asked him why he didn't call the SPCA," Kevin recalled. "He was very vague. I didn't really get a clear answer."

Then, Kevin offered the most controversial statement of his testimony. Holm asked him if Craig had said anything else.

"He told me not to speak to anybody or any detectives," Kevin claimed.

"What about?" Holm asked.

"About what happened that day," he responded.

The remark, Kevin testified, seemed strange, since all Craig had done, to his knowledge, was hit a dog and bury it.

Cohn elicited from Kevin that he had originally told Marriscolo that Craig asked him to throw out the tennis shoes and shovel that he had left at the Palo Alto home. It wasn't until eleven days later that Kevin contacted Marriscolo and told him that he had been mistaken about the shovel, that it actually belonged to his father.

Holm and Wagstaffe were both of the philosophy that it's sometimes just as important to let the jury know what evidence technicians didn't find, even if the "negative evidence" seems to help the defense more than the prosecution. "You've got to show the jury that you did everything possible in your investigation," Wagstaffe said. "It enhances your own credibility. It lets them know you are being open, fair and honest."

Besides, if the district attorney didn't admit to the jury that the search for Denise Redlick's fingerprints in the Econoline van, as well as Craig Anderson's fingerprints on the Triumph, was futile, the defense attorney certainly would have. And, then it could have been seen from a completely different light.

Stanley Baker, the fingerprint evidence technician who, with Benny Del Re, examined the van on December 23rd, said that, using the mechanical method of dusting with black fingerprint powder applied with a very fine bristled brush, he lifted seven cards of latent prints—two fingerprints on one and six palmprints on the others—from the inside of the vehicle. But, he said, the only identifiable prints from among those were the middle and ring fingers of the left hand of Sheriff's Lieutenant Mike Dow and two cards of palmprints identified as those of criminalist Del Re.

Baker explained that when the lab first examined the van in December, the technicians were told that they were looking for blood, not prints. "That's why they weren't that careful," he said. The lab also obtained photographs for eight lifts from the van using the more sophisticated laser method.

Holm led Baker through a long explanation of how the lab attempted to match the unidentified prints with Denise Redlick using documents that were given to Marriscolo by Bank of America that she might have touched and personal possessions—including shoes, photo albums, ceramic figurines and a toothpaste tube—from her home. None of the prints lifted from those items matched the prints in the van.

The only known, inked print for Miss Redlick, he added, was a thumbprint from her driver's license application and it also failed to provide a match.

"Mr. Baker," Cohn began, "you've been talking for quite awhile and the bottom line—the bottom line—for all this is that you were not able to identify any fingerprints belonging to Denise Redlick in the van. Is that the bottom line?"

"That's the bottom line," Baker matter-of-factly responded.

"In fact, when you gentlemen went in and took the first prints off the van, four of the prints you took off were belonging to the police officers, isn't that right?"

"Yes, it is."

"You've found cases where a thumbprint was enough to identify someone?"

"Oh, yes," Baker said.

■ CHAPTER TWENTY-FIVE ■

The Prosecution Concludes

Without fingerprints, would the jury be able to connect Denise Redlick to the van? That largely depended on the outcome of a day-long hearing May 16th, in which the defense would attempt to disparage the San Mateo County Forensic Lab's work in analyzing the bloodstains in the van and on the tennis shoes.

The jury had been given the day off so that Capaccioli could consider the complex issue before him.

Earlier in the week, attorney Robert Brower had learned that his trial scheduled in San Francisco had been postponed. He contacted Cohn and volunteered to assist in the Anderson case, after all. Brower and Grunbaum, who had worked as a team in the past, were ready, once again, to attack the credibility of forensic serology.

But Holm and Wagstaffe had completed their homework. They had contacted Rockne Harmon, an Alameda County prosecutor who had squared off with Grunbaum in court before, and asked if he would be willing to be deputized as a San Mateo County prosecutor. If Grunbaum were to take the stand in the Anderson case, Harmon, who had already collected and disected thousands of pages of transcripts of Grunbaum's testimony in courtrooms across the country, would conduct the cross-examination.

It was a juicy offer that the Alameda deputy district attorney couldn't resist.

"I was flattered to be asked," says Harmon, a lean and tan long-distance runner, who cynically credits Grunbaum with "making me famous. We prosecutors are such egotists, we aren't inclined to ask for somebody else's help. I was glad to do it."

Harmon began collecting information about Grunbaum in 1985, when he was called upon to prosecute the retrial of Lawrence Riley, charged with the brutal, drug-related murders of three people. Grunbaum had testified for the defense in the original trial in which Riley was convicted of three first-degree murders and sentenced to life in prison. But the appellate court had overturned the conviction based, in a convoluted way, on the content of the amicus curiae brief that Brower and Grunbaum had filed with the state Supreme Court in People vs. Brown, an otherwise completely unrelated murder case.

In preparation for the retrial, Harmon examined each of Grunbaum's transcripts and compiled a detailed, topical index of his testimonies. What he began to see were "a lot of inconsistencies on Grunbaum's part." Harmon thought he detected that the scientist's opinion changed, in each case, depending upon what the opposing party, usually the district attorney's office, was trying to do. The deputy district attorney went back as far as 1980 to examine letters Grunbaum wrote that were "totally at odds" with what he was testifying now. The bottom line, Harmon felt, was that Grunbaum was milking the legal system for all the money he could because of his own "petty vendetta." Harmon believed that Grunbaum was still angry at the forensic community for not accepting the electrophoresis method that he had spent several years studying and promoting at the University of California at Berkeley.

Harmon and Grunbaum ultimately squared off in Alameda County Superior Court in front of the judge in the Riley case for nearly three days in an extremely acrimonious hearing.

"I took everything he'd done over the past five years and made him eat it," Harmon said. Grunbaum, however, had a different recollection of what happened. Harmon's expertise, Grunbaum said, "is in bullying people."

"He had absolutely nothing to incriminate me with and he did himself a lot of damage," Grunbaum claimed.

Ultimately, there were no real winners in the Riley retrial. The jury found the defendant guilty of three second-degree murders for a maximum of twelve years in prison. Since he had already been in custody for eight years, he was paroled within a short period of time.

And Harmon was angry.

"Because of Grunbaum's vendetta, somebody who butchered three people got out of prison just like that," Harmon said. "Otherwise, he would probably still be in prison today."

On the morning of the bloodstain hearing in the Anderson case, Grunbaum and Brower—who was introduced to Craig Anderson for the first time in court that morning—were conferring with Cohn, when Wagstaffe, followed by Harmon toting two large cardboard boxes of files that obviously contained ammunition against Grunbaum, marched conspicuously into the courtroom.

What happened next is a matter of interpretation.

The prosecutors believe that Harmon's threatening presence forced Grunbaum to retreat. Harmon saw the defense attorney—who had no idea, until that moment, who Rockne Harmon was—and his hired guns suddenly huddle and a heated exchange ensued. The body language told Harmon that Cohn hadn't been advised by his experts that they could be blown out of the water by a visiting prosecutor. Cohn had a lot at stake in this hearing and he didn't want to lose.

But the defense experts denied that any such thing occurred. Grunbaum said he never intended to testify that day, that the key to successfully challenging forensic evidence lies in skilled cross examination of the prosecution's own experts.

"Harmon looked like an utter idiot when he came walking in with all those boxes," Grunbaum declared.

At any rate, the only witnesses during the day-long hearing would be Benny Del Re, the county criminalist who, ironically, had once worked for Grunbaum, and Edward Blake, a forensic serologist with a private lab, Forensic Science Associates, who would serve as the prosecution's impartial expert to validate the San Mateo County Forensic Lab's work.

Wagstaffe, whose razor sharp mind easily absorbs technical detail, had spent most of the previous week studying up for this hearing, while Holm was selecting the jury. Although Harmon wouldn't wind up asking questions, he stayed for the entire hearing, conferring periodically with Wagstaffe on specific points. Likewise, Grunbaum sat in the front row of the gallery behind the defendant, frequently conferring with Brower.

Although spectators had filled the courtroom most days, only a few observers realized the critical significance of the hearing concerning the bloodstain admissibility and were willing to sit through an entire day of technical, complex, and often tedious testimony. Among them were Harry Redlick and Ron Anderson.

Del Re explained how he conducted a double diffusion species test on crusts from the van to determine that they came from a human source since there was some suggestion by the defense that all of the stains—on the shoe and in the van—might have come from a dog. On a tablet of white paper posted at the front of the courtroom, the witness diagrammed how he punched small wells in a petri dish containing a gel. In the various wells, he placed an extract of the stain, an antihuman antisera which should react positively to human blood, a sample of his own blood as a known "human standard," a known dog blood sample and an antidog antisera which should react positively to dog blood.

The contents of the dish were allowed to diffuse overnight. A positive reaction between the stain extract and any of the wells would be indicated, the next day, by a faint white line. What he saw, he said, were reactions between the antihuman antisera and the stain; his own blood and the stain; and the antidog antisera and the dog blood. But there was no reaction between the stain extract and the antidog antisera.

"Therefore, I was able to say we do not have dog blood, but we do have human blood," Del Re said. "All the stains that I examined were of human origin."

His next step was to determine the ABO group type of the stains. To do that, he performed two tests, one to confirm the other. The first, called absorption elution, uses known antisera to identify the antigens on the red blood cells—and, consequently, the blood type—in the dried bloodstain sample. The clumping or agglutination of Type A antisera with the bloodstain cells indicated that the stain, Del Re said, was Type A.

Then, each stain was subjected to a reverse test, known as a Lattes, that looks for a reaction between antibodies in the bloodstain sample and red cells of known blood antigen types that are added to the sample. The binding of an antibody in the sample to a known antigen determines the blood type, he explained.

Del Re testified that, after completing the Lattes test, he concluded that the stains were Type A.

But in his skillful and, at times, abrasive, cross-examination of the criminalist, Brower brought out that while Del Re included unstained "control" threads in an absorption elution test for the bloodstain on the tennis shoe, he did not use a cotton swab to collect a "control" sample from the interior surface of the van where it appeared to be unstained.

"I observed the area," Del Re testified. "It seemed as though it was not stained with anything other than the blood." There appeared to be no paint or metal attached to the crusted samples, he said.

"Doesn't good practice in California in 1985 require that criminalists take controls near bloodstains when the bloodstain is deposited on a nonabsorbent surface?" Brower asked.

"If it's written down, I have never seen it," Del Re responded.

"Who taught you to take a bloodstain from a nonabsorbent surface?"

"Myself," the criminalist declared.

Del Re said that regardless of the missing control, the lattes test confirmed the results of the absorption elution. He explained that the Lattes test is dependent upon antibodies and bacteria that could contaminate a sample cannot create antibodies.

Brower zeroed in on yet another issue, aimed at showing the judge that the San Mateo County Forensic Lab's methods were new and, therefore, not proven. The witness said that of perhaps twenty or so published techniques for absorption elution, he used a modification, with "just slight variations," of the so-called Howard-Martin technique. However, Del Re couldn't precisely describe how his technique varied from the published method.

"I don't recall what type of changes were done," he admitted. "Like I say, my time of absorption may be a little bit longer. My wash time may be longer." Every crime lab, he said, changes methods slightly to work in their own setting. "The principal science behind it is exactly the same."

Brower also asked a series of questions focusing on Grunbaum's pet peeve, the lack of validation of results in crime labs. Del Re participated in a proficiency test in 1982 and his lab had just begun subscribing to proficiency tests again.

"So is it correct to say that you have not done a proficiency test for approximately three and a half years or so at or about the time that you tested this evidence?" Brower inquired.

"That's correct," Del Re matter-of-factly said.

Del Re ultimately had to agree with Brower that there have been cases in which two criminalists, given the same dried bloodstain, came up with different ABO results.

Blake, who had been forced to wait outside during Del Re's testimony, was hired by the prosecution to independently validate the Forensic Lab's findings. But it didn't quite work out that way.

Initially, Blake, who holds a doctor of criminology degree from the University of California at Berkeley and is an expert in forensic serology, said that the Howard-Martin procedure Benny Del Re used was, "in general," similar to what most criminologists in California use to type bloodstains.

When questioned by Wagstaffe, Blake agreed that many crime labs adopt minor modifications of the published methods of conducting tests of dried bloodstains. Most are "rather trivial and no big deal," he said.

Then, Wagstaffe asked about the need for a control in the absorption elution test. Blake said that, in standard practice, a control should be used. If the control has the same reaction to the test as the specimen, it means that the substance in the control area may also be in the sample area so the test results can't be used, he explained. In his opinion, without the control, the test is flawed.

But he contended that the follow-up Lattes test, which Del Re also ran, confirms the results of the first test.

"If the Lattes test had not been done at all, I think that, in my judgment, there is some potential that the test conclusion could be compromised," the witness declared.

In his own lab, he would simply do the absorption elution test, using a control sample, and not bother with the Lattes test to confirm the results of the first test.

"If I had some reason to suspect the accuracy of whether or not my absorption elution test was giving me an accurate result, I would back it up then with the Lattes test," Blake explained. "It's a question of scientific judgment."

Brower, furiously taking notes through the direct testimony of both prosecution witnesses, had stumbled upon something. With a grand flourish, Brower handed Blake a copy of Benny Del Re's bench notes for the Lattes test on December 23rd and asked the forensic scientist if it appeared that the criminalist had incorporated a built-in control, an O blood type cell, which would have provided extra assurance that the results were valid and that the sample was not contaminated.

Blake carefully studied the notes for a minute and looked up, knowing that his answer wasn't going to please Steve Wagstaffe.

"It doesn't appear to me that he did," Blake was forced to reply, catching Wagstaffe by surprise. With Brower's persistent prodding, Blake said that the missing control in the Lattes, coupled with the missing control in the absorption elution, "shows a degree of sloppiness that makes me uncomfortable." However, he added that he did not believe the test results were compromised.

Judge Capaccioli said he was only interested in getting to the truth.

"I want to think on it," the judge explained. "I want to look at my notes. I want to reread some of this material that I was given. But I want to sleep on it."

When the attorneys left the courtroom for the weekend recess, the parting words of Judge Capaccioli were ringing in their ears.

"If I were to rule right now, I would be inclined to rule against the People."

At 11:00 a.m. Sunday, Benny Del Re returned to the crime lab and, using the miniscule quantity of remaining blood sample, conducted the Lattes test again, inserting the Type O control cell. Ed Blake had asked Gary Sims, a criminalist with the Institute of Forensic Sciences, a private lab in Oakland, to be an independent observer. Sims looked over Benny's shoulder and took his own notes.

Cohn and Brower had declined the prosecutor's offer to send their own expert to watch the retest. They felt, Brower said, that "the Lattes test was an inappropriate test to do with the remaining evidence and Benny Del Re was the wrong person to do whatever test ought to be done."

After the weekend recess, Capaccioli gave the prosecution a chance—with the jury again dismissed—to present the new test results in court. Del Re returned to the stand and explained how he conducted the Lattes test, this time inserting the missing Type O cell control, and again concluded that the bloodstain was Type A.

Sims agreed with other witnesses that the Lattes test alone, even with the proper controls included on Sunday, could not provide a definitive conclusion between Type A and Type O blood. But, with the Lattes test and the absorption elution test from December combined, "There's compelling evidence that it's Type A blood."

It was all that Judge Capaccioli needed to hear.

"I am now satisfied that they [the People] have employed the correct scientific tests on the stains in question, and that the tests that were described by Dr. Blake, Mr. Del Re and Mr. Sims were carried out under an appropriate standard and control, and I find and conclude that the test results of the stain found in the van are admissible into evidence."

Now, it was up to the jury.

On Monday, May 19th, the jury began to learn that Craig Anderson had asked several of his acquaintances to vouch for his whereabouts on November 11, 1985, although they later changed their stories.

The most revealing of the so-called "alibi witnesses" was

John Soller, the painting foreman, who recalled that when he saw Craig at the San Carlos store on the morning of November 12th to demand $1,000 that he believed Craig owed him, he noticed deep red scratches running down both sides of the defendant's neck into his shirt ("They hadn't scabbed over yet") and scratches down his arms, four or five lines each. He also detected a yellow and purple bruise on Craig's nose.

"Did you comment to the defendant about these scratches?" Holm asked the long-haired, blond witness.

"Yes, I did."

"What did you tell him?"

"I said, asked him what happened, it looked like he had been fighting a bobcat," Soller gruffly said.

"Did he say anything in response?"

"Just that he had some problems over the weekend. He just mumbled, didn't put anything real clear, just blew it off and walked away."

Soller recalled Craig asking him to step into the little office in the warehouse area of the store.

"He asked me if I could—he wanted me to tell the police that I saw him on Monday afternoon."

"Did he say why?" Holm asked, gazing at the jurors to guess if they were listening closely.

"He said that he had some problems over the weekend and that he needed someone to tell the police that I saw him on Monday."

"What was your reaction to that?" Holm asked.

"I said, 'Well, I can't really do that, because I don't want to get in any trouble.'"

"What was his response?"

"He said, 'It's worth this to me,'" Soller responded, raising his right hand, his five fingers pointing upward, to pantomime what Craig had done.

Soller, in the end, agreed to lie to the cops because "he just hinted to me that it could cause some problems with my job if I didn't do it for him." Soller further testified that Craig paid him $300 that morning and promised to add the remaining $200 to a subcontracting payment.

The witness said he decided to tell police the truth because he saw the posters about Denise's disappearance and "it started getting to me then." He was even having trouble sleeping at night because his conscience was bothering him.

Cohn saw, however, an opportunity to possibly destroy the witness's credibility. The defense attorney made certain the jury understood that there were inconsistencies between what Soller had said at the preliminary hearing and in direct examination at the trial. And, he pointed out that over November and December, Craig gave Soller a total of around $1,000—all of it representing money that Anderson owed his subcontractor for various jobs, not for a bribe.

The jury heard numerous witnesses describe the scratches they had seen on the defendant's arms and Craig's varied explanations for how the wounds occurred. No one, however, could provide a better description than Pat Chavez.

Chavez, a short and round woman with a friendly face who had worked as a registered nurse for six years before becoming the director of the Missing Children's Project and a volunteer with Community Outreach, had interviewed Craig in the Redlick kitchen on the evening of November 14th.

"And did you notice anything unusual about the defendant when you saw him that night?" Holm asked her.

"He seemed agitated. His hands were marked and scratched."

"And did these appear to be what might be termed significant scratches or marks?"

"Yes."

"And were there more than one? Was that more than one scratch that you recall seeing?"

"Yes, there appeared to be two types of scratches on the back of his hand, and they were many."

"Would you describe those?" Holm asked, knowing that Chavez could provide a nearly clinical description of what she had seen.

"One set of scratches were small pin-type scratches. The other type of scratches were long, approximately one and a half inches, grooved scratches."

270

"And, could you tell from your experience whether the pin types were older or fresher than the others, the groove type?"

"The pin-type scratches appeared to be—the series of groove scratches appeared to be over the pin-type scratches."

"Indicating to you what?"

"That they were new scratches," Chavez believed.

"Did this appear to be relatively fresh?"

"Yes, they looked like they were about three days old."

"Can you describe in what direction they were going on his hand?"

"Yes, they indicated—she paused and raised her arms to demonstrate—"they appeared to be coming from the wrist to the knuckle area."

"Could you see up the wrist, up his arms at the time you saw him?" Holm inquired.

"No, I could not."

"Was he wearing something covering his arms?"

"Yes."

"Did you notice anything, any marks on his face or head?"

"Not on his face but I noticed a mark on his neck. He had a groove scratch on his neck."

"Do you recall what side?"

"That would be his right side."

"Is that the side you were looking at?"

"Yes."

"Did he have any marks anywhere else that you recall seeing?"

"I recall a mark on his left ear lobe."

"What kind of mark was that?"

"It looked like a nick."

Although John Soller had already testified that Craig Anderson had paid him to provide the police with an alibi, Holm brought in two more witnesses—Mike Shea and Frank Roberts—to suggest that Craig was covering up his tracks on November 11th.

Mike Shea, the general contractor who sometimes did jobs for Craig, said he often dropped in the store in the morning, staying for around an hour while Craig mixed the paint that he ordered. He recalled telling police officers around the middle of November that he had been at the store on November 11th but now, six months later, he could no longer be so sure.

"I didn't swear to it," Shea declared. "I don't absolutely know that I was in the store on that day. At the time I thought I was. I thought I could have been because I had been in the store so much every day buying paint, doing this job for Craig, and I thought I had been in the store at that time."

"Did he say anything about establishing an alibi for him?" Holm asked.

"Yes, he said that if I was in the store at that time, that I would be a good alibi, because he needed to establish his whereabouts."

"And, did he ask you or say anything to you about what time he needed an alibi for?"

"Sometime around noon, if I was in the store at that time," Shea said.

He was followed to the stand by Frank Roberts, the paint spray equipment salesman who usually dropped in Craig's store two or three days a week. Roberts said he originally told police he had gone to the store and seen Craig there on November 11th but later, distinctly remembering that he had been home that night to watch the Forty-Niner-Denver game, the one with the memorable snowball incident, on television, he realized he had been mixed up about the days.

"Do you have any recollection as to why you said to the police officers that week that you were in the store on the eleventh?"

"Well, I was just . . . I was nervous, I guess. It's hard to remember for me as far as my calls go. I was in the store so many times. I was usually . . . I went back and reviewed my records and then recollected about the football game and realized that I had been there on Friday," he declared.

The courtroom was deadly quiet on the morning of Wednesday, May 21st, when a somber Joan Redlick, her shoulders drooped and her eyes red, took the witness stand.

Joan described Denise's close relationship with her father,

brother and, of course, herself, and then was asked by Holm to describe her only daughter "in your own words."

Her response was not easy to listen to. When the case began, court reporter Olivia Shirley had positioned herself so that her back was to the jury. She wanted to avoid having an inadvertent facial expression, perhaps a smile or a frown, which might influence the feelings of the jurors. She was especially glad she had done so when Joan Redlick testified.

Olivia suspected that the testimony of the alleged victim's mother would be difficult to sit through. So, as Joan approached the stand, Olivia focused on a spot on the floor a few feet away and fixed her eyes on it, hoping she could block out the emotion of what she was about to hear. "This is going to be a rough one," she thought to herself.

Minutes into the testimony, as Joan began describing her daughter, Olivia began to feel her eyes water. She began to hear sniffling behind her. She knew that members of the jury had also been overcome with sadness.

Later, she asked a deputy sheriff who had been in the courtroom if he had noticed how many of the jurors had wept.

"Who could possibly look up?" the deputy responded. He, too, had been deeply affected by what he had heard.

"Denise was the best person I ever knew in my life. She was beautiful. She was kind. She was loving. She was giving. She was one of the gifts of this world.

"Even as a little girl, she never asked for anything for Christmas. She had more joy in giving. She was my best friend and confidant.

"She loved to laugh. Her classmates voted her "best laugh in the class" because her laughter would ring. I can still hear it in my ears. One thing I'll always remember about her was her laughing. Nothing ever got her down so far that she couldn't laugh.

"I'm very proud to have been her mother and I'll miss her and grieve over her until the day I die."

"Was she dependable?" Holm asked his star witness.

"Always dependable. I could always count on her."

"When she said she would be some place, would she be there?"

"Absolutely."

"If she would go some place and might be late, would she call to tell you where she was and what her plans were?"

"Yes, she would," Joan responded.

Joan testified that, as a child and teenager, her daughter never—not once—threatened to run away from home.

Holm led Joan Redlick through a series of questions concerning Denise's relationship with Craig, from the trip to the Bahamas during which they became engaged to the cancellation of the wedding. Joan recalled calling Denise at work on September 30th, and Denise telling her of an incident at the wedding where she and Craig had fought after Craig became angry over her dancing with a high school friend of Mike Redlick's.

"He insisted that he take her home," Joan said. "So they went out of the building and he was pawing at her. He pushed her against the wall. She hit her head against the wall and subsequently lost an earring which she never found. She got in the car and was so frightened at that time, she didn't know what to do."

Cohn objected, "That's an opinion and conclusion."

His objection was readily sustained.

Denise told her, Joan continued, that Craig was hollering at her as they drove down the freeway and that "all of a sudden, he lashed out with his hand and just hit her across the face."

Joan testified how, after the engagement, Denise stopped tending to her personal appearance with her customary diligence and how, after the break-up, she began getting her hair and nails done and wearing makeup again. Denise said that Craig had once told her that "when she went to work, she wasn't dressing up for him. She was dressing up for other people, so he didn't want her to do that."

Joan sadly recalled the morning of November 11th when, unknowingly, she saw her daughter for the last time. She recalled the untouched phone messages from Charles Nan, the early morning phone call to Craig, and the decision to call the police when she and Harry knew for sure that Denise hadn't shown up for work on Tuesday morning. She also described the search for

Denise, emphasizing that Craig never volunteered to distribute leaflets, although all of Denise's other boyfriends had.

"Mrs. Redlick, do you have any idea where Denise is at this point?" Holm asked.

Joan looked at him blankly. "Where her body is, you mean?"

"Objection, Your Honor!" Cohn boomed. "There's no evidence . . ."

Judge Capaccioli instructed the witness to simply answer the question, while Cohn asked that the jury be told to disregard her original answer. "You are admonished not to consider that answer," the judge agreed.

Holm asked again, and Joan replied, simply, "No, I do not."

Cohn wouldn't get his chance to cross-examine Denise's mother until after a lunch recess. Then, he began gently, telling her to ask for a glass of water or to take a break if she should need it.

His cross-examination focused largely on Joan's memory of the tape-recorded phone conversations with Craig. The defense attorney did exactly what Joan Redlick feared might happen if the tapes were allowed in court. Cohn pulled one exchange after another—most of them casting the defendant in a favorable light —from the conversations, asking the witness if, in fact, that was what she or the defendant had said. Joan, however, often said she didn't recall or, more decidedly, it wasn't what Craig had said at all. At other times, however, she had to grit her teeth and agree that her daughter's ex-fiance had, in fact, expressed concern or compassion for Denise and for the Redlick family.

Cohn asked her if, on one occasion, Craig said, "There's no way in the world I could hurt Denise."

"That's what he told me," Joan declared.

"He told you he loved Denise?"

"That's what he told me."

"He told you that he loved you and your husband?"

"Yes," Joan responded. She also admitted that, at one time, she told Craig she loved him, too, "but I didn't mean it."

Then Cohn asked if Craig had said that he wasn't coming by the Redlick house because the police had told him that Joan and Harry were suspicious of him, that he might be involved in

Denise's disappearance, and that he had been told to stay away. Joan offered a denial.

She conceded that, in several conversations, Craig seemed to break down and cry. But she said, "I don't recall," when Cohn asked her if that occurred when she told him that search parties, with dogs that can smell dead bodies, had been called into action.

Some of the answers Cohn didn't want to hear.

"You told him over the phone that you wanted him to call you, didn't you?" Cohn inquired. Joan said she had.

"And you asked him, 'Don't abandon me,' didn't you?"

"Yes. I was trying to keep communications open with him. I thought maybe he would break down and tell me what he did with my daughter."

Joan said she couldn't recall Craig calling the whole ordeal "a nightmare" for him and denied Craig had said that he would do anything for Denise because "they were still best of friends."

Cohn asked Joan if she recalled Craig telling her that he had a poster concerning Denise's disappearance in the window of his store.

"Mr. Cohn, Denise's friends put that picture in his window," Joan responded. Cohn was annoyed at her response, saying, "I didn't ask you that," and trying the question again.

"Yes. He did have a picture in his window," she reluctantly declared.

After nearly one hundred-fifty questions about the phone conversations, Cohn asked the court for permission to play all the tapes, with Holm strongly objecting. During a discussion at the bench, the judge agreed to consider the request—aimed at impeaching Mrs. Redlick as a witness—only if Cohn could show how they might be relevant to the trial.

To consider the request, Capaccioli read a 1971 ruling in People vs. Green, a case involving a defendant who had been charged with providing marijuana to a minor. A witness to the transactions who had testified at the preliminary hearing, became curiously vague at the trial, often saying, "I can't be sure" and "I can't remember" about what had occurred. Even after being shown the

preliminary hearing transcript, his recollections of the actual incident remained surprisingly dim.

The courts found that, in such a situation—where a witness
was "markedly evasive and uncooperative"—the witness' incon-
sistency is justification for allowing a prior statement—or, in this
case, a tape—to be brought into evidence. But Capaccioli said that
Mrs. Redlick was obviously under stress on the stand and that,
although he hadn't personally listened to the tapes, he hadn't seen
where her testimony had been inconsistent and evasive.

The judge said Cohn would have to find the allegedly inconsistent sections on the many hours of tapes ("You're not going to
unload those tapes on me without first identifying precisely what
you want me to listen to.") before he would listen and issue his
ruling. Simple lack of memory would not be enough to justify
playing the tapes.

The prosecutor called the defendant's tape-recorded statements "self-serving hearsay" that shouldn't even be admitted in
any form. If the defendant is going to attempt to have such information put before the jury, it should be by way of his own testimony, subject to cross-examination, Holm argued.

The day after her testimony, Joan Redlick walked into the
courtroom carrying a colorful flower arrangement, a simple,
kind gesture from the mother of a very good friend who had
come to the trial for the first time.

Cohn, who noticed the flowers as the jurors began filing into
the courtroom after their lunch break, discreetly went to the
bench and asked for an immediate in-chambers hearing. Cohn
had been keeping a scornful eye on what he felt were theatrics on
the Redlick side of the courtroom which might prejudice the jury
against his client. To Cohn, the flowers gave Joan the appearance
that she was mourning a dead person.

In chambers, with Brower, the Defendant and Holm also
present, Cohn told Capaccioli that, despite his sympathy for Joan
Redlick, the flowers had to go. Mrs. Redlick, he said, had been
standing out in the hallway with the arrangement in her hands
after lunch, while jurors milled around. She then had brought
them into the courtroom, sat in the first row of the side closest to

the jury box—where she had been sitting every day for the past three weeks—and propped the bouquet on her lap.

"I think it's deliberately done by them to give the idea that somebody is dead," Cohn insisted. The judge hadn't even noticed, but agreed that the flower display was inappropriate and that she should leave it in the corridor.

The delicate dilemma, however, was how to eject either Mrs. Redlick or the flowers from the courtroom without drawing even more attention "to something we shouldn't be wasting all this time on," the judge declared.

After some discussion, Capaccioli suggested that while the jurors were distracted by the formality of rising to their feet as the judge stepped up to the bench, Holm should ask Denise's mother to have someone take the flowers away. The task was quietly accomplished moments later.

Joan Redlick was embarrassed by the entire incident. "I had never been in a courtroom until all this happened and I certainly didn't know anything about what kind of deportment you should have." Much later, she still couldn't imagine why Cohn had been so upset.

The seemingly trivial incident, however, was one that Cohn would later argue had added to the general, overwhelming atmosphere of judicial bias against his client.

In pre-trial motions, Holm had agreed that he would not offer testimony from Craig's former girlfriends concerning their allegations that he had beaten or abused them unless he first notified the court. Cohn certainly didn't want the information to be admitted and the judge would have to decide if the prosecutor had a legally legitimate reason for such testimony. Holm recognized early on that, unless Craig testified and opened the door by claiming, for example, that he had never been violent with a woman, there was little chance of bringing that evidence in.

Nevertheless, four of Craig's former girlfriends had received subpoenas and their names were on the list of ninety prospective prosecution witnesses which Holm had filed with the clerk. Ultimately, only one of them, Lucy Larson, would testify.

All eyes were on the tall and attractive Larson as she stepped to the front of the room and sat in the witness' chair. Holm suspected that Cohn would be on the edge of his seat, waiting for Larson's testimony to tread into controversial waters. In response to Holm's foundational questions, Lucy said she had known Craig for three years and that she had lived with him, off and on, in 1983 and 1984.

Cohn was, indeed, on guard.

"Excuse me, your honor, may we approach the bench?"

"Yes," Capaccioli said. In an off-the-record exchange, Cohn asked the judge to again remind Holm of his commitment not to refer to the allegations of violence. The defense attorney gave Craig a reassuring smile as the attorneys resumed their places.

"Did you ever learn that the defendant was engaged to marry Denise Redlick?" Holm asked.

"No," Lucy said, her eyes avoiding the defendant.

"Did you understand him to be dating her?"

"Yes."

"During the year 1985, did you ever date the Defendant during that year?"

"Yes," Lucy unhesitatingly answered, causing several of Denise's closest relatives to exchange surprised glances.

"Do you have any recollection how many times it would have been?" Holm inquired, sneaking a glance at Craig.

"Well, when I still lived in San Carlos, he came over and would visit a couple times or I would go over to his house and meet with him, and I would go like on a bicycle ride."

After describing their casual dates, Lucy was asked if Craig ever talked to her about Denise. She recalled him saying they had "some kind of a blow-up" after a wedding reception when he struck her.

"When he told you they had broken up over this incident at the wedding, did he say anything to you about her in that conversation?"

"Well, he just said that she was real headstrong and she was kind of set in her ways, and real spoiled. She was a real mama's girl."

Lucy recalled that Craig was "real depressed and real mopey, like he felt as if he did something wrong and he wanted to try to mend his ways," immediately after he and Denise broke up. But she sensed that his demeanor had changed by the end of October when she talked to him again.

"Between those conversations, did the defendant say anything else about Denise Redlick that you can recall?"

"Yeah, he was, he kind of got a real bitter attitude toward her. He said he felt as if she was real spoiled, and she really wasn't worth him trying to get back with her because she wasn't really worthy of him, and that she was nothing but a, I believe the words he said was a 'heartless bitch,' because she just wanted to throw away everything that those two had built up to."

Holm glimpsed at his notes and asked Lucy about her conversation with Craig on December 2nd after she returned from a vacation to Cancun, Mexico and learned from detective Marriscolo about Denise Redlick's disappearance.

"Did you call—when you called the Defendant, did you talk to him about Denise Redlick?"

"Well, I just asked him if those two had mended their ways and if they had gotten back together again.

"And, did the defendant say anything to you?"

"He just said that it was over between them, and he was going his own way."

"Did he say anything to you—did you specifically refer to Denise Redlick, his former girlfriend?"

"Denise, yes."

"Did he say anything about her having been missing during this conversation?"

"No, he never mentioned it," Lucy said.

Finally, the jury learned about the crucial link between Denise Redlick and the Ford Econoline van, a link that the defense would still try desperately to discredit.

Benny Del Re, the county's newly promoted supervising criminalist, spent most of Thursday, May 22nd, on the stand and part of the following day in direct and cross-examination. Del Re, by the end of the rigorous questioning on this controversial issue, appeared weary and tense. But he still managed to answer Brower's sharply-worded, often accusatory questions without losing his composure. The criminalist felt confident that his testing procedures were valid. "My biggest problem was keeping myself from getting emotionally involved," he later said. Dr. Grunbaum, the former mentor whose research Benny had rejected as flawed by the time he left Grunbaum's Berkeley lab in 1978, watched critically from behind the gallery bar as the witness defended his own work.

Del Re told the jury that when he first examined the interior of the van on December 20th and conducted the initial presumptive test, he identified fifty spots distributed primarily on the walls and the ceiling.

"They were very light in color. They were as though somebody had diluted them with water or something like that," Del Re declared. It was like what happens when you take a shower and water splashes on the walls, leaving a little color from the soap suds when it dries. Del Re explained how he tapped two crusts— about one-eighth inch square each—from the ceiling and one from the back inside of the seat belt housing on the passenger's side onto clean white sheets of weighing paper and brought them back to the lab. There, he used the double diffusion test to determine that the stains were human blood and the absorption elution and Lattes tests to identify them as Type A in the ABO typing system.

Holm then showed Del Re People's Exhibit 28, an envelope containing the two vials of blood taken from defendant Anderson in January. Using the same test commonly used by blood banks, Anderson's blood had been typed as Type O.

"And the bloodstains that you collected from the van were ABO Type A?" Holm asked, clarifying the significance for the jury.

"That's correct," the witness responded.

The prosecutor also brought out the two bags containing the Nike high-top tennis shoes, size eleven. Del Re said he detected a thin smear of blood, using the presumptive test, on the back of the right shoe, pointing to the area where the word "Nike" is printed. No further testing was possible. But, on the left shoe, in the area above the top inside eyelet, there was enough blood to identify Type A using the absorption elution method, he said.

Brower may have been defeated in his attempt to prevent the

jury from hearing about the Type A evidence, but he had one more chance to discredit the crime lab's work, this time in front of the jury.

The defense attorney, in cross-examination, quickly resurrected the debate over the missing test controls. Focusing on Del Re's failure to take a swab of an unstained surface of the van for a control test, Brower asked if a person's perspiration, left on a surface that he touches, can leave behind a blood type. The criminalist agreed that the eighty percent of the people in the world who are "secretors" display their ABO type in their other body fluids.

Brower made sure the jury understood that Del Re didn't wear rubber gloves when he collected the bloodstains, since his own fingerprints were among those found when the interior was dusted several days later.

"Because people may have ABO types in their perspiration, is that another reason that controls are necessary when doing an absorption elution test?" Brower asked.

"It can be a reason, yes," Del Re said.

"Isn't it true that in the absorption elution test, that reading the test result is a subjective process?"

"It's a subjective process based on scientific facts and techniques, yes," the witness said.

"Have you ever heard of a case where two different criminalists have analyzed some dried blood and come up with different answers?" Brower asked.

"I've heard it may have happened, but I haven't talked to the individuals involved, so again, it's just hearsay," Del Re said.

Emphasizing to the jury that the defense was objecting to the blood typing test methods, Brower took a step backward to the presumptive test in which ortho-tolidine was dabbed on the fifty stains in the vans to preliminarily identify them as blood.

Del Re agreed that other substances—including horseradish, squash and turnips—can have a positive reaction to the test. However, the criminalist insisted that the intensity of the color would be much less and would take longer to develop than with blood.

The witness also conceded, under cross-examination, that none of the tests could determine how long the stains had been on the sneakers or in the van, whether they may have been there before November 11th, or even if they all came from the same person.

Holm, in re-cross, explained to the jury that there had been some of the blood sample remaining after the crime lab conducted its tests.

"Did anyone from the defense or anyone else ask to try to retest the blood samples that were taken from the van?"

"No," Del Re said.

"Did anyone ask to retest and check your results from the test that you did on the tennis shoes?"

"No."

Brower was still determined to show that the Forensic Lab had not done its job. During a jurors' break, he asked Capaccioli to allow him to question Del Re about the electrophoresis tests that weren't performed. Brower argued that since the Burlingame investigators had taken Joan and Harry's blood samples and conducted tests to identify protein and enzyme marker systems, they should have continued what they began by conducting the same tests on the bloodstains in the van. The prosecution had insisted that there wasn't enough blood sample left to perform the electrophoresis.

"It is our position that if there was sufficient blood to do a Lattes test . . . then it was big enough to do an electrophoresis test," Brower told the judge. Brower said the defense's own expert would be prepared to testify that a Lattes test requires 50 milligrams of sample, while the electrophoresis test requires only five to ten milligrams.

"So, if they did the Lattes test twice, they would have had enough," Brower contended. If an electrophoresis test of the dried blood failed to match the parents' genetic profile, it would cast doubt on the possibility that Denise had been a victim in the van, he added.

The failure of the crime lab to perform a test that, obviously, should have been performed shatters the credibility of the criminalists' work, he said.

"It's our position that when he (Marriscolo) took the blood

and realized that if he did this electrophoresis test, it could exclude the alleged victim, they didn't go any further," Cohn argued. "And, I think we have the right to bring that out."

But Capaccioli was skeptical. Any discussion of the genetic makeup of Denise Redlick would be purely speculative. And, besides, the acceptability of electrophoresis was never even addressed during the day-long hearing on the admissibility of the bloodstains.

Cutting off any further debate on the subject, Capaccioli ruled that the defense could not bring up the crime lab's failure to complete the electrophoresis tests.

It was yet another frustrating blow for Craig Anderson's defense.

On the morning of Friday, May 23rd, the prosecution called its last witness, Tom Marriscolo. Inspector Marriscolo took the stand—for the third time—to explain how the Burlingame police had investigated Denise's disappearance and what steps they had taken to find Miss Redlick, dead or alive.

Holm idly touched his moustache and began, "Good morning, Inspector Marriscolo. Could you tell us who you work for again, please?"

"Burlingame Police Department," Marriscolo smiled faintly, the sides of his mouth uplifted.

"You were the chief investigator in the disappearance of Denise Redlick?"

"That's correct," Marriscolo was serious again.

"During the initial investigation of Denise Redlick's disappearance, were efforts made to contact all the local hospitals to see if Denise Redlick was . . . had gone there?"

"That is correct."

"Were you able to find out any information that she had gone there?"

"No, we did not."

"And were entries made into various computer systems for the purpose of trying to find Denise Redlick?"

"Yes, they were."

"Could you describe what was done in that regard, please?"

"Miss Redlick's name and date of birth were entered into the NCIC system, which is a system that goes nationwide in case you were to show up somewhere. Her driver's license was entered into the DMV file with a hold put on it in case somebody was using the driver's license or she would use the driver's license. The police officer was to check the driver's license."

"And was there ever occasion when the NCIC system . . . let me withdraw that. What is known as a hit in your terminology?"

"A hit is when you get a positive response back on an inquiry."

"So were any hits made on the NCIC system that goes nationwide?" Holm said, his voice rising.

"No, they were not," Marriscolo said definitely.

"Now, the NCIC system, does that refer . . ."

"National Crime Investigation Center"

"Was that system where a person's name, if they were stopped by a police officer, or made any inquiry of anyone, that information would be put in the NCIC system and then they—that name—might come up. Is that right?"

"We would come up with a hit. That's correct."

"And you didn't receive any hits from November 11th until today's date?"

"That's correct."

"What about the Department of Motor Vehicles Inquiry. Were any hits made on that?"

"There was a hit made on the DMV."

"Do you recall approximately when that was?"

"It was sometime either late December, early January, and it was an inquiry made by an insurance company regarding some insurance that the Defendant and Miss Redlick were going to take out."

"This was prior . . . insurance that was taken out prior to November 11th of 1985?"

"The insurance was never taken out, but the application for it was prior to that, that's correct."

"Were there any other hits on the Department of Motor Vehicles computer system?" Holm's voice hardened.

"No, there were not," Marriscolo replied with equal definitiveness.

As Holm continued, the finality of the knowledge that all traces of Denise had completely disappeared, and that she was never heard from after the November 11th date, became indisputably evident.

On cross-examination, Cohn grilled the inspector about tips that the police might not have thoroughly investigated that could have, in fact, led to finding Denise. Marriscolo said any calls—in response to the thousands of posters that were circulated in the state and elsewhere—were prioritized by importance and checked out in that order. "I've had calls in this case as late as last Sunday night," Marriscolo said, adding that he was in the process of investigating it.

"The lead that you got Sunday night," Cohn asked, turning his back on the witness and looking at the jury, "what was that lead?" Without realizing it, the defense attorney had committed the sin of asking a question for which he did not know the answer. Marriscolo maintained his professional demeanor as he replied, although anyone who knew the inspector knew that he was relishing the moment.

"That was a telephone call that I got from the chief of police where he had been informed by another city employee that the remains of Denise Redlick had been taken up to Mr. Anderson's paint store and that two friends of his (Craig's) brother, Mark, knew that that's where she was disposed of."

Cohn winced slightly, but quickly regained his composure.

"In the paint store?" Cohn asked.

"That's correct."

"You investigated the paint store, didn't you?"

"Not Mr. Anderson's paint store in the city, no, we did not."

Cohn went on with the subject, but Capaccioli, mercifully, interrupted, "Mr. Cohn, aren't we in an area now that is very peripheral?"

"Yes, Your Honor," Cohn conceded.

"And I'm wondering," Capaccioli continued, "what the relevance is at this point, not knowing what this witness is going to say to your questions. But you go ahead. There's no objections, Mr. Cohn."

To the relief of courtroom observers, who were cringing in disbelief, a few questions later Cohn changed the subject. Later, he would complain that Marriscolo's tip—revealed in dramatic fashion in the courtroom—was a set up. The tip hadn't been among the dozens presented to the defense as part of the routine trial "discovery" process which requires the prosecutor to turn over the fruits of its investigation, so that the defendant can adequately prepare his case. Furthermore, both the district attorney and the inspector knew that the tip was false, Cohn complained.

Marriscolo, who grinned like a Cheshire cat when he stepped off the stand, claimed he had only done his best to truthfully respond to cross-examination.

Wagstaffe, who silently observed the exchange between Marriscolo and Cohn from his seat in the gallery, later said that many police officers wouldn't have answered Cohn's open-ended question so specifically.

"I think Tom set him up," Holm agreed with Cohn's observation.

"And Cohn bit," Wagstaffe declared.

At the end of Marriscolo's testimony, Holm announced, "The State rests."

■ CHAPTER TWENTY-SIX ■

The Defense's Case

The big question being debated both in the media and the courtroom, before and during the trial, was, "Would Craig Anderson testify in his own behalf?"

Carl Holm was asked by a reporter, as he wound down his own case, if he expected to have an opportunity to cross-examine the defendant. "Ask Mr. Cohn," Holm responded with a smile.

But Cohn wasn't saying.

Technically, it didn't matter if the defendant took the stand. Capaccioli had instructed the jury that a defendant in a criminal case has a constitutional right to determine if he should testify and the jury should not draw any inference from the fact that he decides against it. The defendant may simply rely on the state of the evidence and, if the prosecutor fails to prove beyond a reasonable doubt every essential element of the charge, the defendant's lack of testimony can not be used as a factor in finding against him in any of those elements.

But anyone who had heard the evidence in the case of Denise Redlick would be left with inevitable questions that could, in fact, only be answered by Craig Anderson.

Why, for example, had he not told the police about his stop at the Seedlocks' home on Monday, November 11th, using Mrs. Seedlock as an alibi witness, if he wasn't doing anything illegal?

Why did he offer several inconsistent explanations for how he had acquired the scratches on his hands and neck?

Why didn't he offer the three receipts for sales transactions for November 11th to the police before the search warrant was served if, in fact, they were genuine?

And, why didn't he simply dig up the dead dog that he had buried to legitimize his story? Cohn told reporters that Craig couldn't do that because there was no dog. Frances and Kevin Seedlock had misunderstood or misinterpreted what Craig had told them. If that were so, why couldn't Craig face the jury and vindicate himself?

Brower would later contend that, from what he could see, Craig's defense wasn't carefully thought out.

According to Brower, on the day before the prosecution rested, Cohn turned to Brower and asked, "Do you think I ought to have Craig testify?" Brower responded, "Have you prepped him?" As Brower recalled it, Cohn responded, "Well, no."

Moments later, Cohn asked the judge if the trial proceedings could be delayed to give him all day on Friday to meet with his client and his investigator to go over the testimony of the scores of prosecution witnesses. Cohn claimed that it had been "quite a tedious procedure to see the defendant." But Capaccioli took offense at the suggestion that the defense attorney had difficulty seeing his client. According to officials, all Cohn ever had to do to meet with Craig before or after court was to knock on the door to the hallway where the holding cell was located.

"Have you ever knocked on the door?" the judge asked.

"I've tried the door and it's been locked."

"But you've knocked on the door and we've opened it."

"One time and that was this morning."

"When was the first time you knocked on the door and it was ignored?"

"I didn't knock on the door."

Capaccioli said the jury had been promised that it would be in session on Friday to compensate for the Memorial Day holiday the following Monday and speed the proceedings along. Furthermore, Holm had informed the court as early as last week that he would finish his case that day, the judge declared, "So your request is denied."

On the morning of Tuesday, May 27th, after the three-day trial recess, Judge Capaccioli announced the first defense witness.

"Let the record show that all the jurors are present in their places. Good morning, ladies and gentlemen . . . You may call your first witness, Mr. Cohn."

Cohn stood ready, "Mr. Brower is getting him. Thank you, Your Honor. Your Honor, due to the fact that Mr. Brower took the cross, I'm going to let Mr. Brower proceed with the whole blood situation."

As the witness took the stand, the clerk said, "State your name, please?"

The witness responded, "Paul V. Holland. H-o-l-l-a-n-d."

"Thank you. Be seated in the witness chair, sir," the clerk replied.

Capaccioli motioned to Cohn and Brower, "You may proceed."

Brower stepped forward, "It's Dr. Holland, isn't it?"

"That's correct," Holland replied in a curt, clipped tone.

"What is your current occupation?" Brower asked.

"I am the medical director, the chief executive officer of the Sacramento Medical Foundation Blood Center."

"Dr. Holland, have you ever testified before in a criminal matter?"

"Yes, once before."

"Have you ever testified in front of a jury in a criminal matter?"

"No, I have not."

"What I'm going to do is qualify you as an expert, and I'll be asking you background questions first."

"Fine."

As Brower made the witness' background clear, Holm looked troubled. Before Holland's present position, he had been chief of the blood bank department at the National Institute of Health, where he also taught graduate courses for twelve years and, along with his job at the Sacramento Blood Center, was a clinical professor in hematology at the University of California at Davis Medical Center. With Brower conducting the questioning, Holland also revealed he had passed examinations and been state board certified in internal medicine and the specialty of blood banking. He was the associate editor of *Transfusion,* the primary journal of his medical specialty.

Holland said that, although he was not involved in typing of dried blood in his day-to-day work, he had extensive experience in typing of fresh blood and was familiar with the similarities and differences.

When either side in a case offers a witness as an expert—as in this case—the other often chooses an opposition expert. Holland was being offered as an expert in typing of fresh blood samples and the three tests performed on the samples. He planned to testify that the ouchterlony double diffusion test and the absorption elution test on the stains from the van and the shoe—both determined by the San Mateo County criminalists to be Type A— were both set up incorrectly and that the results were, therefore, invalid. In addition, he said that the procedure used for typing the defendant's own blood sample—determined to be Type O—was also wrong.

Holm objected to Holland's qualifications as an expert. "In fact, throughout our experience, it's been all with fresh blood samples, isn't that correct?"

"That's correct," Holland said.

Holm insisted he could only accept Holland as an expert in whole blood testing. Capaccioli also appeared concerned about the witness' expertise in the area of evidence at hand. Holland had to concede that he had never participated in absorption elution or Lattes tests of dried blood.

After hearing all of these doubts, the jurors were sent into the hallway to await the outcome of a brief hearing during which the judge probed Holland's expertise further.

Holland was testy about his credentials being questioned, "Can I make a comment?" he inquired in a less than friendly tone.

"I'm trying to find out if you can give me an opinion," Capaccioli said, a trifle irritable.

Holland continued without waiting for Capaccioli to finish, "I think it's very relevant. The tests that the serologists are doing, the tests that the technologists at the blood bank are doing, the tests I used to do. . . . There are some combinations and permutations in-between. I have to treat it a different way whether you have to put the stain body on and take it back off. The bottom line is the same."

Capaccioli looked skeptical, "Techniques—as I understand it —I know blood begins to deteriorate the moment it leaves the body, and dry blood is different from fresh blood."

Holland was forceful, "That's why it's more important to run stringent controls, so you say that they are there."

Capaccioli was becoming irritated, "The question is, have you run enough of these—or participated in enough of these— yourself to give an opinion to this jury?" Turning to Brower, he almost pleaded, "Just tell me what he's going to testify to."

Brower used two Defendant's exhibits to explain, "He's going to testify that the ouchterlony double diffusion test that was run on the van and on the shoe was set up wrong. That is, the items are in the wrong place, and, as a result of their being in the wrong place, there is no answer . . . the absorption elution test on both the van and the shoe are invalid because the standard did not work. As to the fresh blood, he will testify that the typing of Mr. Anderson's fresh blood was wrong."

Capaccioli scratched his head, "Has the jury heard any testimony about Mr. Anderson's fresh blood?"

Brower persisted, "That it was typed O."

Capaccioli nodded, "I see what you mean."

Ultimately, Capaccioli decided that Holland could testify to interpret the procedures used in testing the blood stains. However, his demeanor won few points with the judge.

"Do you want me to show you how it should be done properly?" Holland asked the judge, referring to the absorption elution test.

"No, I want you to step down. You are a witness. You are not running the place yet."

When the jury returned to the courtroom, Holland would use marking pens to draw sketches of petri dishes representing the way that Benny Del Re set up the tests, using the criminalist's notes as a blueprint. One test at a time, he showed how, in his opinion, the results obtained by the San Mateo County Crime Lab should be discounted.

Holm began his cross-examination of Holland by asking him how much he was being paid to testify for the defense. Holland said his fee was $250 an hour, including the four hours spent consulting with the attorneys out of court.

The prosecutor also pointed out that Holland had made certain assumptions about Del Re's notes without ever talking to the criminalist who ran the tests.

But much of what Holland said during his two hours of testimony was so technical—so bogged down with the scientific minutia of antigens, antibodies and complex cell reactions—that the jurors appeared to be overwhelmed by the information.

Holland was followed to the stand by Raymond Morris, a commercial photographer who, at Cohn's request, had taken pictures at 10:00 a.m. that day of the area around the building at 1633 Old Bayshore where Denise was last seen. Morris described each of the eighteen photographs which he had printed in the nick of time. Some were taken from the building—looking out toward surrounding streets, while others showed the parking lot from various angles. The photos ostensibly showed that it would be difficult to carry out a kidnapping for the purpose of murder in such a bustling, highly visible, business setting.

Holm objected that the witness' photographs were irrelevant.

"This may sound like a stupid question, Mr. Morris, but were you at the area on November 11th, 1985?"

"No."

"And, did you know the subject of this controversy here took place on a holiday, Veteran's Day?"

"No," Morris acknowledged that, although Monday had been another holiday, Memorial Day, Cohn had specifically asked him to wait until Tuesday morning, a regular business day, to take the photographs.

And with that testimony—to the surprise of the entire courtroom—the defense rested. Craig Anderson, despite his claims that he had been unjustly accused and unfairly maligned by the media, did not take the stand in his own behalf.

Holm called one rebuttal witness, Benny Del Re, to once again explain certain fine points of the blood tests and to testify that there was no doubt in his mind that the blood on the tennis shoe was human—not dog, that it was definitely, in his opinion, Type A, and that Anderson's own blood was Type O.

Brower, by then, had departed, not knowing that the criminalist would be called again. That left Cohn to tread into technical territory in which he was not well-versed. He did the only thing he could—try to make Benny look foolish.

"Isn't it true that you had to do a brand new test in May to make up for the phony test you did before?" Cohn asked him, referring to the weekend test the crime lab was forced to perform.

Capaccioli interrupted before Holm could, calling the question improper. "You should cross-examine, not argue with, the witness," he said.

Cohn tried again.

"You did a test a week ago, is that correct?"

"Yes, I did," the witness said.

"By that test, were you trying to cover up for the other two tests?"

"Objection . . ." Holm began.

"Argumentative! Sustained!" Capaccioli cut him off. Cohn, with a lofty air, snapped, "No further questions," and returned to his chair.

Cohn discussed afterward how he felt—with the evidence the prosecution had presented—his client was "sure to get an acquittal." Putting Craig on the stand, he contended, was a no-win situation. It would have become a contest between Craig and the witnesses who said Craig had tried to get them to offer his alibis.

Then, Cohn discussed, there was the matter of the former girlfriends, four of whom were on the list of potential witnesses and were, apparently, available to testify. Cohn believed that he could have kept their testimony about Craig's earlier alleged acts of violence out of the courtroom ("The law says that I should have been able") but he had no way to know for sure what would happen if Craig had been subjected to cross-examination.

Cohn was also afraid that Craig might be asked something about his past relationships with women that he didn't want his parents to know, or something about Denise that might make her look bad if he answered those questions truthfully. That meant Craig might be put in the position of being tempted to lie "about something that had absolutely nothing to do with the case."

"It was a calculated risk," he admitted of his decision to keep Craig from testifying. "I went over it thoroughly with Craig, from all sides. It's a hell of a lot of stress on a person charged with murder to put him on the stand. He had been in jail all this time and he was angry. By the time an experienced lawyer got through with him on cross-examination, he was bound to look bad."

Holm and Wagstaffe were disappointed. They had looked forward to interrogating the Defendant during what, they anticipated, would have been many hours of cross-examination. Once he denied kidnapping and killing Denise Redlick, the prosecution would have been free to probe, in depth, his activities on the day of Denise's disappearance.

"A glib defendant can walk himself out the door," Wagstaffe said. "That's exactly what happened in the case of a San Mateo teenager, accused of killing his parents, in 1983." During the first trial, the Defendant was "a smart ass" on the witness stand. Fortunately for him, the jury was hung. But, on his retrial, the Defendant was transformed into a perfect gentleman, carefully answering each question with a "No, sir," and "Yes, sir." "That the second jury acquitted him was not a coincidence," Wagstaffe said.

Wagstaffe didn't believe, from what he had seen, that Craig Anderson was bright enough to handle the pressure. "He clearly wasn't someone who had put together a brilliant plan for murder," the assistant district attorney declared. "He and his attorney both knew he would flub it."

At any rate, Cohn gambled that the circumstantial nature of the case—combined with the points he planned to make in his closing argument—would prevent Craig Anderson from spending the rest of his life in prison.

■ CHAPTER TWENTY-SEVEN ■

Verdict

Superior Court Judge Walter Capaccioli was more tolerant than many judges when it came to accommodating spectators and reporters in his windowless courtroom on the eighth floor of the Hall of Justice.

But, as he looked down at the overflow crowd that had gathered to hear closing arguments in Craig Anderson's murder trial at 10:00 a.m. on Wednesday, May 28th, he was concerned.

"I notice some people standing in the back," Capaccioli observed. "I prefer to have everyone seated. It's distracting during arguments to have people standing along the walls."

"May I sit on the floor?" came a female voice from one side of the courtroom.

"No, I don't think that's appropriate," the judge insisted. "We'll get you another chair. There are limits to everything in this world and I think we've reached the limit here."

When chairs had been found for everyone and the jurors were in their places, the courtroom business finally began. But the spectators weren't to hear the attorneys' arguments just yet. First, Nathan Cohn read excerpts (approved in chambers by the judge earlier that morning) from Joan Redlick's testimony, contrasting them with excerpts from the phone conversations she had taped with the defendant before his arrest. Cohn felt that the tapes cast a shadow over Mrs. Redlick's entire testimony, showing that she had been less than truthful in cross-examination.

Cohn read the court testimony in which Joan denied that

Craig told her he was staying away from the Redlick household because the Burlingame police had told him that Joan and Harry believed he was involved in Denise's disappearance.

Then, he read from the transcript of Joan's telephone conversation with Craig on December 7th, in which Craig told her that everything Inspector Marriscolo had said to him had been negative. According to Craig, the inspector "put his face right in my face and said, 'You better believe that her parents have made a decision that you had something to do with their daughter disappearing.'"

Next, the defense attorney read from Joan's testimony denying that Craig ever claimed that he and Denise were still "best of friends," even after they broke up.

But, on November 20th, Cohn pointed out, Craig had told her over the phone, "You know, Joan, whether or not Denise and I would have been together again, we were still best friends. Your best friend doesn't just disappear and you don't hurt. Denise was my best friend, you know, for a long time."

Finally, Cohn read Joan's testimony where she denied that Denise was planning to surprise Craig, before their break up, with an especially pretty picture of the two of them taken at a friend's wedding.

Cohn pointed out that in the November 20th phone conversation, Craig and Joan talked about that very photograph. Craig confided that when he and Denise first split up, he was in shock and had taken his pictures of Denise off his mantel. But, in what seemed to be an expression of his love for Denise, he confided that he would save his pictures of Denise forever.

"I don't care who, or when, or how, or why, if I ever get involved with anyone in the future, I'm never going to let anyone take those away from me," Craig had said.

Cohn hoped the brief excerpts from the transcripts provided the jurors with a glimpse of Craig Anderson as an emotional, caring, warm human being. Without Craig's testimony, the jurors knew him only as the quiet, passive, unexpressive murder suspect who sat in court everyday in the same blue-gray suit with his eyes mostly fixed on the floor.

"Those are the points, Your Honor," Cohn said, "We'll rest, Your Honor."

Judge Capaccioli looked searingly at the jury, "Ladies and gentlemen, at this time, I'm going to—in a moment—invite the People to make their closing argument followed by the argument or summation of the defense.

"Closing argument—as I indicated yesterday—is a summation where each side is given an opportunity to evaluate and discuss the evidence that has been introduced to assist you in arriving at you verdict.

"With that, I'll invite Mr. Holm to make his opening argument."

Holm, who had devoted an extraordinary number of hours to this case and felt closer to the victim's family than in any other case he had ever tried, knew that his remarks that morning were as important as any evidence he had presented over the last three weeks. As he moved toward the podium, he began an emotional, heartfelt plea.

"Ladies and gentlemen, we are here today—and we have been here for the last few weeks—because that man right there," Holm went on, whipping around to point a menacing finger at the accused, "Craig Anderson, could not take no for an answer. He could not accept the fact that Denise Redlick was no longer interested in him, that she didn't want to have anything else to do with him.

"Denise Redlick, a woman, a beautiful woman, you've learned about who her parents are, will never see her again. Her mother, her best friend, will never hear Denise's laughter, her laugh that she remembers so vividly and will always remember until her dying day.

"Her father, Harry Redlick—excuse me—will never again be able to collect those Hummels with his daughter, Denise. They will not be able to share those memories of their trip to Europe that they took together in November of 1984. They will never see the smiling face of Denise Redlick again, nor will her friends because we've shown, unfortunately, that Denise Redlick is dead at the very hands of that man right there.

"As I told you, in this case you would come to know her, but never see her in person. She was loved by everyone who came in contact with her. She was a woman that all of the witnesses would describe as warm, loving, vivacious, upbeat, happy, interested in the welfare of others, close to her family, had a remarkable relationship with her brother, her nephew, Matthew."

As Holm went on to remind the jurors of the terms in which witnesses had described Denise, he paused, cleared his throat, and appeared to shed a few tears. He later denied that the tears were generated for courtroom effect.

"She was a person who enjoyed life," Holm continued, "A person who was dependable, who always told her parents if she would be late, who always indicated if she was going some place else."

As he spoke of Denise, a number of spectators—obviously moved by the prosecutor's remarks—were seen dabbing tissues and handkerchiefs at their eyes.

Holm continued, "Back on November 11th, 1985, she thought she had eliminated the one thing that the evidence has shown was dragging her down and suffocating her. That man, again, the Defendant. But, unfortunately, the evidence has shown that it was the Defendant who eliminated her."

Then Holm turned to the circumstantial facts of the case, knowing that emotion alone would not bring in a guilty verdict. Calling attention to Craig's shattered alibis for where he had been on November 11th, 1985, Holm called the defendant's behavior "indicative of his consciousness of guilt." When a defendant gives a false statement—as he did when he told the Burlingame police that Fred Brooks and others could vouch for him—it can be considered in determining guilt.

The evidence of Denise's death, Holm argued, includes the lack of activity on her credit cards, bank accounts and automatic teller card after she vanished, the many personal possessions left in her room at home, and the 70,000 posters distributed as far away as Australia that failed to turn up any trace of Denise Redlick.

"The evidence clearly shows that Denise is dead and that man, the Defendant, is the one who did it," Holm said, gesturing at Craig for the third time.

Holm called attention to Craig's derogatory comments about Denise, like calling her "a spoiled little bitch" and a "heartless bitch" and callously telling a friend, "I split with that chick," well after Denise's disappearance had been publicized. He recalled the wedding where Craig slapped Denise for dancing with another man and how he "didn't lift a finger" to help her many friends, including several of her former boyfriends, search for her.

"He claims, through Mrs. Redlick, that he loved Denise. That's balderdash. There's no evidence of any affection for her. All he could care about is himself and the boys that she was dancing with and showing some interest in. He was a possessive, extremely jealous individual who was not about to let anybody else have her," Holm claimed.

Holm then turned to the testimony of the Seedlocks at whose home Craig suddenly appeared on Veteran's Day to wash the inside of the rental van. He pointed out that it's odd for anyone to spend half an hour scrubbing the inside of a rental vehicle unless he is "trying to cover something up. "And what was that something? Blood." As for the van, it was rented to catch Denise off guard since she had made it clear to Craig a few days before that she wanted nothing else to do with him.

Craig, Holm contended, could easily have cleaned out the van at his own home, just six blocks away from the Budget rental agency. "Why is he doing it at the Seedlocks'? Because he doesn't want anybody to notice him."

Holm drew a chilling scenario for the jury: Denise opened the door of her father's sports car as the Defendant sneaked up behind her, snatched her and pushed her inside the unfamiliar vehicle. He tried one last time to convince her to stay with him and, when she refused, he killed her. "If he couldn't have her, no one could," Holm insisted. The scratches that witnesses recalled seeing on Craig's hands and neck were inflicted on him by Denise in her struggle to survive.

Benny Del Re, the county criminalist, testified that, although he was able to obtain enough of a sample to test only three of the spots in the van, many other spots had a positive reaction to the presumptive test for blood. It was as if someone sprayed water on one large bloodstain and it splashed up on the walls of the vehicle. One of the spots that the criminalists could test, resulting in its identification as human, Type A—the same as Denise's blood type—was on the passenger's—not the driver's—seat.

As Holm moved to the final moments of his argument, he paused and moved closer to the jury.

"Ladies and gentlemen, I'd like to focus a brief moment on Denise Redlick. Sometimes we lose sight of why we're here in these cases. A delightful human being was robbed of her life by the Defendant. I want you to reflect for a minute on the enormity of what that means. I'm not asking you for your sympathy for Denise because, in a court of law, sympathy has no place. I'm not asking you for your passion for Denise, either, because you don't make decisions in a court of law based on passion.

"John Dryden, an English poet, once wrote, 'Murder may pass unpunished for a time, but tardy justice will overtake the crime.' All I'm asking for is justice. And justice in this case calls for a murder conviction.

"You all agreed that you could look the Defendant in the eye and tell him that your verdict was 'guilty' if the facts were so. You also agreed that you would be able to find someone guilty of murder even though no body was found, as long as the facts were there.

"Well, the facts are here for you to do just that, and I stand before you without any reservation or any hesitation on my part."

Holm paused, and then continued, his face grimly set, his voice like steel, "I ask that you convict the Defendant of murder."

The courtroom was hushed as Judge Capaccioli announced a ten-minute recess.

When court reconvened, Capaccioli announced, "Mr. Cohn, you may proceed."

Nate Cohn stepped forward.

He knew how important his closing argument in this case would be. After presenting only two witnesses—the blood expert and the photographer—and scoring a doubtful number of points on cross-examination, it was up to the defense attorney to eloquently and cleverly convince the jurors of his client's innocence.

Cohn looked every inch the veteran, criminal defense attorney in his charcoal gray, three-piece suit with his pocket watch chain dangling from his vest. He walked confidently to the podium, removed his glasses to make better eye contact with individual jurors and proceeded.

"Your Honor, Counsel, ladies and gentlemen of the jury, now comes time for the . . . for me to basically argue the case. We call it arguing; it's really a summarization of what we believe the evidence has shown. What we lawyers say here at the podium is not evidence. If, somewhere along the line, Counsel or I tell you something about the evidence that you don't recollect, you go by your own recollection. I'm sure I'm not going to do it intentionally, and I don't think Mr. Holm is going to do it intentionally.

"You have a job to do. You are now basically all judges, and you have a very serious job to do. You've been called to serve on a jury of probably the most serious charge that can be made against any person. That's murder in the first degree.

"You all promised at the beginning of the matter when you were interrogated in *voir dire,* you promised that you were going to follow the law of the Court, and you were not going to let prejudice or passion, or sympathy, or anything like that influence you, that you'd call it as you saw it, and also that you wouldn't do anything other than bring in a verdict of not guilty unless the prosecution proved all the material elements of their crime . . . of the crime . . . beyond a reasonable doubt and to a moral certainty.

"This is a unique and different case. I've been practicing for thirty-nine years, and I have never seen one like it. I don't suppose Mr. Holm has ever seen one quite like it. You've got a charge of murder. Nobody knows where the alleged victim is. Nobody has proved that the alleged victim is dead. Nobody has proved what happened to the alleged victim.

"Now, in a case like this, the Judge will instruct you that our first job will be to determine one basic . . . two basic issues. Now, that's the first thing you have to do, you have to, before you can go any further about everybody thinking about what Mr. Anderson may have done or may not have done, before you even go into Mr. Anderson's alleged statement to Mrs. Seedlock, before you go into the alleged statement of these other people . . . The

302

Judge will instruct you that the prosecution must prove what is known as a *corpus delecti* before you can even consider any admissions or any other evidence."

Cohn, elaborating on his theme of a non-existent victim, said that while circumstantial evidence can be used to prove murder, it must be evidence that can be interpreted in only one way. But, in this case, the possible interpretations were numerous, he contended.

"Now, there's no evidence in this case that Denise Redlick is dead. There's no evidence in this case that Denise Redlick was killed."

Then, Cohn offered his explanation for why he had chosen not to present witnesses in rebuttal to the prosecution's seemingly thorough case.

"I had quite a decision to make whether or not to proceed to put on a case in rebuttal of the prosecutor's case, or to rest, and I figured that there was no case, and it's like trying to prove something that never existed. You are trying to prove that it never existed, and we don't have to do that. We do not. We are not here to do that. They have to prove every material allegation . . . that Denise Redlick is dead, not missing, not kidnapped, not runaway, not suicide, not anything. They have to prove she is dead beyond a reasonable doubt."

Again, Cohn reiterated this.

"There's no evidence in this case that Denise Redlick is dead . . . She's missing, that's true. Now, it can be interpreted two ways. She could have been kidnapped by some people. It's been done. It's been known. Thousands of people are missing every week, every month. That doesn't mean they are dead. That's not proof beyond a reasonable doubt that they are dead."

Later, at least one juror would call this position taken by the defense as one of arrogance.

"There's absolutely no proof in this case that Denise Redlick is dead.

"This is not a murder mystery and you aren't watching a television show," Cohn declared. "This is real life. You've got this young man's life, his whole future, in your hands. You've got to be sure beyond all reasonable doubt and to a moral certainty before you do anything except find him not guilty."

Cohn attempted to convince the jury that the prosecution—despite the vast number of witnesses—had really presented very little of substance. A large number of the witnesses, he pointed out, were in court only to testify that they did not bleed in the van. "Then, the prosecutor spent a half day explaining why technicians were scientifically unable to find fingerprints in the vehicle," he added.

"Now, don't be taken in by this," Cohn said forcefully. "I'm not trying to play games with you. I can actually show you that the district attorney has provided me with more evidence in our favor than you may realize, and that will clear up a lot of things in everybody's minds."

Cohn attacked the value of the bloodstains. The lab technician, he said, was able to extract only four, one-eighth inch drops "of what he claims is blood" from the van. But no one knows where those drops came from, how long they had been there, or even if they all came from the same person. Those spots that couldn't be subjugated to any more than a presumptive test, could have come from any number of sources, including various vegetables that cause the same chemical reaction.

Even if the blood is Type A, so are forty percent of the people in the United States. That means that—among the jurors—approximately five people might have Type A blood, he insisted.

In fact, Benny Del Re had to retest some of the samples in the middle of the trial because the original tests "were no good."

Cohn began to explain "why I called in Mr. Brower, the first time I've ever had another lawyer help me on a case," but Holm immediately interrupted.

"This is objectionable," the prosecutor insisted. Judge Capaccioli agreed. "It's immaterial why you called Brower," the judge chided Cohn.

"All right, I'll let the jury decide why I called him," Cohn, undaunted by the disruption, responded. Instead, he went on to give specific examples of how the evidence presented by the prosecution could lend itself to various interpretations, not all of them pointing to a verdict of murder. Cohn noted that Denise's car was unlocked, although friends and relatives testified that she always—absolutely always—locked her car doors.

"Now, I don't know about you, but I don't know anybody who never ever does one thing all the time," Cohn said. "Anybody can make a mistake. Anybody can forget. There's no reason to say she's dead because she didn't lock her car."

When Inspector Marriscolo admitted that there had been some tips about Denise Redlick that weren't completely pursued, "their case went down the drain," he asserted. "That one issue wiped them out." Many, many people disappear and some of them are found because an anonymous tip is pursued, he argued.

Cohn noted that, in the neighboring courtroom just a few months earlier, a man was put on trial for hiding, for seven years, a woman he had kidnapped and used as his sex slave. "Suppose someone else—perhaps the woman's boyfriend—had been charged with her murder," Cohn said. "It would be a terrible thing to do to an innocent person."

Cohn suggested that the witnesses who remembered Craig calling Denise a bitch didn't prove a thing. "If you put everyone in jail for murder who said his girlfriend or wife was a spoiled bitch, you wouldn't have room anywhere to walk in the jails. That's ridiculous."

Cohn went on to claim that there was no way that Craig could have known that Denise was going to be visiting her cousin, Lori, at the travel agency around noontime on November 11th. And, there was no way that Craig could have waited in the Budget van for more than an hour for Denise to come out of the agency and not be noticed by anyone who was in or around the building that day, Cohn declared.

"If you are going to premeditate something, are you going to go get a van with 'Budget' written all over the sides? You mean to tell me, with people walking back and forth all morning, no one saw anything? That's just not possible with that particular van," Cohn insisted.

On top of that, testimony revealed that Craig used his own name and address when he rented the vehicle, Cohn added, which would not have been a particularly brilliant maneuver for someone planning to carry out a murder.

"Anybody in the world with an ounce of intelligence, or even without an ounce of intelligence," planning to kidnap and kill Denise Redlick would have planned to do it differently, he said.

"Mrs. Seedlock," Cohn cleverly announced, was "our best witness." The woman said that she hadn't seen any scratches on Craig, unlike other witnesses who saw the suspicious scratches a day or more later.

"What that proves is that when he went home that night and was working on his bathroom and working on the outside of the house, he got the scratches," Cohn claimed. "Can you say beyond a reasonable doubt that he had scratches on him at that time? You can't do it."

Cohn discussed how Kevin Seedlock said nothing about Craig telling him about a dog until February—nearly two months after the original interview with the police. Then, he only did so to "build up his mother's story. That's all bull." According to Cohn, Kevin Seedlock also destroyed his own credibility when he said Craig told him to "get rid of the shovel and the tennis shoes," only to tell the police later that the shovel actually belonged to Walter Seedlock, his father.

And, then there was the testimony about Craig slapping Denise, a fact that Craig himself never denied nor lied about, Cohn argued.

"Look, I don't believe a man should strike a lady. I never had and never would. But it happens, and maybe some of it is because of the fact that we're getting more equal, even though I don't like some parts of it. Young men don't look at women the way I looked at women when I was a kid. They look at them as just another person. They get teed off, they have a thing. A woman will strike him and he'll think nothing of striking back.

"Some young fellow strikes his girlfriend . . . fiancee . . . and they break up. Does that mean he's going to kill her? That's absurd."

Cohn then attempted an unusual tactic for a closing argument. He recalled several people testifying that Craig, after November 11th, had a bruise on his nose, implying that he suffered the injury in a struggle with Denise. But the defense attorney contended Craig had a mark on his nose all the time.

306

Cohn asked his client to stand up in front of the jury "so you can see he has a blue spot on his nose right now."

"Any objection, Mr. Holm?" Capaccioli asked the prosecutor.

"It's totally irrelevant," Holm responded.

"I agree," the judge said.

"Evidence of a blue bruise?" Cohn said, seemingly surprised that he was being denied the chance to parade his client before the jury.

"You should have done it during the trial, Mr. Cohn," the judge responded. Then, thinking he had heard Cohn mutter something under his breath, Capaccioli reprimanded him. "Keep your personal comments to yourself," he sternly told the defense attorney, who sheepishly dropped the issue.

In wrapping up his ninety minute closing argument, Cohn asked the jury not to hold anything he or Mr. Brower ("He's not the most warm human being in the world, but he's a good lawyer") did during the trial against the Defendant. Looking directly at the eight women and five men who would decide Craig Anderson's fate, Cohn eloquently pleaded, "You have quite a very serious obligation. I, personally, under the evidence in this case, there's no way . . . there's no way that a jury should bring in a verdict other than not guilty.

"There's no evidence of anyone being dead. There's no evidence of anyone being killed. There's no *corpus* in this case.

"Hundreds of cases you read about all the time in the newspaper: little boy found in Ukiah, seven, eight years after he disappeared in Bakersfield . . . little girl over in Oakland disappeared from a shopping center, found in the back of a van in San Francisco with two nuts . . . girls found all the time. As I said, the girl tried next door disappeared for seven years. She was a love object for some nut that picked her up and put her in a car. He's in jail. He and his wife kept her captive.

"There's been no proof in this case that Denise is dead. A couple of drops of Type A blood, which is forty percent of the population, doesn't prove anything.

"When this case is over, whatever your verdict, the District Attorney can rationalize it and say, 'all I did was present the evidence. The jury is the one that found him.' The judge can say,

'Well, I told everybody the law, and I kept everything legitimate, and kept a case going right, and I didn't allow anybody to do anything wrong, and only the evidence that was admissible was admitted. The jury is the one that was responsible.'

"Remember one thing, you've got a very, very important thing to do. You've got to . . . you are the ones, the buck stops at your responsibility. You cannot find this young man guilty on this evidence. You can do it conscientiously.

"There's no evidence here that you can do this on.

"Thank you very much. I ask you to bring in a verdict of not guilty on all counts."

Now, Holm had his last opportunity to tie up any loose ends of a very difficult case. Although he had made his most important points earlier, this was his only chance to reverse any damage Cohn had done to the prosecutor's case in his closing argument.

"Ladies and gentlemen, I'm not going to belabor the points that have been argued already, and I'm not going to rehash all the testimony in this case in order for you to be refreshed on it, because you were all paying attention to that testimony, I believe, and if there's any doubt about your recollection as to the testimony of any other witnesses that you heard, while the Court Reporter doesn't like it, that's why she has these notes for you to be read back."

His words brought a faint smile to many of the jurors' lips.

Holm pointed out a number of what he felt were contradictions between prosecution witnesses' testimony and Cohn's interpretations of what those witnesses had said. It was interesting to note, he said, that the defendant, according to witness Rossana Hanak, had been calling Denise at work several times a day up until the very day of her disappearance. Then, he made not one single call to her at the bank.

"Doesn't that suggest to you that the defendant knew full well where Denise was and that he was responsible for her absence?"

The defense attorney, the prosecutor declared, was trying to make it seem that there had been "a grand conspiracy" to frame Anderson for murder. But Holm insisted that the only "reasonable interpretation" for the circumstantial evidence—the scratches, the bogus alibis, his strange behavior at the Seedlocks' house, his calling Denise a 'bitch,' his paying Fred Brook $500—is the guilt of the Defendant.

Holm reminded the jury that Cohn made a lot of promises in his opening statement concerning things he was going to prove— like that the defendant rented the van to take debris to the dumps —but never did.

And, the prosecutor made certain that he placed some doubt in the minds of the jurors about the credibility of the only significant witness—and only issue—generated by the defense. Dr. Holland, "the hired gun in this case," admitted he had "zero" experience in testing dried bloodstains. He was "vague and ambiguous" about how the test was run, because he really didn't know how to run it, according to Holm.

"All he knows about is how you deal with real blood, whole blood, fresh blood. We don't have that in crimes. You have dried blood, and Mr. Del Re, with his experience, knew a lot more about it than anyone else, and you look at those documents and you will see the reactions that took place, that it was human blood, not dog, and it was Type A." The criminalist said he didn't need a control from the van because he didn't see any contamination. The bloodstain he flicked off the ceiling was not tainted by the metal roof. The Lattes test, he said, was a double-check because there is no bacteria—and consequently no contamination— involved when checking for antibodies.

"Mr. Cohn says that we're building a stack of cards to do this dastardly deed. The only dastardly deed that took place in this courtroom is the fact that the defendant killed Denise Redlick, not anything else."

Holm brought his argument to a close.

"Ladies and gentlemen, you look at all the evidence. You don't look at it in a vacuum. You don't take one piece and analyze that all by itself, and then disregard it, or what have you, and then look at another piece and disregard it. It's a mosaic. It's like a puzzle. You put all the pieces together. You look at it as a whole. You use your common sense, and when you do that, you will understand that actions speak louder than words.

"The defendant professed his love for Denise as I mentioned before. He was interested in her, he says. He felt sorry for her, the family, wished that he was still a member of the family.

"What efforts did he undertake to do something to try to find her? Where's the explanation from Mr. Cohn for that? None. And his lack of actions speaks, as I say, louder than words, because when you combine that with all the other evidence, it's clear in this case that the Defendant is guilty of first degree murder of Denise Redlick.

"He's guilty of kidnapping Denise Redlick, and guilty of the special circumstance.

"At the end of this case, you will be given various verdict forms. There will be two verdict forms for murder in the first-degree. Two verdict forms for murder in the second-degree. Two verdict forms for voluntary manslaughter. As I said, His Honor, under the law, is required to give those instructions. But there's no heat of passion. There's no evidence whatsoever of anything involving voluntary manslaughter.

"Listen carefully for what it requires. You will be given two verdict forms on a special circumstance as to whether the killing was committed during the commission of a kidnapping, and you will be given two verdict forms for kidnapping. One will say guilty and one will say not guilty. The one dealing with the special circumstance will say true and not true.

"You will be told that the first thing you do is you look at it and evaluate the evidence regarding first-degree murder. You have to decide was there an unlawful killing of a human being. That's obvious. The evidence shows that conclusively. Was there malice aforethought? Yes, there was. What does it require? It only requires intentional killing. It does not require ill will or hatred. Although it's certainly evident in this case, but it doesn't require for second degree, or first, you must find deliberation and premeditation.

"Where is that in this case? Getting that van, hiding himself. Mr. Cohn says how did he know she was going to be at Lori Voyeyer's in the morning or around noontime on Monday? We know how. You can infer the fact is he used that van to follow her, to stalk her.

"Why is there ninety five miles on that van? Look at the documents in the records of Craig Anderson's rental—ninety five miles is how far that van was driven. You have that here.

"If you decide for whatever reason that there isn't a first-degree murder, then you decide, if you are unanimous, then you sign the non guilty verdict.

"If you find it to be true, you all sign it here, and you forget the rest of the instructions dealing with count one, or the murder.

"If, however, you decide that there's insufficient evidence of that, then you go to the instructions, or the form for second-degree murder, and you decide that.

"If you conclude that that's not here, then you go to voluntary manslaughter. If you conclude that there's no evidence or not proof beyond a reasonable doubt of any count, or that the defendant is not involved, then you sign the verdict form not guilty.

"But that's not what's going to happen in this case, because you were sworn to follow the law. You all agreed that you would take it as your duty to evaluate this evidence and talk among yourselves and discuss it and use your common sense and, if you do that, you will find that we have proven beyond a reasonable doubt and to a moral certainty that the defendant is guilty of the murder of Denise Redlick, guilty of kidnapping Denise Redlick and responsible for the killing of Denise Redlick during the commission of a kidnapping.

"Thank you very much."

In every criminal trial, what goes on outside the presence of the jury is often as intriguing, as dramatic, and as important as anything that the jurors see. Special hearings in the courtroom—like the day-long session on the motion to eliminate the dried bloodstains evidence—and discussions in the judge's chambers may be part of the official trial record and may determine precisely what occurs in the jury's presence. They may also be critical factors in subsequent appeals. Jurors often wonder why they are told to show up at a certain time and then wait outside the courtroom doors until they are called into court by the bailiff, often hours later. The plight of the juror is a frustrating one.

In the Redlick case, the subject matter of one of those privately discussed issues—sometimes in the courtroom, but more often in chambers—was the attentiveness of one of the jurors.

The potential problem surfaced during the first week of the trial. At Cohn's request, Capaccioli had called one juror into his chambers and, in the presence of both attorneys, received her assurance that she was paying attention to the evidence. Then, on Friday, May 23rd, Cohn claimed—based on the observations of Shirley Anderson—that the juror again appeared to be falling asleep. Mrs. Anderson had taken minute-by-minute notes that morning, indicating when the juror had closed her eyes, when her head had dropped, and when she actually seemed to doze. The judge said he would watch the juror more carefully after the weekend recess and, if Mrs. Anderson's observations were correct, "I would have no hesitancy to substitute her."

Now, the day before the jury would begin its deliberations, Cohn was raising the question again. During a break in Cohn's closing argument, the juror was again called into chambers, where the judge asked her if she felt she had missed any of the evidence. "I don't think so," the embarrassed juror responded.

"Do you have any doubts at all in your mind as to the fact that you were or were not able to hear everything that went on or see everything that went on?" Capaccioli asked her.

"No, I don't have any doubt," she responded and was subsequently sent back to join the other jurors—unaware of the dilemma—waiting in the hallway.

But, after she left, Cohn said Mrs. Anderson had taken more notes about her apparent drowsiness and the judge agreed "she was fighting it all morning." Holm stayed out of it, saying he hadn't been watching the woman at all.

"We really don't need the lady because we have an alternate," Cohn declared. "I hate like heck to have her deliberate. It's like having eleven jurors. She's liable to go in there and not know what the heck anybody is saying."

Capaccioli decided to have all the parties—Cohn and the Defendant, and Holm—think about the matter during lunch and return to his office at 1:20 p.m. to work out a solution.

But when Anderson joined the attorneys and the judge in

chambers after lunch, the defense had decided to keep Juror No. 1.

"So you're withdrawing your request to have her discharged?" Capaccioli pointedly asked.

Craig, without hesitation, said, "Yes," he was.

Capaccioli thought he had heard the last of the debate over the sleepy juror.

Judge Capaccioli began reading the tedious, but necessary, jury instructions—hammered out earlier in the week in conferences with the attorneys—at 9:45 a.m. Thursday. Many of the jurors took notes as the judge went through the lengthy, technical explanations of the charges and the legal issues surrounding them.

The jurors learned that to find the defendant guilty of murder, they must agree that Denise Redlick was killed with malice aforethought, meaning that the defendant manifested an intention to kill her. That, the judge explained, does not require a lengthy period of deliberation or an ill will or hatred of the person killed.

But, if the killing was preceded and accompanied by a clear, deliberate intent on the part of Craig Anderson to kill which was the result of deliberation and premeditation—that it did not occur in the sudden heat of passion, for example—then it is murder in the first-degree.

Should they decide that the killing occurred with malice aforethought, but that the evidence is insufficient to establish deliberation and premeditation, then it would be murder in the second-degree.

And, Capaccioli said forcefully, "If you are convinced beyond a reasonable doubt that the defendant murdered Denise Redlick, but have a reasonable doubt whether it was first or second-degree, you must give the defendant the benefit of the doubt and return a verdict in the form of latter.

"Furthermore, the jury is charged with the task of determining if the murder was committed while the defendant was engaged in a kidnapping," although the jury would not be informed that the special circumstance could make the difference between

313

a sentence with the possibility of a parole and without the possibility of a parole.

The required elements of kidnapping, Capaccioli said, are that the victim was unlawfully moved by the use of physical force, compelled by another person to move because of a reasonable apprehension of harm, moved against her will and without consent, and that such movement was for a substantial distance.

Finally, at 11:10 a.m., he was finished and the jurors were instructed to follow bailiff Peter Kutch to a room in the interior hallway behind the courtroom, adjacent to the judge's chambers, where they would begin their deliberations.

At the same time, Cohn, Holm and Defendant Anderson again joined the judge in his chambers at Cohn's request to discuss the problem of the one juror's attentiveness.

"This morning, she had her eyes closed during some of the instructions and I went out to make sure that I wasn't the only one," Cohn declared. "Craig's mother and his sister saw the same thing. I talked to three ladies out there—just spectators who aren't part of Craig's family—and they noticed the same thing.

"Instructions are the most important part of the case and, at this time, I'm asking that she be relieved and that the alternate be placed," Cohn said.

Capaccioli was annoyed by this last-minute demand.

"Mr. Cohn, I brought her in here yesterday because of your concerns. I've talked to the woman on two other occasions in the past," the judge said. "When your client decided to withdraw his request, that solved the problem." Then the judge looked squarely at Anderson, who had been silent. "What's your position, young man?"

"I would agree with Mr. Cohn if he thinks that's in my best interests," Craig said.

Capaccioli pondered the delicate situation for several moments. "I haven't seen any signs that the juror had been dozing through the instructions. If she didn't get the instructions, they know they can be reread at any time, as many times as they wish them reread. So, at this time, I'm going to deny your request."

With that statement, Capaccioli ended all arguments.

Joan and Harry Redlick remained at the courthouse, fearful that they might miss the verdict if they returned to San Bruno. They had lunch with Holm and Wagstaffe and then went back to the district attorney's office, prepared, if necessary, for a long wait.

The two prosecutors had talked, as the trial unfolded, about how they would feel, and what would happen, if they lost the case. "What will it do to Joan and Harry," they had wondered?

"We'd never had a case where we had gotten so close to the victim's family," Wagstaffe later said. While, in some ways, that was a benefit to the district attorney's office in preparing the case, it also "placed incredible pressure on Carl," he added.

By noon, the jury had elected its foreman—Juror No. 8, Daniel Apfelbaum, a marketing and sales manager for a telecommunications company. Word came to the attorneys that the jurors had ordered sandwiches delivered to their room so they could continue working through lunch. At 1:30 p.m., the jury dispatched a note to Capaccioli indicating that they had a question. The foreman had written, *"Need instructions on Penal Code Section 190.2 (kidnapping with intent to commit murder). A better definition is needed to determine this special circumstance to be true or not true."* Then, at the bottom, the foreman wrote, *"P.S. Also need a better definition of Penal Code Section 207 (kidnapping)."*

Capaccioli met with Cohn and Holm. The note did not bode well for the defendant. It seemed that the jury might have already decided on the more significant charge—murder. If the murder change had been rejected, it would be unlikely that the jury would need more information concerning the special circumstance attached to it.

Cohn voiced his objection to reading the instructions on the special circumstance, arguing that the district attorney's evidence had been insufficient to prove that the kidnapping—if, in fact, there even was a kidnapping—occurred during the act of a murder, if there even was a murder. It was an objection he had voiced from the beginning.

But Capaccioli determined that the instructions should be reread. The attorney and the defendant gathered at the jury room door where the judge reread the relevant instructions.

When the jury room door was closed again and the deliberations resumed, Anderson, Holm and Cohn returned to Capaccioli's chambers, where the defense attorney was eager to get something on the record.

Once again, it was the matter of Juror No. 1. And, Cohn was admitting that he may have made a serious error in judgment in advising his client on Wednesday. When Craig had said he would not ask for removal of the juror, Cohn had failed to tell the Defendant that, on appeal, it might appear that Craig was fully accepting that juror when, actually, the defense was objecting to the entire jury, arguing that the case should have been transferred to another county. Cohn conceded that he shouldn't have allowed Craig's consent to keep the juror and that he didn't want his client to be in a position where he might feel he had not been competently represented.

"So, at this time, I'm asking that Juror No. 1 be removed because I did not give Craig that (information) yesterday and that she be replaced by the alternate juror who is present and ready to replace her."

But, with the jury already deliberating for several hours and possibly already having reached a verdict on the most significant charge, Capaccioli again denied the request.

Then, at 2:50 p.m., the jury sent out a second note. A verdict —after the jury had spent less than four hours behind closed doors—was in.

Marriscolo had returned to his Burlingame office after deliberations began, but he didn't get much work done.

He had a knot in his stomach "from wondering over and over, if we had done everything we could," he said. "But I was okay because a lot of the guys were coming in to talk about the case, asking a lot of questions about how everything went. It kept my mind off the jury."

Tom had felt good about the jury throughout most of the trial. He felt reassured by little things—that the jurors seemed comfortable making eye contact with and saying "hello" to Carl and him in the hallways and the elevators, that they seemed to pay careful attention when he stood during his testimony to indicate on a map all of the areas where the police had searched for Denise, and that several seemed to stare at Craig during Joan's testimony, as if to ask the question, "Why doesn't he look up?"

At 2:55 p.m., Marriscolo picked up the phone and recognized Holm's voice immediately. "We've already got a verdict," the prosecutor said. "Get down here as fast as you can."

Marriscolo rushed out the door and realized he had forgotten his jacket. As he jogged back upstairs to the detective bureau, he ran into Commander Chase, who saw the frantic look on the inspector's face.

"Where are you off to in such a hurry?" Chase asked.

"The jury's in!" Marriscolo shouted, as he headed out the door to his car.

"Oh, God, no!" exclaimed Chase who, stunned by the news, quickly headed for his own car.

Marriscolo drove the eight miles to the Redwood City courthouse alone, his heart pounding and his mind racing.

"All the way down there, I kept thinking either we did such a thorough job that the jurors had absolutely no doubts or that, damn it, we left something out."

Earlier in the week, Brower began to feel that there was a potential for violence in the courtroom. Brower claimed that one day, while Grunbaum was sitting behind the Andersons in the courtroom, Harry Redlick had pointed his forefinger at the defense team's consultant, as if to form a gun with his hand, and made gestures as if he was firing shots. He also claimed that as he and Grunbaum walked to the elevator on Tuesday, Harry had suddenly taken a swing at the former professor, missing him and accidently striking Brower instead.

In a conference call with Holm and Capaccioli, Brower cited these examples and suggested that security be tightened. In fact, unprecedented security measures prevailed as a crush of spectators and reporters gathered to enter the courtroom. Sheriff's deputies searched purses and used a metal detector to scan spectators as they passed through the heavy, mahogany doors. Eight deputies were positioned around the courtroom as the defendant was led in to take his seat alongside Nate Cohn.

Before joining Wagstaffe to take the elevator up to the court-room, Holm slipped into the district attorney's office restroom, looked in the mirror, and said a silent prayer. He privately felt that the swift verdict was a favorable omen for the defense, but he displayed none of that to the other attorneys he passed in the hallway, many of them dropping their work to go hear the verdict.

Marriscolo stepped off the elevator, looked down the long hall, and felt a lump rising in his throat as he realized it was empty. The possibility that he had missed the verdict made him feel nauseous. But he opened the door to find the courtroom bulging with spectators waiting for the judge to come in. Even the extra chairs, set alongside the gallery rows, were occupied. The gallery was eerily quiet, as the observers waited.

The jurors filed quietly into the courtroom from the inner hallway, their faces revealing nothing about their verdict as the foreman gave the three sheets to the bailiff, who quickly strode across the courtroom and handed them to Capaccioli. The judge read them and silently handed them to his clerk, who faced the courtroom.

Every eye turned toward her as she read.

"We, the jury, in the above entitled cause find the defendant, Craig Anderson, guilty of the crime of murder in the first-degree in violation of Penal Code Section 187 as charged in count one," Gensel read as spectators gasped.

Craig Anderson blinked and bowed his head slightly.

Because of what happened next, few in the courtroom noticed when the clerk read the second verdict, finding Anderson "not guilty" of kidnapping and, as a result, not guilty of the special circumstance that would have guaranteed that he would serve the rest of his life in prison, without possibility of parole.

Instead, all anyone could hear were the sobs of the murder victim's mother, as Joan Redlick heard the pronouncement—without any doubt—that her daughter, her "best friend and confidant," was dead.

Few in the courtroom would also notice that, at the opposite end of the row, Shirley Anderson was also quietly crying.

Craig—still devoid of expression—was led back to the fourth floor jail by the deputies. The jurors filed out of the courtroom and hurried to the elevators, escaping several reporters who ran behind them, asking for comments on the verdict. One juror turned and stated they had agreed not to comment about their deliberations.

Deputies separately escorted the Anderson and Redlick families from the courtroom. Although Joan and Harry lingered in the hallway, Craig's parents—who had shunned reporters from the day of their son's arrest—disappeared.

Joan, overcome with emotion, was consoled by relatives and friends who had made it back to court in time to hear the verdict. Harry, despite obvious anguish, fought back tears and patiently talked to reporters whom he had come to regard as allies in the search for Denise.

He thanked the public for its support and the prosecution for its extreme diligence.

"Justice obviously prevailed," he declared.

Standing nearby, Cohn, never one to refuse an interview—even in the wake of defeat—was visibly stunned by the verdict. He wasted no time in telling reporters, who gathered around his imposing figure, that his client had not received a fair and impartial trial.

"The evidence was absolutely ridiculous," Cohn said. "There was absolutely no proof that anybody was killed." He blamed the jury's surprisingly swift verdict—less than four hours including lunch—on the damaging effect of pre-trial publicity.

"In no other county would this kid have been found guilty," Cohn insisted. Jurors, he said, had been conditioned to think of Craig Anderson as guilty long before they had even been called to serve on the panel.

"There wasn't one person on the jury who hadn't already heard about this issue," he declared, although it was not entirely true. Several, during *voir dire*, had said they had seen nothing about the case in the media. Reporters wanted to know how Craig had reacted to the verdict.

"He didn't believe it," Cohn said. "He thought he was going to get acquitted and so did I."

Holm was reserved in his jubilation over the verdict. Returning to his office, he met privately with Harry, Joan, Carolyn and John. Wagstaffe had gone to make phone calls to tell witnesses and other key figures of the trial's result. Marriscolo found a quiet corner, surprised himself by crying, and then called his wife to tell her what happened.

Finally meeting with reporters, Holm speculated that the jurors probably felt that Redlick had voluntarily gotten into Anderson's vehicle, eliminating the possibility of conviction for kidnapping or the special circumstance. However, in finding Craig guilty of first-degree—rather than second-degree—murder, the jury clearly agreed that the killing was premeditated.

"Anytime a defendant fails to testify in his own behalf, it probably hurts his case, no matter what the judge instructs the jury," Holm said. Asked about Craig's placid behavior throughout the trial, even as the verdict was read, the prosecutor shook his head.

"There were times you'd like to go up to him, slug him in the chops and say 'Wake up!'" Holm declared.

"I felt like saying, 'React to SOMETHING, you zombie, react!'" Wagstaffe added.

Often, at the end of a successful trial, the prosecutors crack open the champagne and celebrate. There was no such jubilation in this case. No one could escape the fact that, for Joan and Harry Redlick, the ordeal was still far from over.

Commander Chase had tried, from his first interview with Craig on November 12th, to let Craig Anderson feel that he had one person he could trust in the Burlingame Police Department. Where Inspector Marriscolo always played the heavy, letting the ex-fiance know that—at least in the detective's mind—he was a suspect, Chase had attempted to leave the door open for Anderson should he ever decide to confess.

On Friday, May 30th, the day after the verdict, Chase went to the jail with a single purpose in mind. It was his desire to obtain from Anderson the details needed to find Denise Redlick's remains.

Apparently Craig was expecting a visit from his attorney when he entered the inmate's side of the partitioned visitor's booth. He had no time to react before Chase blurted out what he had planned to say.

The way Craig recalled it, in a formal grievance filed with the jail sergeant later that day, Chase said, "I didn't come here to gloat over our big win, but I told you, four months ago, that we would put you so far away, they would have to pump the light in. Do you want to talk to me now?"

The way Chase remembers it, Craig turned red, clenched his fists and gave the commander a hateful, scurrilous look before demanding, "Get the hell out of here," and retreating to an adjacent booth.

Anderson had closed the door on the Burlingame Police Department and the Redlick family for the last time.

CHAPTER TWENTY-EIGHT

Twenty Five Years
to Life

"My heart goes out to Joan and Harry Redlick. Their daughter is missing and presumed dead. I did not know that a murder conviction was possible without a corpse (proof of a murder).

What will the judge, jury, district attorney, et al. be able to do for Craig Anderson should Denise Redlick surface alive?"

—From a letter to *The San Mateo Times*
published June 6, 1986

For the family members of murder victims, the trial of the accused and the subsequent sentencing of the convicted murderer is a cathartic experience. After months—and, in some counties of California where the judicial system is especially sluggish, years —of grieving over the violent and wasteful ending of a life, the trial serves as a final chapter. Family members may never completely recover from their devastating loss but, at least, they can feel that their personal tragedy has reached its conclusion, allowing them to rebuild their own shattered lives.

For Joan and Harry Redlick, that was not to be. The trial and the guilty verdict represented a beginning, not an end. The jury had confirmed what they had grown in their hearts to believe—

that their daughter was dead. But not knowing where her body lay nor how she had been killed meant that the sleepless nights were far from over.

"To this day, no one has ever said to me, 'Your daughter is dead'," Joan said to a friend one day. More than ever, she was convinced that she would never see Denise again. There no longer were any fleeting thoughts of Denise calling from a telephone booth, crying, "Mom, please come and get me," or, perhaps, a police officer from some remote village contacting them to say, "We've found your daughter and she's alive and well."

The dreams were absolutely gone. Only the nightmares remained.

In California, a Victims Bill of Rights allows surviving family members to participate in the convicted assailant's sentencing hearing. While some choose to send letters to the judge, others prefer to make a public statement in court. Many others decline the opportunity to be involved.

Many times, during the months since Denise's disappearance, Joan and Harry had said that their only desire was to find their daughter's body and, at last, give her a proper funeral and burial. After Craig's arrest and throughout the trial, Nate Cohn had objected to publicity in which Denise Redlick was portrayed as a murder victim, arguing that the jury was being unfairly conditioned to believe something that had not been proven. But now, with Craig's conviction, the parents could make a legitimate, court-sanctioned appeal to their daughter's former fiance to help them find her remains.

On the morning of Friday, June 20, 1986, the courtroom was once again packed as the sentencing hearing commenced.

Joan and Harry Redlick, their prepared statements in hand, were sitting in the front row of Judge Capaccioli's courtroom when it came time for Craig Anderson—dressed now in orange, jail-issued coveralls, his hands in cuffs secured to a chain around his waist, like any other convicted inmate facing sentencing—to leave the relative comfort of the San Mateo County Jail and be sent to a state prison.

But first, defense attorney Cohn—still finding it difficult to believe that he had lost—made his motion for a new trial. Before coming to court, he had filed several declarations contending that Craig had not gotten the fair trial to which he was entitled. He continued to argue that the circumstantial evidence did not add up, beyond a reasonable doubt, to murder.

"The prosecution never proved the *corpus delicti,* " Cohn had argued in one document filed with the court. "There was no proof beyond a reasonable doubt that (a) Denise Redlick was killed or (b) that she was killed by unlawful means."

The sole evidence, he stated, consisted of "four drops of blood obtained from a van operated by the defendant and one drop of blood obtained from the canvas shoe belonging to the defendant."

Even then, he said, the bloodstain analysis was inconclusive. "Forty percent of the population could have left the drops of blood in the van which were the subject of the tests," he added. The stain on the tennis shoe, he said, could have just as easily occurred when the defendant was playing basketball, football or participating in some other recreational event.

The judge erred, Cohn contended, in not allowing the defense to cross-examine Benny Del Re about why the electrophoresis tests—which possibly could have created a more specific genetic profile of the bloodstains—were not completed.

"The only reason could be that the prosecution did not wish to take the chance that they would have to exclude their evidence," Cohn contended.

Furthermore, Cohn claimed there were other reasonable explanations why Denise Redlick had not used her credit cards or bank accounts (perhaps she had been kidnapped or joined a commune, he suggested).

His declarations repeatedly attacked Holm's strategy. The prosecutor had contended that the defendant had kidnapped and killed Denise because, if he couldn't have her, no one else could. Yet, Cohn felt there had been no evidence that the defendant ever made such a statement.

The defense attorney even suggested that the speed with which the jurors deliberated—finding Craig guilty "in a ridiculously short period of time" without even asking to see any of the exhibits—was indicative of Craig's inability to obtain a fair trial in San Mateo County.

"The deduction is simple," Cohn wrote in one declaration. "The jury was biased, prejudiced and inflamed against the defendant from the moment they were selected to serve. The jury was inflamed throughout the trial by the actions of the Redlicks and their friends, by the district attorney and by Inspector Marriscolo.

Cohn accused Holm, the prosecutor, of misconduct for, among other things, gesturing towards the defendant in a demeaning manner during the opening statement and closing argument, for having Charles Cantrell of the Budget Rent-a-Car Agency testify about the stain on the floor of the van that he thought was blood when it had been clearly determined by the criminalists that the stain was not blood, and for allowing the alleged "tip" about Denise's body being buried in the Anderson Paint Co. to pop out in court without any previous notice to the defense.

Cohn also contended that there had been juror misconduct. Cohn's investigator, Charles Bates, a retired Northern California FBI director who had gained national fame for his arrest of newspaper heiress Patty Hearst on bank robbery charges after her abduction by the Symbionese Liberation Army, had tape-recorded interviews with two jurors. One of them, had said that the jurors discussed the fact that the defendant did not testify—although they were instructed not to consider his lack of testimony—and that, despite the judge's stern admonition, they had discussed the case during their lunch hours before they began deliberating.

According to the transcription, the juror, who described himself as the "last to hold out," said he felt "everyone wanted to get out of there" because the trial had taken so long.

"It was his impression everybody had their minds made up when they went in there," Cohn told Capaccioli.

After Cohn made his oral arguments for a new trial, Holm got his chance to respond, flatly denying all of Cohn's accusations.

Holm pointed out that Bates' transcribed interview with another juror gave quite a different version of what happened during deliberations. This juror denied there had been any discussion of the case before deliberations officially began or that the jury had considered the lack of testimony by the defendant.

The deputy district attorney was enraged at Cohn's suggestion of prosecutorial misconduct.

"Mr. Cohn still cannot get through his head the fact that the four or five hours that it took for the jury deliberation was based on the strength of the case and not any bias or prejudice that this jury supposedly had as a result of publicity," said the prosecutor. "All of these jurors indicated that they had minimal knowledge of this case and, if they had any knowledge, they could put it aside to decide the case."

The judge, who had read Cohn's declarations and the transcripts of the interviews with the jurors, swiftly denied the motion for a new trial.

After that, the formal sentencing was ready to begin.

Harry Redlick, his shoulders slumped and his hand gently resting on his wife's shoulder, stood and read from a carefully prepared statement. He repeatedly looked at the defendent who sat, unresponsive, with his head bowed.

"As I sat on Sunday in St. Robert's Church during the Father's Day Mass, I was overcome with a feeling of loneliness because my daughter was not at my side," Harry said, as he began to weep openly. "And, I was even more remorseful because I then realized, as I saw the many fathers with their sons and daughters approach the altar for a special prayer, that there would be many more lonely Father's Days for me because Denise would never be at my side.

"There is not a day—there is not an hour—that goes by that Denise is not in my thoughts and it is a terrible burden to bear, a burden that I shall have to bear with my family forever."

Then, it was Joan Redlick's turn.

"The devastation the prisoner has brought upon my family is impossible to put into words. My family has been cut in half. I no longer have a daughter. My son, Michael, no longer has a sister. My grandchildren will never know their Aunt Denise.

"She was a shining star, the very light of all our lives. She was all things good, kind, caring and everloving to everyone around. There is a great sadness in all of my family. My eighty-year-old parents miss her and mourn for her every day as they had a great love for her and she for them. There is no punishment in the world that could make up for the taking of a life, the life that was really just beginning.

The world is a lesser place for her not being here any longer. Not only did the prisoner kill my daughter, but, just as impardonable, he has hidden her away and refuses to tell us where she is. This adds to the cruelty of the act. It makes him twice guilty. He has no defense and no remorse.

"To Craig Anderson, I want to say this," Joan went on, deliberately facing the man who nearly became her son-in-law. "You came into our home. You told us you loved our daughter, told us you loved us and wanted to be a part of our close and loving family. We believed you and we treated you as our own son, but you made Denise unhappy. You struck her and she had no choice but to leave you.

"Craig, this was all your own doing. Yet you cannot face the fact that she left you forever and you killed her to end your own misery.

"As a mother, I say to you, if there is still a conscience somewhere inside of you, listen to it and do the only right thing you can do now. Confess your guilt. Let us bury our daughter. Free yourself of that great burden you carry and will carry for the rest of your life. Make your peace with God for your own sake. Eternity lasts forever."

The stonefaced defendant did not respond. He sat staring at the floor as if he had simply not heard.

Finally, Capaccioli was ready to pronounce the sentence. Under California's sentencing law, a first-degree murder conviction is an automatic twenty-five years to life sentence. San Mateo County Probation Officer John J. O'Connor, who prepared a sentencing report for the court after interviewing Anderson for several hours, calculated that Anderson would receive credit for having served one-hundred-twenty-one days in jail and an extra sixty days for good behavior, one-hundred-eighty-one days in all.

Although he had made no comment in court and had chosen

—on the advice of his attorney—not to testify at his trial, Craig Anderson had plenty to say in the statement that he submitted to O'Connor.

"The facts surrounding my case are very simple," Anderson began. "It was decided by the Burlingame Police Department to point a finger at one individual, rather than continue to pursue other leads regarding the disappearance of my ex-fiance. Once they made the commitment, they had to stick with it, to avoid looking like fools within the community.

"We all know Denise Redlick is missing from the area," he went on. "She was last seen by her cousin at a location in Burlingame and it is possible that foul play was involved with her disappearance. I had broken an engagement with the missing woman in October, 1985, and only saw her three times after the break-up. Many theories as to what might have happened are still unsolved. It is the feeling of her parents that she would not leave the area without telling them. I have different ideas regarding the situation.

"Denise and I were still good friends and I feel very strongly that she left the area because of pressure at home. I pray that she has not met with foul play and will return home, or at least contact someone regarding her whereabouts. I am still very much in love with Denise and greatly respect her parents."

Craig continued that he was very distraught over Denise's disappearance and, rather than help search for her, he occupied himself with his business activities and work around the house.

"I am very upset, and deeply hurt, by all the accusations which have led to my guilty verdict in Superior Court. I know in my heart that I could never harm Denise Redlick," he said.

The convicted murderer said that, as his trial neared, he had been able to see that he had already been convicted by the news media. He was shocked when he did not get a change of venue to another county.

Craig said that "behind-the-scenes politics," with Harry Redlick using his friendship with the mayor of San Bruno to help set up a reward fund, "were staggering."

"From that moment on, the local television stations and newspapers were flooded with pictures and information regarding Denise and our recent break-up. I feel that my privacy and good standing within the community were seriously damaged," he wrote. "Many violations of my civil rights occurred, included with those of my family."

"My conviction was based on the fact that I was not chained to my office door during the entire day which Denise Redlick disappeared. I did nothing which could be conceived as elements required to prove a first-degree murder conviction. However, the Burlingame Police Department collaborated with the district attorney and painted an imaginary picture of an alleged crime with no solid evidence to back the allegations.

"I am appalled that a modern day police force could be so ignorant as to the current facts regarding the hundreds of disappearances of people each month in the United States. I am even more shocked by the gullible nature of some people in this county," Craig claimed. He added that the Burlingame Police Department singled him out to cover up the department's lack of modern training in tracking missing persons. Numerous tips received by the police "that could very well lead them directly to a healthy and happy Denise Redlick" still have not been followed, he said.

"I find it very hard to accept, knowing that I am faced with the prospect of a lengthy prison term for an alleged crime which I did not commit," he said.

In closing, Craig said he was "deeply hurt" by the suffering of the Redlick family and his own family as a result of the "current situation."

"To this day, I would do anything for the Redlick family," he said. "If I had any involvement with the disappearance of Denise Redlick or any information concerning her disappearance, I would have told the authorities long ago. Unfortunately, I have been caught up in a nightmare which, for me, started in October 1985."

On July 11th, Craig Anderson was bussed, with a dozen other convicted county inmates, to California Medical Facility at Vacaville, the state Department of Corrections facility for evaluation of newly transferred prisoners.

And, on August 6, 1986, Craig Anderson, now state prisoner

D34209, was transported to Folsom State Prison in the grassy foothills near the state capital of Sacramento where he began serving the remainder of his lengthy sentence.

More than three hundred people—family members, friends, and even strangers—gathered in St. Robert's Church on the evening of Sunday, November 10, 1986, to memorialize Denise Redlick—one day short of the one-year anniversary of her disappearance.

As the many guests entered the church where Denise had received first communion, been a bridesmaid for several weddings, and often attended Sunday services with her parents, they were given formal programs titled, "A Celebration in Memory of Denise Redlick's Life and of Her New Life in the Resurrection."

During the candlelit one-hour service, there was no specific mention of Craig Anderson or the murder trial and conviction. The Reverend Paul Rossi, in the Celebration of Mass, asked the mourners to thank God for Denise, who was "a gift to all of us." He reminded the church guests that supporting the Redlick family over the past year was only a small part of what needed to be done. The months and years to come, he said, would be just as important.

"When someone dies so young, and in such a tragic way, something dies within all of us," he said.

Michael Redlick welcomed the crowd of mourners, thanked them for their support during the difficult year, and set a tone of joyfulness, rather than sorrow, in memory of his missing—and presumably murdered—sister.

"In thinking of Denise, we must think of all the positive, uplifting joy she brought to everyone she came in contact with, and that feeling should always stay with us," Michael said. "We must take comfort in the fact that Denise's suffering ended the moment she was united with God."

Those who spoke, including Charles Nan, Chris Morganti, Michele McKindley, John Kristovich and Lori Voreyer, maintained their composure, although their words brought tears to the eyes of many in the church. They asked the mourners not to be sad in the wake of a tragedy, but to be happy for the way in which

Denise's death had brought out the goodness in so many people who were drawn to help the Redlick family in one way or another throughout a difficult time.

Lori, the final speaker, emphasized, "We must not make the memory of Denise Redlick a sad one. That is the least we can do for her. We must not forget Denise and the way she was. We must not be afraid to speak of her. Among all else, we must try to learn from her. Let us try to be more Denise-like—happy, laughing, helping and giving.

"Let the spirit of Denise Redlick live on through us," Lori declared.

For memorial gifts, Joan and Harry Redlick chose a charity that they thought their daughter would have liked—the non-profit, Make-a-Wish Foundation, which fulfills the dreams of dying youngsters. Within two months, the foundation had received more than $1,600 in memory of Denise. "We can't believe it," the grateful executive director, Pat Keller, told a reporter. "The donations keep coming in. Denise must have been a very well-liked person."

Keller said the beneficiaries included Johnathan, an eight-year-old with brain cancer who was taken by limousine on a shopping trip to buy the computer and software he wanted for Christmas; Nancy, twelve, suffering from spine cancer, who was able to have a remote control television installed in the ceiling of her room where she was confined to bed; and Christina, six, who went on a shopping trip to a toy store. Christina died of cancer the day after Christmas, but "her parents tell us she had such a fun-filled, last two weeks," Keller said.

"This is one small positive note in our seemingly ongoing tragedy, a very bittersweet ending to a beautiful life," Joan Redlick said when she learned of the donations in memory of her daughter.

Compared to the intense interest in Craig Anderson's first trial, his second trial went barely noticed.

On December 1, 1986, Craig was returned to San Mateo County Jail from Folsom to stand trial on charges of soliciting the murder of Michael Brunicon.

Dressed in a handsome, dark blue suit and tie, he looked tan and fit as he entered the courtroom for the start of his trial. In contrast to his detached and disinterested appearance at the Redlick trial, he seemed self-confident and attentive.

"There's the fat little detective," Craig cracked, as he walked past Marriscolo to take his seat to the left of Nate Cohn.

"At least I can go outside and get exercise any time I want," the investigating officer retorted with a polite smile.

Holm and Cohn selected a jury of eight men and four women. Among those testifying for the defense, as they had at the preliminary hearing earlier that year, were Brunicon, Lucy Larson, Doug Rees, Emad Musa and, of course, Richard Weeks.

This time, Craig testified in his own behalf. Even his critics later conceded that he performed well. He testified that he would never have been jealous of Lucy's relationship with her estranged husband because he never considered his own relationship with Lucy to be a permanent one. In fact, while he was dating Lucy, and even while she was living with him in San Carlos, he was dating other women, he said.

Craig said that on the night that Richard Weeks came to his house wearing a police wire, the visitor was drinking a bottle of peppermint schnapps, his eyes were red, "and he was just obnoxious, to put it bluntly."

"Were you frightened of the guy?" Cohn asked.

"Heck, yes," Anderson replied. He thought that the piece of paper Weeks mentioned that police officers had found was not a physical description of Brunicon—which he denied having ever written—but, rather, the police report Lucy had filed with San Carlos police alleging that Craig had beaten her.

"You gave him $300 to get him out of the house?" the defense attorney asked.

"I sure did," Anderson responded.

Holm, savoring the opportunity to go one-on-one with Anderson, cross-examined the witness for nearly three hours, grilling him about the tape-recorded exchange with Richard Weeks, about the conversation overheard by Doug Rees, about the alleged phone call to Emad Musa, and about his alleged demonstrations of jealousy over Lucy.

"I want to get a complete picture of this," Holm said, facing Anderson. "You're saying that these people lied . . . that they are conspiring to bring this charge against you?"

"I feel that," Anderson convincingly replied.

The jury was told by Holm during closing arguments that they had two choices, "The question is whether or not the defendant has been subjected to a sophisticated conspiracy to frame him for the charge of solicitation to commit murder—as he unconvincingly claims. Or, is he the jealous ex-boyfriend . . . that the evidence suggests he is?"

Holm, playing off Anderson's own testimony, argued there was no evidence that Anderson was set up. Rather, he was "an outrageously jealous man" who solicited a murder because he was angry that the woman he was living with had, for a few days at least, returned to live with her husband.

Holm felt the testimony of key witnesses Weeks and Rees was corroborated by others. To believe Anderson, the jury would have to believe that all of the witnesses lied, he contended.

Cohn, who had cleverly brought Anderson's prior conviction to the attention of the jury after securing the judge's ruling that it would not be brought up by the prosecution, offered a different conspiracy theory. He claimed the district attorney's office was pursuing the solicitation case only because they were so unsure of themselves in the murder case.

"This case is ridiculous," Cohn argued. "This is an attempt by Holm and Marriscolo to protect themselves. If Miss Redlick were to walk in here, these two gentlemen would be embarrassed. That's why we're here.

"They're covering their tails," he claimed. "It's as simple as that."

Cohn, drawing attention to his client's favorable appearance, added that Anderson, "as good looking as he is, had no trouble getting dates.

"But Mr. Holm here would have you believe that Mr. Anderson would go ape because Lucy Brunicon wants to go back to her husband. It's a good story maybe for the movies or for TV or for a good romantic magazine."

The jury began deliberating at 9:30 a.m. on Wednesday, December 10th. After a lunch break, they met again until 4:40 p.m., but were back on the job at 8:45 a.m. the next day. In an hour, they announced that they were done.

The verdict: not guilty. Shirley Anderson, seated next to Craig's father in the front row, wept as she heard the verdicts read. Anderson appeared to take a deep breath of relief.

One juror, in describing the deliberations, said the corroborating evidence of solicitation just wasn't convincing enough.

"We asked in the jury room, 'Weren't we led along a path and then just dropped?' " one juror explained to reporters.

Cohn couldn't wait to tell reporters, in the hallway, that his client was able to convince the jury of his innocence because the intense publicity had subsided. Unlike his murder trial in May, Craig Anderson, this time, was tried on the evidence, not on the publicity, he claimed.

"All I can say is that I got twelve people who, somehow, had not been brainwashed," he declared. "People in this county were embarrassed by what happened (in the first case) and, finally, they decided to be fair with Craig.

The defense attorney added that San Mateo County shouldn't even have gone ahead with the case, that it was a waste of money. If he had been convicted, the maximum possible sentence of six years would have run concurrently with the murder conviction, Cohn told reporters.

"He's a liar," snapped Holm—who wasn't accustomed to losing—when told of Cohn's comment. "The sentence can be served consecutively; it can be served concurrently. It depends on the judge."

None of this really mattered, however, to Craig Anderson.

Within twenty-four hours, he was back on a blue and white San Mateo County Sheriff's bus, headed up the Peninsula and east through the valley to return to his home, a dismal forty-eight square foot cell that he shares with one other inmate at Folsom State Prison.

Like most of California's other eighteen prisons, Folsom is grossly overcrowded. The prison houses 7,000 men, nearly twice the capacity for which it was built. While prisoners with a propensity toward violence are housed in the new, state-of-the-art section of Folsom, built in 1986, those who are considered better security risks—like Anderson—live in the old granite stone prison, built in 1880. Although cells in the newer prison are bigger, at eighty square feet, and more modern, with electronic doors rather than bars, the older prison is considered a more desirable place to be incarcerated, according to prison spokeswoman, Cammy Voss. Of the average one hundred thirty stabbings a year, around seventy-five percent occur in the newer section.

The area where Anderson is housed contains five tiers of identical cells. His cell contains a bunk bed, a sink with hot and cold running water, and a toilet. Like all Folsom prisoners, he has shelf space and a locker to store up to six cubic feet of personal property. He is permitted to have a television, radio or tape player —if he can afford to buy one.

During his initial CDC evaluation while at Vacaville, Anderson had expressed hope of being assigned to a job that utilized his bookkeeping and accounting skills. Apparently he made a favorable impression upon prison authorities because, shortly after he arrived at Folsom, he was assigned to work as a clerk-typist in a prison office—a prestigious, sought-after position. "The clerks are normally well-respected by other inmates," Voss said. Anderson has the potential to earn up to $130 a month.

As a prisoner at Folsom, Craig Anderson can enroll in a variety of vocational programs, earn a community college degree, and participate in a number of recreational activities, including boxing and softball teams that compete against visiting teams from the community. He is entitled to meet with visitors five days a week in a large, open meeting room well-stocked with vending machines. Should he marry while in prison, he would be eligible for forty-eight hour conjugal visits in any of the prison's ten two-bedroom, motel-like units where inmate's children are also welcome.

Yet, despite efforts to reward well-behaved prisoners with certain privileges, prison life is regimented, monotonous and dull. The prison uniform is a long-sleeved chambray shirt and blue jeans. Showers are limited to a maximum of five minutes a day. Prisoners may embrace or kiss their visitors only at the beginning and conclusion of their visits although they may hold hands in between. And, the daily sack lunch, distributed at breakfast—which begins at 5:30 a.m.—contains a predictable sandwich, bag of chips, fruit and cookies.

In his Vacaville evaluation, Anderson's correctional counselor observed that he "appears eager to program in a positive manner, hoping to maintain a low profile in an environment that initially has created considerable anxiety." Apparently, he has succeeded in his predictably difficult adjustment. According to prison authorities, Anderson has been "almost disciplinary free" since his imprisonment, an impressive accomplishment considering that an untucked shirt is worthy of at least one demerit, and is "doing very well in his work assignment."

His straight, blond hair and blue eyes have earned him the nickname "Malibu" among his peers.

According to Voss, the first date that Anderson can appear before a three-member panel representing the state Board of Prison Terms, which determines when prisoners are eligible for parole, is March 12, 2002.

At that time, Anderson will be forty-four years old and will have spent nearly one-third of his life behind bars.

Epilogue

Like most summer days in the Santa Clara Valley, August 12, 1987, was sizzling, close to 95 degrees by mid-afternoon. Adding to the disagreeable atmosphere, the tranquility of the valley's rural areas was being shattered that summer by a housing boom, fueled by thousands of new jobs in the south Peninsula's prosperous computer and electronics industries. The pear, prune and cherry orchards that once surrounded metropolitan San Jose were being consumed by tractors and backhoes. Once fertile farm land had become prime residential real estate.

On the boundary line between the upper middle class cities of Saratoga and Cupertino, where Stelling Road narrows into a country lane and finally dead ends at Prospect Road, the grinding of chain saws signaled the demise of yet another orchard. Developers had already plotted land just south of Prospect Creek on the other side of Prospect Road, which serves as the dividing line between the two towns, for construction of upper-priced custom homes. And, they were just beginning to prepare vacant land to the north of the creek for a master planned community comprised of hundreds of affordable and nearly identical houses on compact lots. But first, the creek—a drainage canal for runoff that flows from nearby Stevens Creek County Park in the Santa Cruz Mountains—had to be cleared of dense trees and shrubs that clung to the bone dry creekbed and its eleven-foot high banks.

Jerry Castro, an employee with the sub-contracting firm hired by a developer to clear the creek, was felling trees with a

337

chain saw when nature called. He wandered westward about one hundred feet to find a place to urinate. Castro had been standing still for several seconds, a few feet from the base of a shady oak, facing the north bank of the creek, when his eyes fixed on a brownish-gray object a few feet away.

Castro shivered as he realized that the object was not a rock. It was a human skull.

He took a step forward and then thought better of it. Instead he hustled back to his supervisor and reported, in an excited mixture of Spanish and English, what he had seen. Within minutes, a small group of workers clustered around the skull. As they apprehensively moved closer to examine it, they saw that the upper jaw appeared to be in tact.

"We better leave it alone," one of the men said, volunteering to jog back to the developer's trailer and call the Santa Clara County Sheriff's Office.

Lieutenant Mike Lombardo, who happened to be on patrol in the area, was one of the first officers to respond to the radio dispatch. Lombardo. a former detective who had observed more than seventy-five homicide scenes, knew from experience that construction workers in the valley sometimes inadvertently uncovered Ohlone Indian "mounds" yielding tools, shells and human skeletons dating back as far as the late 1700s. Construction projects in the valley had sometimes ground to a halt for weeks— and even months—as the Bureau of Indian Affairs sent its representatives to evaluate the significance of the discovery and assist in carefully relocating the remains to new burial sites.

Lombardo knew that his visual examination of the skull would be important in determining who else should be called to the scene.

The construction workers, whom Lombardo thought looked slightly annoyed at having their tightly scripted work schedule interrupted, met the deputies on the shoulder of the road above the creek bed. From there, they could see the skull resting on its left side on a pile of leaves about thirty feet away. Lombardo and his partner that afternoon, Captain David Thomas, then climbed down the southern embankment and walked toward the skull, which sat—completely exposed—on a plateau about three feet above the very bottom of the drainage ditch.

Lombardo squatted in the dry grass to get a closer look.

"I don't think we have to worry about this coming from an ancient burial ground," he said to Thomas. "I can see fillings in the molars."

Just a foot or so to the right of the skull, Lombardo also observed what appeared to be part of a pelvic bone.

He had seen enough to know that it was time to notify the detective bureau.

Within a hour, the creek bed was filled with investigators. They had tied yellow ribbons to trees to cordon off the area from all but official observers. While two patrol deputies stood guard at the top of the creek on Prospect Road and two detectives interviewed the construction workers, evidence technicians Danny Aulman and Frank DeLuna snapped 35mm photographs, made precise measurements of the creekbed, and began excavating—first by hand, then by trowel and, finally, with shovels—within a four-foot radius of where the skull and pelvic bone had been found. It didn't take long to uncover two vertebrae, a leg bone, three arm bones and three ribs. Digging lower, Aulman uncovered an additional vertebrae.

Within a few feet of the skull, the technicians also found pieces of what they believed to be nylon pantyhose, caked in dirt, a pair of gray trousers, and a few clumps of brown hair.

As the early evening shadows closed in, Detective Sergeant Ken Kahn was forced to call a temporary halt to the investigation.

"We've got to come back here and try again," Kahn told the technicians. From experience, Kahn knew that, unless the upper jaw provided an extremely unusual or distinctive pattern, it would be crucially important to find the lower jaw of the victim for a positive identification to be made. He and Aulman agreed to return the next morning, before it became uncomfortably warm, to continue the grim search.

Their return visit to the site paid off. About ten feet east of where the skull had been located the previous day, at the base of the oak tree, Aulman found the lower jaw. It was missing two teeth. Carefully sifting through the dirt, Kahn eventually found one.

Nearby, they uncovered what they thought might be more related evidence—a piece of dark-colored sweater, a small remnant of gold-toned carpet, a hair brush, a piece of light-colored plastic and one gray belt. The deputies placed each item in its own brown evidence bag, labeling where and how it had been found.

Before they suspended their exploration of the creekbed, they had uncovered additional pelvic and rib bones and vertebrae.

They found nothing else to indicate how the person might have died. All of the bare, well-weathered bones were delivered to the coroner's office, where Dr. Angelo Ozoa, assistant medical examiner and veteran of four thousand autopsies, was able to determine that the victim was a white female, roughly twenty to thirty years of age. He detected no fractures of the skull, spine or other bones and saw no evidence of bullet perforations or any other violent trauma.

The cause of the victim's death, Ozoa stated in his report, could not be determined.

At 3:30 p.m., Kahn punched a teletype in the United States Department of Justice message system, alerting police department "unidentified bodies units" across the country to the discovery of the remains of a white female, mid-twenties, with light brown or dirty blond hair, including information about the items of clothing found nearby. Preliminary examination of the remains, the teletype said, indicated that the body had been in the creek bed "at least six months and possibly as long as two years."

But, with the weekend approaching, the teletype was unnoticed by many police departments. It was tossed in baskets with dozens of other similar cross-state and cross-country messages. For three more days, the victim found in the creek bed remained a Jane Doe.

On Monday, August 17th, Kahn was at his desk when Sergeant Donald Tam from the patrol division called him.

"You know those remains they found last week off Prospect?" Tam asked.

"Sure. Still unidentified," Kahn said, pulling the telephone closer to his ear.

"Well, I was thinking about something." Tam mused. "Sometime in 1986, around April or so, the Burlingame Police Department got us to help them search for a body out by Stevens Creek Reservoir. They were looking for a woman, in her twenties, I think. That creekbed (where the bones were found) is just a mile or two, as the crow flies, from where we were looking."

Kahn's curiosity was piqued. The detective hung up and immediately contacted the Burlingame Police Department. He was informed, by the watch commander, that the body of the missing woman, Denise Susan Redlick of San Bruno, had never been found, although her presumed murderer had been convicted.

"I think we might have found her," Kahn declared.

Late that afternoon, Kahn and Marriscolo compared dental charts over the phone. The description of the dental pattern of the skull seemed to fit the dental chart that Marriscolo had obtained for Denise Redlick just a few days after her disappearance.

But what really seemed more than a mere coincidence, Marriscolo told Chase after the call, was that a pair of gray slacks and a gray belt—similar to things Denise had been reported wearing—had been found within a few feet of the skull.

"I knew this day would come," Marriscolo told his supervisor, shaking his head.

Early the next morning, Sergeant Kahn and Sergeant Dave Pascual drove up the Peninsula to Burlingame where they obtained Denise Redlick's dental X-rays. Then, the two Santa Clara detective sergeants met Marriscolo, Collopy and Officer Becky Galvez, who happened to be in training that day with the detectives, at the Santa Clara County Coroner's office. The officers watched as Dr. John Hauser, chief medical examiner, and Dr. Ozoa, the assistant medical examiner who had examined the bones, compared the charts.

They were a perfect match. The search for Denise was over.

An hour later, Kahn and the three Burlingame officers stood on the edge of Prospect Creek and looked down into the gully where the remains had been found.

"It's incredible," Collopy thought out loud. "It's so close to the road."

But, two years ago," Kahn told him, "this area would have looked quite different." Most of the land was still covered by orchards at that time, he said.

As they stood on the ledge above the dry creekbed, several cars drove by, reminding them that probably thousands of vehicles—many of them winding their way up the road to the Saratoga Golf and Country Club—had passed along this route over the past twenty one months.

The Burlingame officers scurried down the bank and walked in and along the creekbed, attempting to piece together what might have happened on November 11, 1985.

As they drove away, Marriscolo looked lingeringly back at the creek and knew that his most difficult task lay ahead.

For months after the trial, Joan had prayed that she and Harry would be able to give their daughter a proper burial. But there had come a time the next summer when she had begun to accept the uncertainty of her daughter's fate.

When Joan saw Tom Marriscolo walk into her office on the afternoon of August 18th, she assumed he was there on business and had stopped in to see her at her job. But, looking at him more closely, she didn't notice that little grin on his face that had always erased the tension during those long days of 1985. When she saw Kevin Collopy and an unfamiliar young female officer trailing him, she knew they were not making a social call.

As Tom approached, Joan slowly rose from her desk and walked toward him. Silently, he embraced her and, after a moment, said softly, "We've found her."

Together, they cried, and then Marriscolo drove her home to break the long-awaited news to Harry.

By late that night, word of the discovery of Denise's remains had been released to the media. Denise's friends, some of whom first heard the news on radio, began arriving at the Redlick's house. Turning away requests for on-camera interviews, Harry and Joan pleaded, "This is a time for our family and close friends." Later, Harry would tell a newspaper reporter that the discovery of their daughter's remains was "a shock, but we are also relieved."

"It's bringing it all back," he said sadly. "At least now we'll be able to give our daughter a decent burial."

Denise's funeral was finally held on the morning of Thursday, August 20th at St. Robert's Catholic Church. Although Denise's parents announced—through the newspapers—that it would be a private service, more than one hundred people attended.

Standing before Denise's draped casket, the priest asked the mourners to support Harry, Joan, Michael and Lynn Redlick in their sorrow as they had supported Denise's loved ones through the difficult times of the past.

When the service concluded, Denise's closest girlfriends each selected a single rose for remembrance from atop the casket. Then Michele slipped outside. "This isn't Denise at all," she thought, choosing to remember, instead, her best friend's giggle.

Denise was buried in Holy Cross Cemetery at the foot of San Bruno Mountain just south of San Francisco, with a simple, flat granite memorial that reads:

Denise S. Redlick
1962–1985
Our loving daughter

Nate Cohn, upon learning that Denise Redlick's remains had been found and identified, expressed disappointment.

"That's too bad," he said. "I was hoping she had just gone off somewhere." Still, he insisted, evidence of her death did not prove that Craig Anderson was responsible.

"It might even be helpful to us if they find evidence that someone else did it," Cohn declared.

Informed of Cohn's reaction, Marriscolo was incredulous.

"There isn't any new evidence," he said disgustedly. "We'll probably never know how he killed her."

Marriscolo felt that the location of the remains only strengthened the prosecution's case. On the day before the funeral, the detective drove a calibrated police car from the Seedlock house to Prospect Creek, a distance of twelve-and-a half miles which was well within the ninety-five miles logged on the Budget van's odometer. The discovery location was also in the midst of an area one of Craig's friends had told the detective Craig enjoyed driving. It was also close to the community college where Craig had reportedly taken classes, jogged and played tennis.

"We never had any doubt that Anderson was guilty, but this just reinforces our case," Steve Wagstaffe insisted. "I would be shocked if the verdict were reversed."

Cohn knew that the finding of Denise's remains wouldn't be considered by the appellate court, since an appeal is based strictly on the Superior Court trial record and not on anything that occurs after the trial. Anderson's appellate brief, filed soon after the trial, had argued that the defendant couldn't get a fair trial in San Mateo County, that the *corpus delicti*—the "elements of a crime" —had never been proven, and that the purely circumstantial evidence failed to preclude, as required by law, every reasonable hypothesis of innocence.

After Denise's remains were found, Jeffrey Bryant, the deputy attorney general handling the appeal on behalf of the district attorney's office, asked the appellate justices to take into evidence Redlick's death certificate, which had not been part of the Superior Court record. His request was denied.

Ultimately, it didn't matter.

On September 24, 1987, five weeks after Denise's funeral, Craig Anderson's hopes of having his jury trial verdict overturned were destroyed. A three-member judicial panel unanimously affirmed Anderson's first-degree murder conviction, discounting every one of the prisoner's arguments.

Concerning the denial of a change of venue, the justices wrote that although some jurors were aware of Denise Redlick's disappearance, few had heard of or recalled any connection between the defendant and the disappearance. Those who did said they could set that knowledge aside and fairly consider the case in the courtroom.

Besides, the defendant's acquittal on his solicitation charge provided further evidence that he was, in fact, able to obtain a fair trial in San Mateo County, the appellate decision said.

The justices also found that the circumstantial evidence in People vs. Anderson—despite the lack of a body, weapon or confession—was more than enough to justify conviction.

"The prosecution supplied a convincing motive for (the) defendant's murder of Denise Redlick; defendant's jealousy and refusal to acknowledge that Denise should be free to go her own way. The circumstances of their relationship, the broken engagement, defendant's physical assault on Denise in September and defendant's bitter statements to friends regarding Denise in October all corroborated this motive."

Although he could have appealed further, asking the state Supreme Court to consider his case, no such appeal was filed. Anderson's attorneys have said that the law firm hired to represent him in his appeals didn't submit the proper documents in time.

It was not the only legal blow that Craig would be dealt.

In February, 1988, a Superior Court civil jury of six men and two women awarded Harry and Joan Redlick $1.8 million—including $1,166,754 in general damages and $650,000 in punitive damages—in a wrongful death lawsuit against Craig Anderson. The lawsuit said that Anderson had caused Denise's parents permanent emotional and psychological damage that would require continued treatment, care and therapy.

Denise's parents said that if they should ever receive any money as a result of the judgment, they would donate it to a charity that Denise would have cared about.

They are not, however, expecting to ever receive a cent.

"It won't bring Denise back," Joan said of the award. "It's just something we were advised to do."

In his official report concerning his "examination of skeletal remains," Dr. Angelo Ozoa had estimated, based on the weathering of bones, that the victim had been dead six months to one year before the remains were found.

Later, Shirley Anderson asked Nate Cohn if that didn't mean Craig couldn't possibly have murdered Denise since he had already been in custody for months at the earliest possible date when she could have been killed?

Cohn thought it was an idea worth exploring.

In a petition filed in San Mateo County Superior Court, Cohn asked for a new trial in light of the evidence that "Denise Redlick met her death after the defendant was convicted." The report, he argued, "proves that defendant Craig Anderson could not have killed Denise Redlick."

As soon as they heard about Cohn's motion, the prosecutors dismissed it as utter nonsense.

"Coroner's estimates are always just that—estimates," snapped District Attorney James Fox.

"In my estimation, there is absolutely no grounds for a new case," said Marriscolo upon learning about Cohn's latest tactic from a reporter.

Superior Court Judge Walter Capaccioli, who would otherwise have heard Cohn's petition to reconsider the legality of Craig's incarceration, had been appointed by Governor George Deukmejian to a vacancy on the California Court of Appeals, Sixth District, in San Jose, not long after presiding over Craig Anderson's trial in 1986.

It had been more than two years since Margaret Kemp had presided over the preliminary hearing on the murder charges in People vs. Anderson. One June 15, 1988, Kemp, now a Superior Court judge, was assigned to hear Cohn's motion.

This time, only a handful of spectators—including the victim's and the defendant's parents—were in the gallery. From Folsom Prison Craig Anderson sent word to the judge through his attorney that he had waived his right to attend the hearing. No explanation for his surprising decision not to appear was given.

Holm, who had been promoted to assistant district attorney the year before, subpoenaed Dr. Ozoa. The medical pathologist testified that his estimate of the time of death was "based purely upon the appearance of the bones, which is a very difficult process." At the time he examined the remains from Prospect Creek, the victim had not been identified. Had he known the presumed date of Miss Redlick's death, it would have helped him "narrow down the estimate," he said.

"I would probably have said that the age of the bones was consistent with the time of her death," he went on. The primary purpose of his estimate was to help police officers identify the remains from among the many files of missing persons.

His analysis was a simple visual examination. No further, more exact testing was possible.

Cohn objected to much of what Ozoa said. The defense attorney felt that it was ridiculous to talk about the date of her disappearance as if it were positively the date of her death since there was no proof of that.

During the testimony of the pathologist and deputies who collected the evidence at Prospect Creek, Joan Redlick had been waiting in the hallway and had, therefore, been spared hearing the description of her daughter's remains. Wearing a white dress and looking pale, she walked slowly to the witness stand, containing the anger she felt over having to testify once again.

Her brief statement, however, added credibility to the prosecutions's insistence that Denise's disappearance and death were, in fact, simultaneous events.

Holm asked Mrs. Redlick if she remembered what her daughter had been wearing the last time she saw her. She described the grey slacks and the coat sweater and recalled offering her daughter her own grey belt to wear.

Holm reached for a brown paper bag and handed it to the witness.

"Please open the bag and identify the item inside," Holm instructed her.

Joan slowly opened the package and took a deep breath. There was her once shiny, new grey belt, the one she had given Denise to wear, now dull and coated with dirt.

"That's my belt," she stiffly declared.

Holm asked the judge to deny the petition. Clearly, Dr. Ozoa's indication of the time of death was little more than an educated guess. Mrs. Redlick's testimony tied the day of Denise's disappearance with the date of her death, he added.

But Cohn said there are thousands of grey belts. "Even if this one did belong to Denise," he insisted, "there is no indication of how many days she was wearing it before she died."

"There has been no evidence to show these records are correct," Cohn contended. "There is no evidence to prove that Mr. Anderson is in jail legally."

Kemp, however, was unimpressed. To merit a new trial, the newly discovered evidence must "completely undermine the entire structure of the case." There was, she said, "no credible and convincing evidence" to justify Anderson's release.

Later, Cohn told reporters he still planned to file a lawsuit in federal court claiming that his client's civil rights had been violated throughout his case. But no such lawsuit was filed and, for Craig Anderson, the only hope of release from prison became future parole, undoubtedly many years away.

Not long after Cohn's motion was denied, with Craig's legal problems beginning to accumulate, Craig became desperate to find an attorney willing to accept his case *pro bono*—for free. Indigent prisoners can usually obtain legal assistance in appealing their criminal convictions but there is no system for them to obtain free legal advice in civil matters. At Folsom, as in most prisons, inmates often share information about generous, competent lawyers they can trust. Craig had met another convicted murder from San Mateo County, David Roundtree, whose trial court attorney had, coincidentally, also employed Dr. Ben Grunbaum.

"Why don't you get in touch with this guy who's helping me, Robert Brower?" Roundtree suggested.

In late June, Anderson, using Roundtree as a reference, wrote Brower a long letter explaining the unusual aspects of his case and asking if Brower would be willing to help him. When Brower received the letter, it was clear to him that Craig didn't even realize that the attorney to whom he was turning for help was the same attorney who had assisted Nate Cohn in challenging the bloodstain evidence during his Superior Court trial.

Before responding, Brower looked further into Craig's case and eventually agreed to help the inmate sort out his legal affairs. He said he had never billed Anderson or his family in 1986, and he decided to get involved again, *pro bono*, because he felt there were interesting issues involved.

"Besides, Craig has no assets," Brower said. "He's broke."

Brower subsequently appealed the $1.8 million wrongful

death judgement to the First District Court of Appeals in San Francisco. However, in April 1990, the appellate court upheld the judgment, concluding that it was not excessive. In its opinion, the panel of three justices wrote, such an award—particularly the punitive portion—must be viewed in light of the defendant's wealth and the gravity of the particular criminal act.

"How much does it take to deter first-degree murder when the risk of long prison term alone was not enough?" the appellate justices asked in their written report. "The answer implies an award severe enough to be felt now and long after any release."

Presumably, only one person knows what happened to Denise Redlick. A jury of twelve men and women unanimously decided that person is Craig Anderson.

A half dozen of the murder trial jurors who were unwilling to be interviewed immediately after the trial, discussed their deliberations, still with some hesitation, in 1990. Without exception, they all recalled the trial as one of the most emotional and difficult experiences of their lives. And, they all felt—well beyond any reasonable doubt—that they had made a decision with which they can live.

Said one juror, "There were so many unanswered questions on the part of the defense." Among those pondered by the jury were why the defendant would have rented a van—rather than a pickup truck—to haul debris from remodeling his bathroom and why he found it necessary to so thoroughly clean out the interior of the vehicle.

By the time a foreman was selected, most of the jurors had decided that Anderson was guilty of murder. The only real question, they said, was the kidnapping charge.

"I can recall sitting in that room and most of us feeling that he must have kidnapped her but we didn't feel there was enough proof," one juror explained. "There was still the possibility that she could have gotten into the van of her own volition, but when she refused to reconcile with him, he refused to let her go. No one will ever know what really happened unless he finally decides to tell."

Several mentioned that they were thoroughly unimpressed

by the prosecution's expert witness on blood testing. "He had never even done one of those tests." said one juror. A few remarked on the little things that bothered them—like the painting (on velveteen of a semi-naked woman) hanging above Craig's bed, as shown in a photograph taken by the Burlingame officers during the search of his house. "The guy obviously thought of himself as a swinging bachelor," the juror declared.

Another juror recalled the difficulty that one member of the panel, who happened to have a son around Craig's age, had in reaching a verdict that would send the defendant away to prison for many years.

"We talked about it and decided it was a matter of justice, not sympathy," he recalled. Jurors don't send people to prison, conceivably for life, "unless you feel, deep down inside, that what you are doing is right."

Nate Cohn, who has represented approximately twenty-five murder defendants in his long career of civil and criminal law, considers this case the most frustrating one of all.

"It was like not being able to swim, falling into a pool of water and all of a sudden it turned to molasses," he said. Everywhere he turned, something went wrong. To this day, he remains convinced that if he could have tried the case in another county, "he would have walked."

"I make it a practice of not trying to figure out if the guy I'm representing is guilty or not," Cohn said. "They tell me their story and I try to get them the best deal I can. If I can win on a technicality or because of some mistake, then that's just fine." However, if Craig had told him, "I killed the girl," he would have taken a completely different approach, perhaps one based on a psychiatric defense, he discussed. Justice, he explained, means different things to different people.

"If you give me a smoking revolver, a guy in a room with a body, with all the doors locked from the outside, and he says, 'I didn't do it,' I've got to take his word for it," Cohn insisted.

Tom Marriscolo ultimately devoted more than one thousand one hundred hours to Denise's case including four hundred sixty eight hours of voluntary, uncompensated overtime. In reflecting on the trial, he believes that if Craig had taken the witness stand

and explained what really happened on November 11, 1985, he might have been convicted of second-degree rather than first-degree murder and he would be facing far less time in prison, perhaps being eligible for parole in just a few more years.

"He was the best I've ever seen, of all the suspects I've ever interviewed, at sticking with his story," Marriscolo said.

Anderson, who has declined all requests for interviews, has now been in custody for five years.

The lengthy statement of denial that Anderson submitted to his San Mateo County probation officer will be among the many documents that a three-member panel representing the state Board of Prison Terms will consider when he appears for his first parole hearing in the year 2002. There are also certain to be many letters, from people like Holm, Marriscolo, Wagstaffe, Denise's friends, and, of course, Harry and Joan Redlick, protesting his release. But there will also likely be letters of support from Craig's relatives and family friends.

According to Phyllis Scott, a Board of Prison Terms spokeswoman, the panel usually "wants to see some acknowledgment of responsibility" for the commitment offense. But a confession or lack of confession is not given any more weight in the consideration than any other document.

"Practically speaking, lack of remorse does make it harder for a convicted murder to secure a parole date," said Assistant District Attorney Steve Wagstaffe. "Most of them do admit their crimes by the time their first parole board hearing comes around," he said.

Wagstaffe clearly remembers the surprised reactions of people who knew Craig from high school or through the painting business when they learned that Craig was a murder suspect.

"They all said, 'It can't be! He's just not that type of guy!' " Wagstaffe recalled. "They never would have guessed it in a million years."

Those who thought of Craig as a friend remain shocked by what occurred. To many of them, he was generous, polite, well-mannered and always charming.

They certainly did not think of him as a person capable of lethal violence.

Even after Craig's conviction, probation officer John M. O'Connor spoke to seven personal references, man and women, who uniformly described Craig as "even-tempered and always in control of himself and of his life in general" as well as "kind, considerate and generous." That is the Craig Anderson who, in a debased sub-culture filled with men whose lives have been marked by corruption, immorality and venality, will impress parole officers when the time comes.

"He had the whole world by the tail," said Doug Rees, Craig's one-time business partner. "The future couldn't have been brighter for anybody. If you have as much going for you as he did, it's hard to imagine throwing it all away over a relationship gone sour. Life goes on and you just have to try to make things better."

Like others who knew Craig well, Rees, in the beginning, "Hoped he didn't do it. But the evidence was there."

But, then, observed several people who were interviewed for this book, there must have been two Craigs.

Wagstaffe believes it was Craig's overwhelming ego that caused him to commit an act that didn't coincide with the Craig that most people thought they knew. "A guy like that just doesn't let a woman tell him, 'No.'"

Craig Anderson, Commander Chase said, "was a hero to himself." He was the high school jock, he was a successful businessman and heir to a prosperous paint manufacturing company and he even drove a Mercedes. "He didn't like any chinks in that image and he certainly couldn't handle rejection," Chase declared.

Through counseling and participation in support groups like Justice for Murder Victims, Joan and Harry Redlick are still learning to cope with—although certainly not accept—the tragic death of their daughter. But every joyful occasion within their close family—a young couple's wedding, an older person's birthday party, or the birth of a baby—brings the painful reminder that Denise is not there.

And, as Joan Redlick sadly observed, "the most agonizing realization of all is that someday everyone who knew Denise will be gone or have forgotten her."

Warning: Someone You Love May Be Dangerous!

by Jennifer Boeth Donovan

- Over half of all murder victims are related to or acquainted with their killers.
- At least half of all rape victims—and sometimes experts say as many as eight out of ten—know their attackers.
- The majority of nonsexual assaults are committed by someone known to the victim.
- Most child molesters are family members, neighbors, teachers, youth group leaders, or other adults who had ongoing contact with children they victimized.

Both law-enforcement officers and criminologists agree that statistically you are most likely to be harmed by someone you know, perhaps even by someone you love. "You are more apt to be killed, injured or physically attacked in your home by someone related to you than in any other social context," says psychologist and family violence expert Richard J. Gelles, Dean of the College of Arts and Sciences and professor of Anthropology and Sociology at the University of Rhode Island.

353

How can you recognize in advance that someone close to you may be a threat? Are there reliable early warning signals? Even knowing, how can you protect yourself or your loved ones from someone you know?

There are no easy answers since every relationship is unique, but there are some common denominators. And there are ways to protect yourself once you learn them.

Sometimes the signs are obvious. During a bitter divorce fight, for example, if a husband who repeatedly blackened your eyes or broke your jaw during marriage spits out: "I'll see you dead before I give you a divorce," you'd better take him at his word, says Hugh McDonald, former chief of detectives for the Los Angeles County Sheriff's Department.

He recalls one woman who didn't. The morning of the day that her ex-husband shot her to death in the parking garage of her apartment building, Dorothy C. had confided to her attorney how frightened she was of her husband. Still she agreed that afternoon to meet him alone at her apartment to discuss a bitterly disputed property settlement.

McDonald says she should have left town temporarily, making sure that the ex-husband had no way of finding out where she was. But a job, children and other commitments can make that nearly impossible.

"If a person cannot disappear," McDonald says, "at least she should stay as far away as possible from the one person who is threatening her. Never make plans to meet him or her alone; make all appointments in the office of your attorney."

(Janet Parker Beck, in the book *Too Good To Be True*, believes that Denise Redlick like many other murder victims, simply couldn't believe that the man she had lived with and loved could actually kill her. Her unwillingness to face this cost her her life.)

The tragic morals of such stories, according to McDonald, is that "every person is capable of murder."

In most of us, the social and internal controls that allow us to live together as civilized human beings remain in proper working order. The first warning sign that they are failing is usually a dramatic change in behavior. A talkative person may become morose and withdrawn; a normally tranquil individual may turn garrulous and hyperactive; someone who has always been prompt may start arriving late for work, missing appointments or simply disappearing for hours at a time.

Any behavior that is uncharacteristic or thoroughly inappropriate to the situation should not be ignored, but treated immediately as a red flag—a signal that there may be other danger ahead.

"I hear it over and over; 'he just wasn't acting normal,'" says Sergeant Sandra Sublet, a Dallas police officer.

Gwen T., for example, had been married for two years before her husband first struck her. She was stunned. When she tried to defend herself, he slapped her. Just as quickly, he apologized, begging her to forgive him, says Sublet, "and of course she did."

Months passed before Gwen found her husband in the same sullen mood. She had almost forgotten the slap, having long since convinced herself that it had been a meaningless, once-in-a-lifetime thing. But when she started probing to find out what was bothering him, she felt a sharp twinge in the pit of her stomach and had a strong premonition that danger lay ahead.

"Don't be silly," she chided herself, ashamed of being afraid of her own husband. She redoubled her efforts to cheer him up.

Sergeant Sublet met Gwen about two hours later in the emergency room of a Dallas hospital. She was told that X-rays revealed her husband had broken her arm in addition to covering her face and body with bruises.

The Dallas police officer calls "nitpicking" a common early warning sign of physical abuse. "It starts with little things, but it easily escalates into life-threatening violence," she warned.

Donna Schultz of the National Crime Prevention Council in Washington, DC, cites these red flags: "erratic, unpredictable behavior, belittling remarks, inflexibility, a tendency to blame others for situations beyond their control, cruelty toward animals or children, possessiveness or jealousy, and abuse of alcohol or other drugs.

"If you see any of these in someone close to you, be on guard," she advises. "If you see them in someone you are dating, call it quits."

Red flags can be verbal as well, a Florida psychotherapist points out. "Does he ask embarrassing, personal questions? Does he make suggestive remarks or tell off-color jokes just to make you uncomfortable?" Claire Walsh asks women students at the University of Florida, where she heads a sexual-assault recovery service and sponsors a campus rape-prevention program. "Those are red flags. Sexual assault may be ahead."

Other danger signs that Walsh describes include "initiation of too much physical contact too soon, an explosive temper, lack of concern for you or your feelings, pressure to make you modify your own sexual value system, and sexist language and attitudes."

She urges women to remember the first safety lesson they ever heard: "Stop, look and listen. Stop believing that you have control of the situation; look at a man's behavior and attitudes as they really are, without making excuses for him and listen to your own inner feelings. If you sense danger, act accordingly. Provide your own transportation; double-date or date in groups. Don't put yourself in an isolated situation where you couldn't get help readily if you needed it."

Unfortunately, such advice is easier to give than to follow. Most women manage to talk themselves into ignoring or discounting warning signals rather than taking positive action.

It is a foolish response and a very common one; you may have behaved this way yourself. Someone is acting strangely, speaking or behaving in a way that makes you uneasy. But because it is someone you love or someone you have known and trusted, you discount your feelings and give yourself a tongue-lashing. "Oh, don't be silly," you say. "He's my husband (or boss, or neighbor, or best friend's brother). He'd never do anything to hurt me." Crime-prevention authorities warn that the "Oh, don't be silly" response can be as dangerous as it is common. Even murder victims rarely think they are in any peril until the final moments. "They don't believe that a spouse, a lover or a family member could ever kill them," observes Marcus Wayne Ratledge, author of a book called *Don't Become The Victim.*

Psychologist John T. Monahan suggests that we stop trying to identify violence-prone people and focus on what he calls "violence-prone situations." And, more and more police officers and crime-prevention experts are calling a gut-level sense of impending danger one of the most effective weapons we have to protect ourselves from someone we know. The National Crime Prevention Council encourages people to trust these feelings. "The primary thing we stress," says crime-prevention specialist Donna Schultz, "is to go with your instinct. Nothing is more reliable. If you're getting bad vibes from someone, get away. Seek help. Don't wait for proof."

Gelles offers a more pragmatic yardstick. "If he hits you once, the chances are he's going to hit you again. If he slaps you once, he's going to punch you the next time and hit you with an object the time after that."

An uneasy feeling about someone you know may only be a starting place, a signal that you should pay closer attention, seek more information. You can do both without accusing anybody of anything.

Donna Schultz says, "We must learn to express our feelings. We've got to take control of what we will and won't permit to protect ourselves, and to set an example for our children, so they can grow up knowing that they don't have to become victims."

Reprinted by permission of *Woman's Day Magazine*

■ ACKNOWLEDGMENTS ■

Just before a 9:30 p.m. deadline for the one-star edition of The San Mateo Times on November 13, 1985, Sergeant James Eldredge of the Burlingame Police Department walked into the news room with a press release, concerning a "missing person," in his hand. As I read the brief announcement about a woman who vanished under "mysterious circumstances," I felt an involuntary shiver.

The release gave a brief physical description of the missing woman—5'7", one hundred and twenty seven pounds, blond hair, brown eyes, twenty-three years old—who was last seen, it said, walking to her car in a parking lot at 1:40 p.m. on November 11th. Attached to the one-page, typed, handout was a photograph—the smiling face of a beautiful young woman who, I immediately realized, I had known fifteen years earlier as a sweet, slightly mischievous, giggling youngster. As a teenager, I had been a baton twirling teacher for dozens of little girls at the recreation center in my hometown, San Bruno, where Denise Redlick had also lived and gone to school. Denise was one of several students who came to my home, with one of her little girlfriends, for private lessons. Although I hadn't seen Denise in many years, I would sometimes run across her picture, taken in my living room, in a box of old photographs from my high school days. To think that this innocent child had grown up to become the victim of foul play—perhaps a kidnapping or even murder—was extremely disturbing.

The story about Denise's disappearance ran in a back section of the paper that day. Missing persons are not an unusual phenomena on the Peninsula and the information and photograph ran as a courtesy to the Burlingame officers who were asking for public assistance. But, as the search for Denise became more intense and the investigation into her disappearance unfolded over the coming months, it became front page news. What happened to the Redlick family touched many lives. Parents grieved for Harry and Joan Redlick whose loss could never be replaced. Young women who saw Denise's picture on television, in the newspapers, and on posters at shopping malls wondered if they, too, could be vulnerable to foul play. Men who read of the romance that turned sour and then, as police claimed, to violence, thought of the pain that can accompany unrequited love.

In the months ahead, the story touched me deeply. In May 1986, I was

Acknowledgments

assigned to cover Craig Anderson's trial while courthouse reporter, Terry Robertson, was occupied with other breaking news. I felt the tension each day as the Anderson and Redlick families—brought together by love and torn apart by a tragedy in less than a year—took their seats on opposite sides of the courtroom. Where many murder trials in San Mateo County in the 1980s revolved around themes of drugs and prostitution with the only truly debatable question before the jury being the degree of murder, this was a trial that had no certain conclusion. Until the verdict was read, it seemed that Craig Anderson still had a very good chance of walking away from the charges forever, even if Denise's body—along with evidence linking her fate to her former fiance—eventually was found.

After Anderson was convicted and sent to prison, I would occasionally think of Denise Redlick and wonder how long her grieving parents would be forced to wait to bury her. The answer came on August 18, 1987, when Burlingame police Commander John Parkin called to announce that her remains had been found.

It was then that the outline for this book began to take shape in my mind. A newspaper reporter tends to think in terms of twenty-inch, sometimes forty-inch, stories and I had never expected to embark upon a literary project of this scope. But it seemed that the details of this case needed to be published. As Joan Redlick said when I first sought her cooperation, "Janet, you were meant to write this." Over the year that I spent compiling this story I often removed from my files the little snapshot of an eight-year-old Denise and wished that I had known the delightful young woman that she had become. With the birth of my own daughter the same month that I signed a contract with New Horizon Press, the subject matter took on a special significance in my heart.

Diana Onley-Campbell, program director of the National Coalition Against Domestic Violence, read the completed manuscript for *Too Good To Be True* and found in it chilling examples of the classic symptoms that too often, in intimate relationships, end in violence. Women should be wary, she said, of any man who insists on isolating her from friends and family; emotionally abuses her; uses his manhood as a privilege by acting like the "master of the castle"; and intimidates her through his actions, gestures and voice. These, Onley-Campbell concluded, are all things that seem to have happened to Denise Redlick.

Dozens of people, most of whom are mentioned by name in this book, allowed me to interview them about this remarkable case and to share with me, often tearfully, their memories of Denise Redlick. I am especially indebted to Carl Holm and Steve Wagstaffe and to the Burlingame Police Department, including Chief Fred Palmer, Commander Tom Chase and, especially, Sergeant Tom Marriscolo, for sharing with me thoughts and

359

Acknowledgments

documents that went beyond the public record. Without their help, this book could not have been written.

Others who are not mentioned in the book, but deserve credit for assistance with important details include court reporters Olivia Shirley and Sandra Bettencourt, and reporter Terry Robertson, whose own articles helped me recreate several events that I did not personally observe.

To Harry and Joan Redlick, who allowed me to probe into their personal tragedy, I can only say it is my sincere hope that my daughter will grow up to trust, respect and love her father and me as much as Denise did her own parents.

My agent, Elizabeth Pomada, and my editor and publisher, Joan Dunphy, deserve special thanks for believing in this project and giving me a chance.

But, most of all, I am grateful to my husband, Jim, who has always seen in me the ability to turn literary dreams into reality. His words of support and encouragement prodded me along during the many frustrating periods when this book seemed an impossible goal.

—Janet Parker Beck